# Scenes In Our Parish

Elizabeth Emra Holmes

In the interest of creating a more extensive selection of rare historical book reprints, we have chosen to reproduce this title even though it may possibly have occasional imperfections such as missing and blurred pages, missing text, poor pictures, markings, dark backgrounds and other reproduction issues beyond our control. Because this work is culturally important, we have made it available as a part of our commitment to protecting, preserving and promoting the world's literature. Thank you for your understanding.

# SCENES IN OUR PARISH.

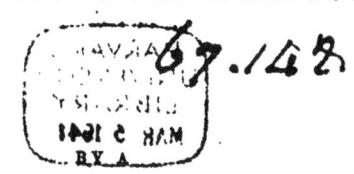

BY A

"COUNTRY PARSON'S" DAUGHTER.

"Needs no show of mountain hoary,
  Winding shore, or deepening glen,
Where the landscape in its glory,
  Teaches truth to wandering men.
Give true hearts but earth and sky,
And some flowers to bloom and die;
Homely scenes and simple views,
Lowly thoughts may best infuse."
KEBLE'S CHRISTIAN YEAR.

FIRST AND SECOND SERIES.

NEW-YORK:
PUBLISHED BY HARPER & BROTHERS,
NO. 82, CLIFF-STREET.

AND SOLD BY THE PRINCIPAL BOOKSELLERS THROUGHOUT THE
UNITED STATES.

M DCCC XXXIII.

TO

THE LIVING COMPANIONS

OF

MY PLEASANT WALKS;

AND

TO THE BLESSED MEMORY

OF

THE DEAD.

# CONTENTS.

## FIRST SERIES.

| | Page |
|---|---|
| Introduction, | 5 |
| An Old Couple, | 8 |
| Christmas-Day, 1829, | 18 |
| The Graves of Infants, | 24 |
| Mary, the Sailor's Widow, | 31 |
| The Last of the Family, | 42 |
| The Dorcas Meeting, | 50 |
| Blind Sarah, | 56 |
| The Strawberry Feast, | 65 |
| The Laying of the Foundation Stone, | 71 |
| The Vestry, | 80 |
| Whit-Monday, | 89 |
| A Day of Gloom, | 98 |
| A Tale of Low Life, | 111 |
| A Party of Pleasure, | 122 |
| Conclusion, | 129 |

## SECOND SERIES.

| | |
|---|---|
| Introduction, | 139 |
| The Evening School, | 144 |
| A Walk in a Wet Day, | 152 |
| One Half Hour to Poetry, | 162 |
| The Ladye Elizabeth, | 169 |
| Alice Grey, | 175 |
| The Crew's Hold, | 183 |
| The Confirmation, | 195 |
| The Woods, | 202 |
| The Day's Work Done, | 209 |
| A Visit to the Old Court, | 220 |
| Extract from a Letter describing a Country Funeral, | 230 |
| Remembrances of an Ordination, | 233 |
| One Page in my Life, recorded on the 31st of October, 1831, | 240 |
| Conclusion, | 256 |

# INTRODUCTION.

> "But is amusement all? Studious of song,
> And yet ambitious not to sing in vain;
> I would not trifle merely, though the world
> Be loudest in their praise, who do no more."
>
> COWPER.

My little book is nearly finished, and I am told I need write an introduction for it. But who are you, gentle reader, to whom I must introduce myself? You must be at leisure just now, or you would scarcely think of spending an hour on a first volume, written by a nameless author. Common civility expects me to thank you for your condescension; and to express a hope that I may render the time we shall pass together, in some degree, agreeable.

Do you love the country? Thither I will wander with you; not, indeed, through such scenery as our native land *can* show, in some of its most favoured retreats: I may gaze with you, on the silver mirror of no Rydal lake; I can take you to no Walla Crag; nor, southward to the Gothic ruin, where the grass grows in the deserted aisles; and the ivy hangs in heavy wreaths round the arches, which once echoed gloriously to the Te Deum, as the music pealed from the vaulted roof, and stole over the placid Wye: I can linger with you in no such silent and beautiful wood walks; and I may pause on no such height with you as the cliff at Piercefield: yet, come with me. "God made the country;" here are wild flowers, and clear waters, such as none but God could make: and for the stories connected with our walks;—Can you stoop to the common concerns of life? For if you enjoy nothing but romance and glowing fiction, I forewarn you that we had better part;—I never saw a knight, or a lady,—a titled lady I mean,—in my life; and the fairies of our forest forsook their haunts here, in the same day on which the first coal-pit was opened.

But have you a heart that can sympathize with human hearts that throb, and ache and flutter, as itself has done? Can you feel for sojourners here, who know the wear and tear of this "work-day world," as you have known it? Will you take interest in the recital of

> "Familiar matter of to-day,
> \* \* \* \* \* \*
> Some natural sorrow, grief, or pain,
> Which has been, and may be again."

Above all, do you like to observe God's ways, the book of his nature, and the lines of his providence? Then let us ponder over the mysterious pages together; and if we bring to the perusal, simple hearts, however dim our eyes may be, I doubt not, we shall study them with profit.

It is needless for me to ask, What your principles are? If you do not like me the better for my title-page, I candidly advise you to close my book. I do not say thus, I trust in haughtiness; in times like the present,

> "Oh! what have I to do with pride?"

but because I feel, that I have not the ability to combat *your* principles, and *my own* will admit of no compromise.

Are we agreed then, thus far? Yes; and I hear you ask me, Why I wrote? To that question, I simply answer, because in a life of much leisure and much retirement, it has been my greatest pleasure to do so. Hitherto, it has never been any thing but an amusement, a relaxation from duties and employments, all pleasant in their way, but not one half so pleasant as this. But you add, Why do you publish? A deservedly popular writer, (I do not remember her exact words, but this, I am sure, is her meaning,) says, "All women who publish, do so, either for money or fame." It would not become me to say, she is wrong: you cannot expect me to say, she is right; attribute to me which motive you please. But as I allow you thus much, believe me when I add, that having written, and having published; I humbly and earnestly trust that some advantage, far beyond either fame or riches, may arise, both to the writer and the reader. It will be so, if I should be made the means of directing any one eye to that light which is from above; or any heart to that "peace which passeth all understanding." Is it possible that so weak and contemptible an agent, should be so honoured? Yes!—

> "All is in his hand, whose praise I seek,—
> \* \* \* \* \* \* \*
> Whose frown can disappoint the proudest strain,
> Whose approbation, prosper even mine."

# AN OLD COUPLE.

John Anderson! my Jo! John! we climb'd the hill thegither,
And many a canny day, John! we had with ane anither;
Now we maun totter down, John! but hand in hand we'll go,
And we'll sleep thegither at the foot, John Anderson! my Jo!
                                                    BURNS.

PERHAPS in times so prolific as the present, in all that genius and fancy produce, gorgeous or lovely, the very simplicity of an unadorned story like mine, may render it valuable by way of contrast—as the green leaves of the jessamine, themselves scentless and unvarnished, render

"More conspicuous, and illumine more
The bright profusion of her scattered stars."

This much I have said, I suppose, by way of apology for my boldness in attempting to write at all; and now I will go on to my tale.

The old man, for whom the prayers of the congregation were desired last Sunday, we missed from his seat in the aisle, only when illness, (his last illness certainly it will be,) confined him to his bed; and until then, in fair or foul weather, sunshine or shower, as regularly as Sunday came, you were sure to see blind Samuel feeling his way, up the rough lane and across the green, to the half open church-yard gate. Latterly, indeed, he came with very feeble steps, and but for the good-natured, though rather rough assistance of some of our school-boys, would sometimes perhaps have been obliged to stop short of his journey's end; but his inoffensive and orderly conduct made him a general favourite; and when once he was within the church, many a friendly hand was willingly offered to lead him round the corner, and up to his accustomed seat; for, in a Christian congregation, how could it be otherwise?—every one was interested for the poor old man; they saw that he was weak and blind, and they knew that he was childless. He had no decent countryman for a son, on whose arm he might lean; no neat, gentle daughter; not even one little rosy grandchild, just old enough to be trusted to "lead grandfather to church, and to sit quiet till it was time to lead him back again." No! poor Samuel came alone. It was his old wife's pleasure, and nearly her whole business on Saturday, to provide for his decent appearance at church. His blindness prevented him from knowing how many necessaries she wanted herself, but he always had a pair of warm worsted stockings, clean and thoroughly mended; and one of his two shirts (for his wardrobe could boast no larger supply) was always made ready on Saturday: and early on Sunday morning, she brought down from the carved chest, where they are deposited, as carefully as if they were last year's purchases, his curious chintz waistcoat, with long sleeves—I never saw but this one of the sort—and his blue coat with very large buttons, which my reader may suppose is a curiosity too, for it was bought more than eight-and-forty years ago. And Hester used to be well pleased when she brushed it, to see how decent her old man—so she generally calls him—looked in it still; but as she reached him the oaken stick, which had been his companion for many years, it has grieved her to think, that blind and feeble as he was, he could have no other support and guide; and she often wept, as she opened the hatch to him and wished him a blessing on his way, that her own still greater infirmities prevented her from accompanying him: labour and trouble have bowed her down, so that, like the woman in the gospel, "she can in no wise lift up herself." But she has fulfilled her duty to him well, and her pleasant task is almost done. He will come up to church no more, as she told me the other day, till he is carried thither; and in the mean time though grace may be given him to show, as the poet and philosopher did, "in what peace a Christian can die,"* there are sad hours of wasting and weariness for him to undergo, and very heavy days of toil and watching; and I am afraid, notwithstanding the parish allowance, and the kindness of friends—of want and privation for poor Hester.

But allow me to fancy that you are accompanying me in

* Addison.

my walk, my kind reader, and as we go along I will tell you some particulars of their simple story. We will turn down this lane, then, on the north side of the church. I am told that this is not a pleasant walk, and I believe it, for those who have told me so are judges; yet if we go out in a mood to be pleased, we generally find something to admire, and I at least—for I am not very wise—always find much to wonder at.

Stop one moment, before we descend the hill. What a lovely gleam of autumn sun-shine bursts across the opposite woods! How distinctly the beautiful forms of the old trees are outlined, and what a splendid variety of tint and shadowing there is still exhibited, even at this late period of the year! Oh! there are lovely walks in those woods! The purest stream, the most luxuriant and picturesque foliage I ever saw. But they do not need my admiration: Bird and Danby have lingered amongst those valleys, and they have immortalized them. As we descend the hill, however, we lose the distant prospect; and the near view, at first sight, offers nothing by way of compensation. If it were April, instead of November, we might gather plenty of primroses in the willow-bed, on the right hand side. They grow amongst the gnarled and mossy roots there, by hundreds and thousands; and I observe it, because I scarcely ever gathered one in any part of the parish beside. Nay, I believe not one solitary straggler ever had the curiosity or the boldness to creep through the hedge to the other side. I cannot at all account for it: the soil appears just the same, and there is the same proportion of shade and sunshine, I should think; so this is one of the many things I wonder at. Earlier in the season we may make a very fair nosegay here of the May flower, and dog roses, and golden cups; the blue blossom of the profuse and balmy ground ivy; and that most lovely of all wild flowers the white major convolvulus, with its broad green leaves and spiry tendrils, and its blossom as pure as sunshine on white marble, that raises itself so loftily to the notice of the morning traveller, and is folded and withered when he passes again at evening, as if it was created for the very purpose of whispering to the gale that passes us, "Man that is born of a woman, so cometh up, and is so cut down," But now the last festoon of its wreathed leaves is sear and yellow, and the rest of the flowers have almost all left us; but there are some lingering hawk's eye daisies and autumn starwort; and there is the vervain, which the "Naturalist," in his interesting "Journal," tells us used to be sacred; and there is one, and only one blossom of that little bright elegant flower, the cinque-foil, whose very name speaks to us of the heraldry of old times, and of its consequences in days that are gone; and yet it smiles there with perfect content, from its lowly bed of deep green moss, and truly, well it may; it never was emblazoned on a fairer field.

Now we will walk more slowly. We have past the low willow-bed, and are beginning again to ascend the hill. Look across the fields—the ground is very irregular here, but you see that it slopes gradually upward, till at the top the hill is crowned by a group of low huts, which, humble as they are, yet rise above the stunted and shattered oaks and elms, by which they are surrounded. That place is called the Holms; perhaps because there are remains of many trees and hedges of *holm* or holly. At least this derivation may serve us until we can find a better. The trees which crest that little point of upland, are indeed, scarcely deserving the name, yet we will look with reverence on them; they are the last descendants of a noble race, for once

> "This was a forest, and a fayre forest;
> In it grew many a seemly tree."

Yes; this was indeed one of the king's woods. A little further away, toward the North-east, you can discover the white gable ends of an old house. It really looks very pretty, peeping through its grove of poplar and chestnut-trees. The eminence on which it is built, commands an extensive view of the surrounding country. On that spot lived the keeper of the royal chase, and it is still called the Lodge. About half a mile to the left, king John is said to have built a hunting-seat, and this very place once echoed with the sound of the bugle-horn, and the cry of the staunch hounds, and the shout of the hunters. We cannot, certainly look round us without feeling that the days of romance and chivalry are utterly past; yet, though one is long coming to the conclusion, and longer still before one chooses to own it, what is lost in romance is generally gained in comfort. To be sure, the country is said to be, from several causes, in a distressed and alarming state. I am no politician, but as an English Christian, "my fathers have declared to me the noble works that our God has done for us in the days of old," and I believe he "will yet arise and deliver us for his honour." In the meantime, whilst I feel very sorry for the distresses of my countrymen in other counties, I am yet bound to be thankful that this parish, though very poor, is not particularly agitated by the commercial troubles of the times. It is not a manufacturing district: and as yet, those who are prudent and industrious have been enabled generally speaking, to escape abject poverty.

There are some, however, the little history of whose days seems but one scene of loss and disappointment; and the lives of the poor old couple, of whom I spoke, are of the number. When they first married, Samuel undertook to supply an extensive factory with coal, and it became necessary for him to purchase a wagon and a team of horses. It was not pleasant, certainly, to go into debt to so large an amount, at the first outset; but he had no choice. It had been his father's business, and was the only one which he understood. The wagon cost more than £40, but the benevolent wheelwright agreed to receive the payment by instalments. The horses—you must not suppose them in very high condition—were paid for immediately, and scarcely paid for, when first one and then another became diseased and died. This was the beginning of troubles. In the meantime Hester met with an accident, which was the immediate occasion of an expensive and distressing illness,—and from the effects of which she never recovered. If my story were not fact, I should fear the charge of improbability in thus heaping misfortune on misfortune; but mine is "*an over true tale.*" About this time, too, Samuel's sight, always weak, failed so fast that it became necessary for him to procure the assistance of a driver for his wagon. Then his heart began to sink, as he has often told me, and the climax of his sentence at this point used always to be, "Then the third horse was dead, and the fourth was dying, and Hetty was bad too!"

But even these heavy and continued expenses might have been borne, but, suddenly, the concern for which he was engaged failed, throwing him, with many others, into a state of great distress. What was to be done? They were not genteel enough to think of the King's Bench. Their principle of honour—do not smile my dear reader at the idea of a collier's honour—and their standard of morality, were very high. They were *His* servants who has said, "Owe no man any thing;" and by his grace they kept his commandment. Every thing—it was but very little—that was not absolutely necessary, was sold; and their best clothes pledged; "for those," said Hester, "have no right to wear good clothes who owe so much as we did then." There are some gay parties, in very high circles, I believe, that would cut rather a shabby figure if poor Hester's maxim were zealously enforced. Their clothes remained unredeemed for fifteen years. Their landlord took the wagon—then much the worse for the wear and tear of some years—as payment for rent; and Hester went round to the other creditors, (the whole of whose demands together amounted nearly to £100,) telling them simply the state of her affairs, and begging them to have patience until she could pay all. Her husband was now blind, but he could feel his way to and from town, with the produce of the little garden which Hester cultivated; and he managed to assist her in many ways, in the business in which she was particularly skilful, that of rearing calves, pigs, and rabbits. It was as a dealer in the last-mentioned pretty creatures, those favourites of all children—to their misfortune poor little things, it is that they are so—that I, then a child, became first acquainted with her. They have told me of losses and disappointments which would make my story too long: suffice it to say, that by constant exertion and strict self-denial, notwithstanding Samuel's blindness and Hester's frequent illness, their debts were all paid at the end of twenty-four years of hard labour, which had brought on premature old age.

During these twenty-four years of toil Hester had very great troubles of another sort. Of her seven sons not one survived the hour of his birth. How great a grief and how bitter a disappointment this was, year after year, a woman's weak pen cannot tell; but no woman needs to be told. "And now," said this childless mother to me, and she wept bitterly at this part of her story, "there's not one to carry home father, not one to carry home mother."

The great debt, as I said, was paid, but the years which it had taken to discharge it, had borne, as they flew, health and strength, and hope away with them; and their daily bread was to be earned by the sweat of furrowed and aching brows, and the labour of enfeebled hands. But straightened as they have oftentimes been, for the mere necessaries of life, they have always found "man's extremity God's opportunity:" to them the promise has been fulfilled, "Bread shall be given thee, and water shall be sure."

Their habits of industry and cleanliness prevent their only lower apartment from displaying that air of wretchedness which great poverty too often, but not necessarily assumes; and why should we wonder at it? "Godliness is profitable for all things." To be sure they are obliged to keep a curious assortment of articles—kettles and pans, an empty rabbit hutch, now used as a cupboard, and a barrel of grain for the pig, all ranged along one side of their sitting room: but the deal table is white and clean, and the few chairs almost bright; and the cups and plates are arranged in seemly order along the shelf; at one corner of which, carefully folded up, like a treasure of known value, lies their bible; and whoever would read them a chapter from that blessed book, needed no other recommendation to make him a welcome visitor.

It was curious to observe in what different ways their sincere and humble attention used to be displayed. Hester's could express itself in many tears and earnest exclamations. But Samuel seldom spoke or moved from the momont when, as the reading began, he reverently laid aside his round collier's hat, until when, as it ended, he quietly resumed it with some expression of assent to what he had heard:—"Ah! that's what we want."—"That's what I told Hetty." And often when it has been a chapter of promise, I have heard him say, slowly, as if the experiences of long years were passing in review across his mind, to prove the truth of it, "Aye, the Lord will provide!" Such, indeed, was the last connected sentence I ever heard him utter. His present illness came on with sudden violence, and has already lasted many weeks; and Hester, bowed down by poverty and disease, and reduced by anxiety and toil to great weakness of body and mind, was crying bitterly at the idea that the parish must bury him. He made a strong effort to speak, and at last said, " She ought not to do so, the Lord *has* provided for me." And HE *has* provided. Notwithstanding their poverty, I really believe the old man has wanted for nothing during his long illness, and Hester throughout that time, has waited on him with the most unremitted attention, and the most sincere affection. I do not mean to say that her neighbours are less friendly than most other poor neighbours; but they have their own troubles to think of; their own pressing necessities to provide for; and though they may have the inclination, they certainly have not found opportunity to give her much assistance. She has risen before day-light, and laboured hard all day, to keep things in decent order, and to provide her dying husband with every comfort which was possible; and she has watched alone with him through the long night. But nature cannot bear long what that poor old man has borne so patiently. It must be over soon. There! we are come in sight of the humble dwelling, which he has inhabited so long, but from which he will soon be borne forth to return no more.

We will not go any further, for the path here is very rough and miry. I cannot think how old Hester will manage to come up this steep lane at the funeral. She will try, I know; for the poor, I am happy to say, still think that friends and relations are those who ought to see the dear form that has been loved in life, laid at rest in its holy grave; and certainly it must have been for the comfort of the sorrowing friends, and not for those hirelings who have nothing of mourners but the name, that the beautiful and most comfortable service of our church was composed. Poor old woman! it will be a weary walk for her, to be sure, but then, one at least, of that faithful pair will, for the first time for many years, be no longer a subject of pity; for "blessed are the dead who die in the Lord."

---

The weather is altered very much since we were together last: it is no longer mild autumn, but cold, and dark, and gloomy—altogether winter. The frost a few nights since, entirely stripped the trees, and now we distinguish them not by the variety of foliage, but the varied character of the dark branches. And what beauty there is in those forms yet! How reverend and even noble the old chestnut looks that almost hides the east window of the church; and with what perfect elegance that tall and fragile birch tree rises beside it! How gracefully all the leafless branches bow together, as the wind sweeps across them; and with what an air of joy they all rise again together when the gust is past! That elastic spring is indeed the only thing that wears any appearance of joy this evening. It is so cold that the lauristinus flowers keep themselves wrapt up, in their red foldings, showing no more intention of opening than they did a month ago. The Michaelmas daisies were entirely withered, and they are cut down; and the few marygolds, small and single, and wet and pale, linger alone along the littered border and tremble at the cold evening gale, as if they dreaded another hail-storm; and indeed the heavy grey clouds, and the sighing of the wind, foretell a stormy night.

Hark! there is a sound fit for such an evening. The bell is tolling for a funeral. It is old Samuel's. That knell has a solemn, but not now a melancholy sound. Come through the gate, to the corner of the church, and we shall see the humble procession pass. Ah! the beautiful service is begun. I know the comforting words well, and the voice which utters them. How deep and musical it is!—" I shall see God! I shall see for myself! Mine eyes shall behold!" Yes, poor Samuel, there is no blindness in heaven. The corpse is borne very slowly, yet the mourner who immediately follows, seems to have difficulty in keeping pace with them. It is poor Hester leaning on her crutches. How painfully she walks; how will she be able to reach home again? and how very desolate she will be when she does. But it will be a comfort to her as long as she lives, that she has performed this last duty—that she has looked into the deep grave, and said, " Good night! good night, Samuel!"—that she has laid him to rest with his fathers and his seven little sons: and, blessed be God, laid him there " in sure and certain hope." But she will weep when she looks on his vacant chair;

the place he occupied for four-and-forty years. She will feel his absence greatly, when she prepares her lonely meals; and she will miss the trembling voice that for so many years has breathed its prayer with her's. And she has not one dear child to console her—not even a near relation; she will be all alone. Well, we must not forget her; we will go and comfort her to-morrow as well as we are able. Poor old Hester!

*Dec.* 2, 1829.

# CHRISTMAS-DAY, 1829.

"———— With thy leave I'll fetch thee flowers that grow
In thine own garden—Faith and Love, to thee:
With these I'll dress it up—and these shall be
My rosemary and bays."

Sir Matthew Hale.

It was a very clear, bright day indeed; quite the beau idéal of a Christmas-day; fresh and cold, but not unpleasantly so, as the wind was hushed. It scarcely waved the dark branches, and the clear purple shadows lay still in the unclouded sunshine, on the unspotted snow. It would have been very pleasant weather for walking, but there had been a thaw, and afterwards a hard frost, so that the pathway to the school was slippery: so our poor clerk found to his cost, for he met with a fall, and came to church looking graver than usual, and his arm tied up in a red handkerchief, under his loose great coat. We are all sorry for him; he is a civil, industrious young man, and he has a housefull of little children. It is well that children's frames are so constituted as not to mind tumbles; certainly they do not, or we should not have assembled so many merry creatures as met both in the morning and afternoon of to-day. What a pretty sight our school-room was! Such a circle of healthy-looking country girls! such a variety of gay colours and picturesque forms, in the way of clothes! For this is one of our high days, when all who have any claim to belong to us, exhibit themselves in their best apparel; and as it is cold, many are decked with shawls or silk handkerchiefs, borrowed from mothers and elder sisters; and many have their black bonnets newly trimmed with gay ribbons, red, green, and yellow. And there was a happy look in almost every face, that it did one's heart good to see. I say almost, for I am sorry to acknowledge that, even amidst our hardy country children, I have known some whose constitutions are unequal to the hardships with which they have to contend; I have seen young faces traced by care; cheeks that ought to have been bright, already faded by want; some poor little ones, to whom Christmas-day was not a *feast* day. Yet it was a happy day even to them. They are allowed, as a particular treat—any thing can be made a treat to simple country children—to go into the boy's school-room to sing; that twice in the year, at Christmas and Whitsuntide, we may have the pleasure of seeing all the children together; and many amusing glances pass between them, as the little shy girls come one after another through the widely-opened door, and range themselves, in decent order, up the west side of the long room, under the windows.

Then the hymns sung on Christmas-day are particular favourites. They know and understand them perfectly, both the words and the tunes; and they sing with all their voices, and as far as can be expected, with all their hearts. They sing as if they rejoiced certainly. And the room is decorated, according to old custom, with sprays of holly and evergreen, and so is the church; and I dare say it is part of the children's pleasure—I am sure it is part of mine—to see the varnished holly-boughs glittering in the sun, and the feathery yew and the dark ivy berries clustering from the sconces and round the pillars. I know there are good people who object to this "*dressing up*" on various grounds, and some prudent ones who think it a needless waste of shrubberies and plantations. But the children who cried Hosanna! did not begrudge the palm-boughs and branches of trees that were strewed in *his* way, the remembrance of whose blessed coming we to-day celebrate with deep gratitude and with fervent joy. O! I love customs hallowed by the use of our forefathers; and when that solemn creed which their wisdom has transmitted to us, was repeated to-day, there were hearts that responded not the less deeply, lips that replied none the less firmly, because it is the fashion of the present day to cavil at it, and because we are threatened that the men "who are given to change" may, before another year, expunge its form of sound words from our beautiful ritual. But we will not darken Christmas-day with gloomy forebodings. I said it was a day of joy. Of joy? Oh! yes, even in such a world of weeping as this, though remembrances that make the heart ache weigh down the mind even to-day.

But for us the holy and spotless table was spread which must in no wise be approached by complaining hearts: nay, if it is possible, we must draw near cheerfully, as well as patiently; and our feelings must not belie our words when we bless God's "holy name for all his servants departed this life in his faith and fear."

I am no judge of music, but the singing at church, in the morning, seemed to me very sweet: and in the afternoon, when the Angel's Hymn, as it is called, was sung, the words seemed verified,—" The glory shone around." The last sun-light of that bright day streamed in through the south windows, quite across the church, lighting up the boughs of fresh evergreens on its way, and reddening the white wall over little Mary's grave, and then reflected back on the marble figure of Hope, and the tablet against the chancel window, inscribed with the names of our member's family; and then the red gleam faded away, and the aisles became more and more shadowy, and the outlines of the pillars were less and less clearly defined, until by the time the service was over, the uncertain day-light had quite given way to the glimmer of the few sconces which were placed at the top of the middle aisle and on the altar rails. No very splendid illumination; yet sufficiently bright to gladden the eyes and hearts of the long and varied procession that presently came up towards it. Look, the children are leaving their seats in the gallery, and are coming up the aisle two and two. At first, as they came down the dark steps, there was a little shuffling and pushing for pre-eminence, but now as they come into the light they appear more orderly. Here they come! a joyous train, and what a variety of faces, and dresses, and sizes: first the tall school-girls, looking almost as much ashamed as they are pleased. They have just arrived at the age when the outward appearance of children outstrips the improvement in manners and understanding; a most awkward and unprepossessing age; and then, seeing that they grow tall, they unfortunately take it for granted that they grow wise also; and just when they most need instruction, leave school. Ignorant as we know these girls to be, we scarcely hope they will condescend to stay with us another year. Yet there are exceptions. Here is one; little grave Betty, with a plain pale face and a tidy nankeen gown: a present, I rather think, for there is something genteel in the cut, though the colour is faded, and her handkerchief is tidily crossed and tied behind. She has a great love of learning; gets by heart all the hymns in all the hymn-books she can meet with, and always when she has said her appointed lessons, comes up shyly, with a countrified curtsey and a modest request, "Please to hear me say my Psalm, ma'am?" She is what our quondam mistress used to call "*a quiet girl.*" It was the chief praise she ever bestowed; and indeed considering little Betty's unfortunate sex, there are those, I know, who would only say,

"Wondrous strange, if it be true!"

Never mind, she is a very nice child at any rate: she is always first in her place, and if her teacher has been ill or absent, there is, when she comes again, a sparkle in the grey eyes and a colour in her white cheek, that makes little plain Betty look almost pretty. But I have said quite enough about her. She has passed the huge basket at the corner of the aisle: has received her cake, and has followed the others into the vestry, and, I suppose, into the snowy church-yard. O no! look, they are gathered in a group round the blazing fire, which throws its quivering and sparkling blaze on the pictures of the Oxford Almanac, and the sprays of laurel and yew with which they are decorated, and brightens the soft folds of the fair white linen surplice which has been thrown across one of the chairs. "Go on, children; make haste home before it grows darker, and slippery as it is, take care that you neither fall down nor fall out by the way." But here comes a petitioner, and I observe that when our children are disposed to be very polite, they will not ask a favour for themselves, but speak for each other—"If you please ma'am, Ann Miles says, may she wait for her brother?" "O yes, brothers are worth waiting for."

And here come the boys; another long and motley procession, not quite so gay-looking as the young ladies, but displaying enough of variety, both of form and colouring to employ a far abler pen in the description than mine. Here are some with clean pinbefores and nicely plaited frills: these have tidy mothers, I am sure: and some with wellfitted velveteen jacket and trowsers, evidently new for the occasion: and some who look very different; whose wild

air and dress, unmended clothes, to hide which, to-day, is
pulled on the father's waistcoat, perhaps of scarlet or spotted plush, and buttons that look like fire-stones; none of it
old, yet none in good condition, all telling more of bad
management than of poverty. And yet the wildest and
most uncouth among them, looks up to-night with a pleasant
smile and a well-intentioned, though not very graceful bow,
and seems, at present at least, disposed to behave himself
"lowly and reverently to all his betters;" and indeed I
trust they are disposed to do their duty by him. How long
the good feeling may last it is not for us to know; we will
take care that it does not fail on our side. The word of life
is put into their hands, and though many of them have the
worst examples at home, we will remember who has said,
"Blessed are they that sow beside *all* waters."

Here come the very little ones: the sexton's three fair
grand-children, with blue eyes and curly flaxen hair.
They always look very neat. I think there must be good
management at home, for there is another baby there, and
the father's wages are only eleven shillings a week. Now
they are all served; all the children at any rate. But there
appears to me a consultation of graver persons gathered
round the great basket. I understand what it is. The
cakes that are left are always divided amongst those who
are so lucky as to be on the spot—clerk, sexton, singers,
schoolmaster and mistress. There is a scarcity I find; this
year they will have short commons, I am afraid: yet they
all looked cheerful and contented; and so the congregation
separated; and the lights were put out, and the church
doors shut, and we all went home. Then came the long
quiet evening, when some of us gathered, as closely as possible, round the bright fire, and listened whilst one and
another dear voice read some passage from *Keble's Christian Year*. Soothing, beautiful poetry! well calculated to
lift the heart above the cares of this troublesome world, and
to light the path with the sunshine of heaven. And then
came the holy hour of evening prayer, and we all assembled.
Not all who had ever assembled there, certainly, but if there
was cause for sorrow, there was more for joy and gratitude; for those who met there loved each other well, and
there was good hope to meet again those who were parted:

there we listened to the word of our hope, and the promise of our salvation, and we joined in prayer to Him who is able to keep us from falling, and to present even us mourners before his presence with exceeding joy; and we lay down to rest with humble and thankful hearts, and our pleasant Christmas-day was ended.

# THE GRAVES OF INFANTS.

"Unhappy loss; nay happy gain be 't said
When by earth's losse, heaven's kingdom's purchased—
Christ's blood the price, God's word the evidence,
Heaven settles crowns on children's innocence—
The branch so soon cropt off, earth cast thereon
Adds turf to twig, and gains possession.
Thy title's good; thy tenure's *capite*;
Death past the fine, Christ the recoverie."

"It is no small advantage," says old Jeremy Taylor, "that our children, dying young, receive: for their condition of a blessed immortality is rendered to them secure, by being snatched from the dangers of an evil choice, and carried to their little cells of felicity where they can weep no more."

———"They," he continues, "are entered into a secure possession, to which they went with no other condition but that they passed into it through the way of mortality, and for a few months wore an uneasy garment." Thus far I read, and then I stopt, and the recollection of some whom I had known thus carried to "their little cells of felicity," recurred to my mind, and it struck me that a relation of some of these real remembrances might interest you, my kind reader. I was standing at my own little room window, and the weather was clear and mild, much such a day, I thought, (only then it was somewhat later in the year) that, now, a long while ago, I went to pay a visit to our clerk's wife and her new-born twins. I had never seen twins; and I remember feeling much delighted—more so, I suppose, than the poor relations could be—when I heard that two had been added to the already large family.

As I went along I could think of nothing but the little brother and sister. I believe they appeared to my mind's eye far more lovely and interesting than any other children could possibly be; and when I saw them wrapped in their long white robes, and lying side by side in the neat cradle, I dare say I much amused the grave nurse by the extravagance of my admiration; and, on my part, I remember being much shocked by her calm avowal, "that though poor Mary might not wish to part with either, now they were come, to be sure she would sooner have had one at a time, if it had pleased God." "Sooner have had one at a time," I said, "what, when they look so beautiful, lying there together!" It was early spring, and when I left the house—(they lived then at an old-fashioned cottage at the bottom of a sloping garden, on the right hand side of the upper road)—some one gave me two or three half opened snow-drops. They were the first I had seen that year; and on my way home, my mind being full of the twin children, as I looked at the fair buds some common-place resemblances naturally enough presented themselves to me. They are as pure, I thought; come into as stormy a world; growing day by day more lovely; and I forget whether then I added, perhaps as soon to wither. But I am sure I did not always dwell on the last point of similarity, for when I visited them afterwards—and I did visit them very often —perhaps sometimes when the poor mother, delicate in her health, and fully occupied with the cares of a large family, could have dispensed with my company—I used to meditate, in a very romantic way, on the delights they would have in growing up together. I thought they would never be separated. I tried to believe that this little brother and sister would never wish for any other love than the pure and holy one of which I supposed nature must have implanted in their minds a double share. I fancied the sister, as she grew up, watching her brother's wishes, with woman's quickest perception, and most earnest desire to please, and the brother ever at her side, her protector, and guardian, and friend; and I usually ended by wishing I had a twin brother. Was I very silly, my patient reader? Did you ever hear of a romantic young lady being otherwise?

One day, when they were about six weeks old, I was much displeased at finding only one lying in the cradle. The other, the mother said, was asleep up-stairs. They disturbed each other, she said, and she had so much work to do that she was glad to let them sleep as long as she could. But her reasoning did not at all satisfy me. I thought it such a great pity to part them: they never looked so pretty as when they were together. I need not have troubled myself, they were not to be separated long. It was when the snowdrops came that I looked first on the little delicate creatures: the snow-drops faded, but the white roses and lilies of the valley opened just in time to strew in the short, wide coffin: death, that stern divider of most fellowships, seemed as eager as myself that here there should be no separation. I forget which died first, but the other little one lay quiet until then, and then perhaps hearing its fellow angel call—

"For they say, that little infants reply by smiles and signs,
 To the band of guardian angels that round about them shines."

—it struggled with the bands of mortality, rejoined its beloved companion, and they flew to heaven together. I saw them once more sleeping; but it was the sleep from which the mother's kiss may not awaken. The disorder which had carried them off having lasted only a few hours, had not in the least marred their beauty. They were still delicately formed and fair children. The eyes were closed, so as to show to advantage the long, soft eye-lashes, and the little dimpled hands were as beautifully rounded as a sculptor would desire to represent them in his pure marble; but they were as motionless as the marble, and as cold. I looked upon them no more, but I remember standing at the garden gate, and listening to the voice which told that "Almighty God, of his great mercy, had taken to himself the souls of our dear brother and sister." They rest together under the chestnut-tree, close to our garden-hedge, and though at the time I was very sorry to lose such pretty playthings, I have long ceased to regret them. When I see how very much evil there is in the world; how much "sin to blight," and how much "sorrow to fade," can I grieve that so many frail buds are transplanted, by the Lord of the garden, to a fairer climate? O no! Jesus said, "suffer the little children to come unto me," and I do believe he said it not only in reference to the group of young Israelites then gathered round him, nor *merely* as an encouragement to Christian parents to trust their living treasures to his care, but that his omniscient eye looked round, at that moment, on the innumerable multitude of those little ones, whom his free grace has, in all ages, called to glory.

Such thoughts always arise in my mind with a feeling of something like joy, as I watch the procession of an infant's funeral. A mother, indeed, cannot at the time comfort herself with these considerations. Rachel will weep for her children. Even when there have been several children, I have seen the remembrance of the lost little one cast a gloom over the mother's brow that the health and mirth of the rest have failed to dispel. So it was with her who has laid her darling close to our altar's rails. You cannot fail to find the grave, for it is marked by a white marble stone, bearing the name, and age, and date of the child's death. The parents came here strangers, and when they left the place, which they did soon after little Mary's funeral, there was not one relation whom the record could interest. But the mother's fancy, doubtless, often hovers round the holy spot, and she feels comforted at the thought, —" the grave cannot be lost, that simple epitaph must preserve it; it cannot be violated, for it is under the shadow of the chancel." She was buried, I well remember, on her birth-day; the day on which, twelve months before, her parents had welcomed their eldest daughter. It was on the first of April, and a very stormy day. The wind drove along before it dark masses of hail clouds, tore off and swept across the church-yard the half-opened leaves of the chestnut-trees, and shook down whole sprays of bud and blossom from the early fruit-trees. Ah! what apt emblems every spring brings with it! But little Mary's mother, though whilst she remained here, she never recovered her spirits, and though the large dark eyes were, during the few times I afterwards saw her, always filled with tears, I trust has since regained her cheerfulness. She had no daughter, but she had two fair and healthy little sons; so she ought to have thought herself a happy mother.

But have you ever observed a grave under the south wall of the church. The briar bush, which is cut down every year, and every year springs up so vigorously, grows close to the foot of it. There is no stone, but the poor lady, who has sometimes come from a distance to our church, knows well who sleeps there. I have seen her, when all the congregation was dispersed, and she thought herself unobserved, go round to the grave, and kneeling by it, hide her face, while the whole slight frame shook with the violence of her emotion. Then she would rise up and go away, and then come back and weep again, and stoop down and gather two or three violets or daisies, or if there was nothing else, some blades of the long grass that grew on the grave. Ah! that poor lady knew well who slept there: it was her son; her only son, whom she loved. I have heard that she was not happy in her married state, and perhaps she had hoped that the birth of this child might be the beginning of better days for her. Perhaps she had been long childless. Perhaps she had set her heart on this fair gourd, and trusted in its increasing shadow to be her shelter; having forgotten that all flesh is grass, and the grass withereth. Perhaps she made an "idol," and found it "clay." I cannot tell; but he was not, and she refused to be comforted.

I am afraid you must be tired, but one story more and I have done; and then we will seek for a livelier scene. The wife of the missionary who came home last spring, brought with her, from the far country where she had been long a sojourner, three noble boys. But they were not *all* her children. Her youngest was not with her. Did he sleep, then, under the stately mimosa, or the beautiful palm-tree, beneath the shadow of the church raised to the name of the Christian's God, in the land of idols? Then, perhaps, his swarthy nurse sits on his grave, and tells how the gentle white lady devoted her child to her Saviour in baptism, and found comfort when he died, and how she, poor heathen as she had been, had learnt submission from the Christian's submission, and wisdom from the Christian's book, and now having faith in Christ, lived in the calm hope of meeting again those her kind instructors, and that her foster-son. No! the Missionary's child is not buried there: he, died on the voyage home: he was buried in the deep sea: so neither nurse nor mother may look upon his grave; but his little coffin was made as neatly as circumstances permitted, and the ceremony of his funeral was conducted with all that attention to order and propriety which it is the last comfort of survivors to pay. All the children, and there were many on board beside his own little brothers, went on deck and stood round the corpse whilst the beautiful service was read; and it was solemnly and affectingly read, by the beloved friend and fellow-labourer who had been a stranger with them in the strange land. It was sad to be obliged to take the *last* look at the dear child even before "the first day of death was fled." There was something inexpressibly melancholy in the plunge with which the lost treasure sunk down, deeper and deeper, to the depths which no line has sounded; and the waves rolled on, and the gallant ship hastened on her course, so that the eye of man might never again know the place of his rest. But Thou, Lord, art the hope of them that remain in the broad sea! So thought his mother whilst she wept in silence; but she looked for the resurrection of the body, (when the sea shall give up her dead) and she was calm.

I have always thought, that of the many troubles which woman's heart feels, the loss of infant children, deep as it must be, is the one which most readily yields to the comforts of religion, and the expressions of many mothers with whom I have conversed, have confirmed me in my opinion. "I did all that lay in my power to do for him," said my favourite Millicent to me, "I should ill deserve to be called mother if I had not, but now he is better provided for." "Mine was a sweet-tempered child," said another, "but none too good for Him who has taken it." "Little dear!" said poor Amy, when last year she buried her youngest of thirteen, "he was as fair a baby as ever the sun shone upon." She wept much, for she was one of those in whose hearts extreme poverty and distress fails to deaden either the warmest or gentlest feelings of woman's nature. "Mine was as fair a baby as ever the sun shone upon, but none too fair for the place he has gone to!" But I have said enough on the subject in prose, I think, so I will finish my chapter with some verses which occurred to me when I was thinking of little Mary's grave.

> Ours is a garden green and fair,
>   And bright with flowers in June,
> And spicy shrubs waft odours there
>   To the high harvest moon;
> But in spring hours we scarce know why,
> Our snow-drops only come and die.
>
> The chestnut's solemn boughs disclos
>   Their thousand blossoms well,
> And hither comes luxuriant rose
>   Her tale of love to tell;
> The snow-drops tremble, and are gone
> From the chill world they glanced upon.

And she was like a bud that died,
  Forgot by all but me,—
But often at our altar's side,
  When her low grave I see,
I think how those first flowers of spring
Fade in their earliest blossoming.

She sleeps not in her father's tomb,
  Nor when their days are past,
To rest them in this shadow'd gloom
  Shall kindred come at last.
Beneath this little marble stone
One infant corpse must rest alone.

O, blessed lot! ere guilt and care
  That smile of innocence belie,
To hide in mother's arms—and there
  Where one has lived—to die.
No dust defiles spring's first-born flower,
No blight is in the snow-drop's bower.

Yet more—'tis to the infant dead
  The blessed word is given;
"Their angels live!" the Saviour said,
  " Round the bright throne in heaven!"
No storm those stainless flowers shall tear,
The snow-drops never wither there!

JANUARY 23, 1830.

# MARY, THE SAILOR'S WIDOW.

> And what her learning? 'Tis with awe to look
> In every verse throughout one sacred book,
> From this her joy, her hope, her peace is sought;
> This she has learn'd—and she is nobly taught.
> CRABBE.

It is just the weather when country people, that is, people like some I have known, who really love the country, and are determined that every body else shall think so, make a point of taking a walk. To be sure it is very dirty under foot, and very gloomy over head, and a cold rain-drop, that has not determined whether or not to become an icicle, hangs from every spray; but there is a feeling of independence with which a thoroughly-bred country woman sets out for a walk in such weather, that she would do ill to exchange for the ease of a luxurious ride; and a degree of pleasure when she considers the exact suitability of her dress to the place and season, which more delicate and costly array does not always afford. The bright, broad pattern plaid, real double Scotch and nearly as thick and heavy as a carpet, is an old friend, has been wet many times, but never wet through, has kept out many hail-storms, and will probably keep out many more; and the snug cottage bonnet,—rather coarse plat, I should guess it was home manufacture—is of far too decorous a shape to think of flying away with the wind, should it blow ever so hard: then the pattens, which, after all, are necessary evils, add a little to one's stature, so that through the degree of self-approval felt, on making a successful effort to leave the fire-side in such weather, the amplitude given to the figure by the capacious foldings of the cloak, and the increased height, this is just the time to feel a person of consequence. And yet the consequence is materially increased by the comfortable contents of the little covered basket. Ah! we are only the bearers of another's bounty. I can guess who has filled it so kindly, and I know who it is for—poor Mary, the Sailor's widow.

If we go the field-way we shall meet with few interruptions; and we will look as we pass the side of the church-yard hedge, perhaps we shall find some of those very fragrant and singular flowers, the scented coltsfoot. Yes; there is one half hidden by its broad rough leaf: it is not a wild plant: we set it in the garden border, on the shady side; but though a winter flower, the little thing did not understand why it was to be deprived of the degree of sunshine, winter could afford, so it broke through all hindrances, forced its tough and knotted fibres through the heavy clods of clay, shot up its broad leaves on the graves, and amongst the nettles and thorns; and in the first gleam of a December sun, lifted up its pale and fragrant blossoms, smiling for joy at having accomplished its purpose. And, really the little flower was right. I have learned, lately, that in so stormy a world as this, sunshine is a thing worth seeking, and to be yet more serious, we should all be wiser, if, like that little flower, we sought happiness in—what ought to be the human soul's sunshine—the light of God's countenance, though it shine amid the thorns and nettles of affliction; aye, and on the very borders of the grave. I am happy to say I know many who understand the secret, and poor Mary is one of them. She has had great troubles, but the Psalmist's God "delivereth out of all." When quite young she lost her mother, and, oh! how much is told in that little sentence! How many kindnesses unperformed! sorrows unsoothed! hours of sickness unattended! Her father married again, and she, a child of seven years old, was sent to a farm-house, to nurse an infant, and to wait upon two or three children younger than herself. Being naturally of a tender and affectionate disposition, she felt her situation more than some older children might have done; and she has told me that she used sometimes to steal away from her little charge, and sitting down under the hedge, hide her face in her pinafore, and cry for her mother; and the sound of the tolling bell would generally awaken a passionate expression of grief, and a wish that it was tolling for her, that she might see her mother. But if the sorrows of children are as hard to bear as the troubles of maturer years, they certainly do not last so long, and He, who, when father and mother forsake, taketh up, raised up for poor Mary, in her next place of service, a kind and watchful friend. Those times were not called so 'liberal' as the present, whether these are wiser and better remains to be proved; and Mary's old-fashioned mistress, besides teaching her the Catechism, and hearing her daily read the Bible, expected her to attend, twice on every Sunday, the ordinances of the church, by God's mercy established in her native land. She did attend—long, perhaps because it was a duty to obey her mistress; afterwards, possibly, because it was a decent and respectable habit; but it has been my lot to know, in more than one instance, that the God of order is often pleased to bless an orderly and regular attendance on the outward means with his inward and spiritual grace. (I wish every one thought so, the churchpath between this avenue of trees would be better trodden.) So it was in her case. She was preserved from the many evils to which she was exposed after the death of her excellent mistress, and providentially provided for, day by day, when ill health compelled her to leave her place, and she applied diligently to learn the trade of a glove-maker. She took lodgings with a respectable young woman, whose husband was at sea; and on his return he brought home with him his brother-in-law, Mary's future husband. I do not wonder the young sailor liked her, so very neat in her person, so civil and industrious, and so pretty as I am sure she must have been then.

Perhaps you can fancy, better than I can tell you, all that happened next; how happy they were together; what pleasant walks they took in each other's company, at twilight on summer evenings; how poor Mary wept at parting, and lay awake listening to the high wind on long stormy nights; and when he came home, how he used to bring her curious things from beyond sea—beautifully polished shells, such as our English fish never heard of; ears of Indian corn; and little pictures of the " *Madonna*," cut curiously at the nunneries; and cocoa-nuts, and a coloured basket from Portugal, and all sorts of things from all quarters of the world; for he made many voyages, both before and after their marriage; and you can fancy that the gifts he brought were very precious, and some of them we may still see hanging in different parts of her neat house, and carefully treasured there; for the hand that gave them is in the grave.

It will be well to walk a little faster. It needs some philosophy to own, that, in weather like this, it is a duty and may be a pleasure to walk at all, for the wind is piercing on the brow of this hilly field, yet the mist hangs so sullenly on the river, and over the beautiful fields beyond, that we cannot enjoy the fair prospect. The lanes into which we next enter are more sheltered, and if we were disposed to loiter, we might even now find wonders enough, and beauties enough, for a long day's consideration, in the leafless hedges and the withered banks. For in the hollows lie masses of snow, that came from the region of heaven, to show us the brightness of those garments which are white," as no fuller on earth can white them;" which comes we know not whence, and will return we cannot tell how; and where it has melted it discovers to us long, shining wreaths of ivy, and beneath the dark leaves the soft green moss, of which nature weaves her velvet inner robe at this cold season, and in which she wraps up her delicate children, young buds, and seeds, and sprouting roots; and of which she forms secret and warm hiding-places, for innumerable glittering insects, through their quiet winter sleep. I like to look at moss, for it reminds me of poor Mungo Park, and the comfort he once derived from the thought that the God who had made so beautiful, and so tenderly guarded *this*, one of his meanest creatures, would not surely be unmindful of him.

But if I do not go on with my story, I shall get to Mary's house, before I have told you all. She married: but a sailor's wife, I always think, must have a double share of sad partings and feverish anxieties. Poor Mary at least found it so. Her husband was long in a French prison, saw dangerous service at the taking of Gibraltar, and was at the siege of Genoa. During many years she had few months of his company, and once he was absent from her for more than three years. All this time she diligently followed her business, living with her sister-in-law. They were fellow-sufferers, for their husbands served on board the same ship; so having like hopes and fears, they were well suited to each other's society; and Mary looks back, with evident pleasure, to the remembrance of those quiet months, and speaks with satisfaction of the regard which was always maintained between herself and her sister, by a scrupulous attention to the discharge of every day duties, and by paying that degree of respect, (which is too often neglected amongst near relations even in more polished society) but which, after all, is perhaps the surest way of securing esteem, and consequently of maintaining real friendship.

But the years passed on, and his country was willing that her weather-beaten servant should rest at last. Samuel came home from the last voyage, and receiving his well-earned pension, brought his wife from the country where she had all her life resided, to our parish, which was his native place. She was our next door neighbour for years, but I was a child then, and knew nothing about her but her name. Her husband's pension amounted to sixteen pounds a year, and she was still able to increase her little income by her business, but the greatest earthly blessing, health, was lost to them both forever. The small house in which they lived is pleasantly situated, and was, I am sure,—for she is one of the neatest women I ever knew—kept in beautiful order. Her husband had no temptation certainly, and I believe never did seek for any recreation but what his own little garden afforded. I never remember meeting them in our walks, but I can recollect when the rulers of our school-room were absent, clambering into the window-seat, and standing on tip-toe, to watch Mr. and Mrs. North, (for they were dignified by their title then, or at least we called them so, being brought up according to the old "regime," and taught to respect our elders) so we used to scramble into the window-seat, as I said before, standing on tip-toe, and stretching head above head, to watch them set out for church. I see them now, in my mind's eye; she in her neat sage-coloured pelisse and straw bonnet, and he in his comfortable great coat and sailor's trowsers, and black silk handkerchief; but they used to walk feebly and slowly; neither had an arm strong enough to support the other, so each leaned on a walking stick; his constitution was rapidly giving way under the hardships which he had undergone; and she, though scarcely past the meridian of life, was evidently sinking under the influence of some unseen but incurable malady. At that time, indeed, comfortable as they were to outward appearance, she had to undergo more than any one knew, except as she sometimes says with tears, her heavenly Father and herself. And she has told me how, for days together, she has watched alone with her husband, when he was unable by any means, to obtain one hour's respite from agonizing pain, how she has risen to wait upon him, night after night, and many times in the night, and month after month; and how, when she had taken pains to prepare nicely their comfortable meal, it was laid aside untasted, because he was too ill, and she too sad, to feel any disposition for it.

Alas! is not this the *real* version of many a story which tells of the happiness of the sailor's or soldier's rest, in his proud native land, when his toil is done? Oh! happy they who expect repose only in that country, where "there is no more sea," and where they "learn war no more!" It was no wonder the anxious wife became weak; no wonder that her weakness increased, so that her hands refusing their accustomed task, her business was laid aside. Then her husband died suddenly, and she ceased to receive his pension; and I have heard her tell, how, on the day of his death, their wedding-day seventeen years before, she found herself a widow with one shilling, and only one; and the expenses of the funeral to be paid. But her landlord is a very clever man in his way, bustling and managing; he bid her "take heart," he would provide for the funeral; so he took possession of her husband's wardrobe, which was much better than that of most poor men, and disposing of the different articles amongst his work-people, without losing a shilling himself, or giving his poor tenant one, he certainly lightened her mind of a heavy burthen. But if one was taken away, many must have been left, and it must have been with a very sad heart that the poor widow applied for the small pittance which yet was all that a parish, overburthened with poor, could be expected to supply; it must have been very reluctantly that she, who had been so long mistress of her neat house, left it to seek lodgings; and she was tempted, perhaps, to doubt the care of her heavenly Father, when she considered that, just when she needed most, her increasing illness entirely put it out of her power to make the smallest exertion on her own behalf. In a short time she went to the Infirmary, and though in patience and humility she submitted to the various trying remedies which it was thought needful to apply, she was, at the end of thirty-six long weeks, sent out as incurable. Incurable, indeed, as to the suffering body, but to the troubled soul the pious labours of one who at that time ministered there in holy things had been abundantly blessed. It would ill become me to praise him. I have known others beside Mary who have blessed his simple and earnest manner of preaching the truth as it is in Jesus; who have experienced his unwearied attention and his laborious exertion, but his record is on high.

Mary returned, patient and cheerful, to her former lodgings, and then our acquaintance with her commenced. She endeavoured, but in vain, to sit up, as she had been accustomed to do; so she took to her bed, and set about discovering the most useful ways of employing herself. She found that she could do a little needle-work sometimes, and the kind widow with whom she lodged agreed to receive this very small requital as payment for her washing. Is there not something beautiful in observing how our God provides for all those little wants of his people which we, in our pride, think too mean to mention? Ah! our Lord did not say in vain, "Your Father knoweth that ye have need of these things." When she was tired of work she could read, and though her Bible and Olney Hymns of themselves occupy most of her time, yet she has many kind neighbours, who lend her various books and tracts, all good in their way, and she likes them all. I speak in the present time, for her employments are much the same as they were; but her hostess, the widow, married, and Mary thinking wisely that brides and bride-grooms are the fittest company for each other, settled herself anew with a very old woman, as clean in her house and person as possible, but altogether deaf and not altogether good-tempered. She was pleased to see her kitchen adorned with Mary's neat furniture, and she certainly liked so respectable a lodger, though she sometimes grumbled a little at the unavoidable trouble she gave; and notwithstanding all her infirmities, she was certainly a very suitable guardian for our poor cripple; a degree of affection subsisted between them; and it was with real concern that we saw the old woman confined to her bed, by what appeared a last illness, and Mary necessarily obliged to seek a home elsewhere. For moving, although our little cart, our lively horse, and our grave man, were always put in requisition, and I am sure ought to have felt honoured in the service, yet cost her some shillings, which she little knew how to afford; and beside, when she and old Sarah parted, she could not find one person who would receive her, helpless as she was, at the very low sum she had been accustomed to pay. "How I shall give more," she said to me, "I cannot tell, but my Lord can tell. Or how I shall find bread to eat (and her lip quivered, and the colour rose on her cheek, and the tear in her bright eyes) how I shall find bread to eat, I do not know, but the Lord knows."

My fancied companion, whoever you may be, feel as poor Mary felt, and I have not told my story in vain. Well, her next removal saw her settled much nearer the church, with a very grave and demure matron, of (as we might read in an old book) a very serious, but not a very sweet aspect. Her handkerchief was always exactly pinned, and I should think she never wore a soiled cap or apron in her life. She had many good points, I dare say, but I never could like her. I was always afraid of offending her, and never in my life met with any one to whom it seemed so difficult to do a kindness. She certainly must have the organ for misunderstanding, if there is such an organ, and if there be any truth in craniology. It would not do long, and we bore all the blame of Mary's giving notice to quit; but indeed we had nothing at all to do with it, except as much as we could, forwarding her removal when it came to the point.

She settled in the Marsh again; sometimes was kindly, and sometimes unkindly treated, and once was left for many days in the house by herself, with half-a-crown's rent to pay out of the three shillings which formed her whole week's income. But when she most wanted a friend, some good neighbour was always sure to come in, and her landlord kindly refused to take the money, which she scrupulously sent. In all her different habitations we have been her constant visiters, and certainly if we have at any time taken pains to serve her, if we have sometimes been exposed to rough weather or unpleasant walks, we have been repaid threefold by her gratitude and her affection. But here we come to one of my country stiles, the last we shall have, luckily, and as it is a specimen of its peculiar kind, we will stop to examine it. No doubt there was here, once, a tolerably passable stile, with straight posts and even bars, as a stile in a civilized country might be expected to have. But some of my compatriots having, I suppose, good reasons of their own, generally demolish every thing that looks like a legitimate boundary. I have heard a story, and that from the very best authority, of a farmer—churchwarden he was in his time, who planted a good hedge one day, rose up to visit it the next morning, and it was gone—the whole hedge gone on the first night. That was twenty years ago: I believe they are much improved since then; still, however, some people call them a lawless set, and hint that they still would thus gladly make "right of common," to turn in their own half-starved quadrupeds to forage in their neighbours' ground: others say that a barge comes down the river at evening, and lying under the shelter of the hill, is ready to receive and carry away, before morning, any thing and every thing that can be smuggled into it—chicken, or knives, or posts, or hay, or stiles, or the great copper boiler. But I do not wish to be suspicious: I would gladly think my poor countrymen "all honourable men." Their antipathy to new gates is certainly an awkward and provoking particular, but the ruder barriers which usually supply their places, are almost almost more fit for drawing; so perhaps it may be from a love of the picturesque.

Am I trifling when I should be serious? Believe me, I do my from heart wish them "to know the way of truth, which they have not known ;" and that "the fear of God might be before their eyes." But I do not believe, considering the population, there are a larger proportion of the worst characters here than elsewhere; and those who are most willing to give our Forest a bad name, have not the opportunities I have, of knowing how little it deserves it. But however this may be, the difficult stile is to be passed notwithstanding; under and on either side, the ground is much|more muddy than any thing we have met with yet, in our muddy walk: so we cannot creep through, and the bars being made of two rough and knotted branches, the lowest somewhat more than two feet and a half from the ground, and the one bending out, and the other as awkwardly bending in; and many twigs and pieces of bark threatening, or that would make good the threat, to tear ladies' delicate clothes, if we had such on. All these circumstances make it doubtful how we shall get over; but we are used to these things; our stern, grave collier, with his candle in his hat, and his full sack of coal on his shoulder, strides across without condescending to notice that it is an impediment: and the upright market-woman, as she gets over, does not lift a hand to the heavily-laden basket, which she poises so steadily on her head: and for ourselves, though our little package requires care; we have only to lean down, and put that in safety first, and then—practice makes perfect—one hand on the rough bough, and a spring, and we are over, pattens and all. And now we are here in the lane, the most melancholy looking lane in the parish, I was going to say; but that word will not do; there is something in that word interesting and "gentlemanlike;" so I am sure it cannot be melancholy, but it is in the superlative degree ugly and gloomy.

The mud, which is the colour of coal-dust, is almost impassable, except that the deep ruts have been in various places filled with flinty black dross, from the smoky lead works below; the ditches are wide, and full of dark-coloured snow, which in some places discovers the yet darker and frozen surface of the stagnant water beneath; the ill-made banks have in many places given way, so that the low briar hedges are shattered and uneven.

But we are almost at our journey's end, that is Mary's house, the lowest and nearest to us: there is nothing shattered or uncomfortable there, for her kind landlord has had it neatly repaired for her, and she is mistress of it herself, paying eighteen pence a week for rent; and old Sarah, wonderful to tell, is quite recovered, and has come to live with her, and take care of her; and for the present, at least, they are both happier than they have been for a long time; and we will delight old deaf Sarah, by making signs and notes of admiration, at the beautiful cleanliness and order of the little establishment, by pointing at the white wall, and gazing at the long rows of various crockery-ware, for I have given up the attempt to make her hear, as a thing quite out of the question; and we shall see Mary's ears of Indian corn, and her curious Portuguese basket, and her bed-side carpet, wrought, she says, to represent the English colours above the French ones. And she will be well pleased to see us; and if we can learn gratitude from her thankfulness, and cheerfulness from her content, we shall have cause to be pleased also, that we left the fire-side, on this cheerless February day, and came through cold and mud to visit the sailor's widow.

*February*, 3, 1830.

# THE LAST OF THE FAMILY.

" Thus they rest"———————
———" They that with smiles lit up the hall,
And cheer'd with joy the hearth,—
Alas! for love, if *thou* wert all,
And nought beyond—Oh, earth!"—Mrs. HEMANS.

"THE last of the family!" I said to myself, repeating the words with which our clerk had just answered my question as to who was going to be buried? "The last of the family! the last of the name!" and then, perhaps, my thoughts might have wandered to very old tombs, with their illegible inscriptions; and to the statues of knights, with the emblems of their holy warfare; and so, to the reclining figures, with the ruffs and peaked beards of the days of the cavaliers; and on to stately monuments of my lord and lady, in the full court dress of the time of George the First; and last, to the plain but massy marble tablet, with the Grecian ornaments of the present day; and I might have fancied the filling up of the vacant space, that told how the last of a mighty race had come to his kindred dead and his long home; and the raising of the last escutcheon, with its death's-head crest, used only, say the old books of heraldry, to show that death has conquered all, into its gloomy abiding place. I might perhaps, but there was no deeper shadow than that of the green chestnut, over the open grave by which I stood; and I well knew that our church-yard was not a place wherein to nurse the recollections of centuries gone by, because seventy years ago there was no church there. Seventy years ago, and where was this chestnut-tree? A slender sapling it must have been then, when the weight of the wood-pigeon could sway it to the very root; and I can remember the old man who planted it. He was father to him who is to be buried to-night, and a very great favourite the old man was with us children, when we followed him about, as he was doing his easy day's work in our garden. To be sure, sometimes we made him angry by scuffling about the gravel which he had been rolling, or by running away with a curious instrument of his, which he used to call his half-moon, and which we found very useful for digging in our own strangely-cultivated gardens: but generally he was very good-natured, and generally, I hope, we were civil to him; and he loved to talk, and we to listen to the story of the days of his youth, when he and his wife danced at the laying of the foundation-stone of the church; and he used to tell us how decently he had brought up his family, and how much he had seen, and how very much he had done, and often concluded by lifting up his hands and exclaiming, "And I had nothing but what these little hands worked for." Oh! what a picture of an old man he was; small in stature, but of really a beautiful face, with flowing locks of shining white hair, and bright blue eyes, and a clear and healthy, but still fair complexion. Oh! what a picture of an old man he was! I have his figure before me now, as on one bright Whit-Monday, when the clubs and their bands of music were coming across the green to church, he stood pulling the bell outside the belfry-door; for, amidst his many avocations, he was bell-ringer; at least if ours may be called bell-ringing, when we boast but of two bells—one great and one small. He was tolling the little bell then, to call the congregation to church; and hearing the glad sound of the procession, and the loyal music, and wishing to be there to spy, he wisely bethought him of the expedient of pulling the bell-rope, which fortunately was long enough, through the door into the church-yard. And there he stood in the sunshine, the fresh wind blowing his long silver hair, pulling with all his might, and his head turned quite the other way, to gaze at the floating flags and the thronging people; and no doubt he complimented himself at thus having found a plan to combine duty and pleasure. He used to look very handsome in his Sunday dress, but perhaps more picturesque in his still more old-fashioned working-day costume, with his brown gaiters and his blue woollen apron; how pleased we used to be to help him, when at Christmas he came to gather sprays of our variegated holly, to help dress up the church; and year after year, it gave our young hearts a momentary pang to hear him say, "Ah! I shall never trouble ye again;" and I remember the very last time he came tottering on crutches, and when we had filled his apron, and tied it up for him as well as we could, as he was slowly going away down the narrow path leading to the church-yard gate, the apron gave way, and all the laurel and holly-boughs fell down. We gathered round him, and filling our pinbefores, carried the evergreens for him into the church, and he said once more, and for the last time, " God bless ye all!" and "thank ye, I shall never trouble ye again!"

Poor old Thomas! he never did; but that is not so many years ago, and he might be called the first of his family,—certainly the first I remember, and the eldest buried under the shadow of this chestnut; the first in point of age I mean, for his grandson Philip died several years before him. But are not any of his own children left? Has not our clerk mistaken? And his son—the man who is to be buried to-night, what is become of all his children? For he had as fair a family, and that not of little delicate ones—not of tender infants, grouped together like a spray of blossoms, of which we are sure that not half can come to maturity. No; his "flowers were in flushing"—all grown up to man and woman's estate. "They were five fair children, beautiful young men and women," said the heart-broken mother; and it was not only the mother's partial heart that thought so; every one says that three of them were very handsome young men, and that the young women were two of the prettiest in the country. And is there not one to come to his funeral to-night? Not one! not one! Philip, the eldest, has been dead almost twenty years, and he was nearly twenty-one when he died. In common with most young men of that age, he was of a joyous and enterprising temper, and in his health possessed of an unbroken flow of high spirits; but he had also, what in men is not so common, a remarkably tender affection to his mother and to his old grandmother, who, in return, were dotingly attached to their handsome and dutiful child. He was one of the first scholars brought up in our parish school, and by all, the very little account I can collect of him, he did it credit. He could read his Bible with ease; he did read it, and from that unfailing source derived that consolation for which he found much need during his lingering and wasting sickness. It was consumption; but consumption is a flatterer, and after many changes, much weakness, and great apparent recovery of strength, he one morning found himself so well, as earnestly to request his mother's permission to join a party of bell-ringers, on occasion, I believe, of some victory. He would not go, he said, if she said "no;" but he earnestly begged her to say, "yes." How could his mother refuse him? and then she had nursed him in his illness so long, and was so pleased to see him better. Dear creature! she could not bear to disappoint him; yet as she tied an additional handkerchief round his neck, and bade God bless him, the tears came into her eyes, and dimmed her sight as she watched him down the road. He promised to come back early, and he kept his word; but it was only to say, with the poor huntsman, in that old and touching ballad,

" O, I am weary mother! make my bed soon,
 For I'm weary, I'm weary, and fain would lie down."

Poor Philip! This happened, I think, in the winter; and he died, says the head-stone, on the 10th March, 1811, aged 21 years.

Then died one whose very name is forgotten. In the leaf of the old Bible it was perhaps written—doubtless it was engraven in his mother's heart, but the first record was worthless to the strangers into whose hands it fell, and they have erased it; and for the second, love is stronger than death, and we will trust that the spirit which cherished the memory of her lost ones to the brink of the grave, has ere this recognized them in that land where remembrance is exchanged for presence—where "an enemy never entered, and from whence a friend never went away."*

Then, but with the space of some years, they lost their daughter Elizabeth. She was for some time our next door neighbour. She came a bride to the pleasant cottage afterwards inhabited by the sailor and his wife, and she lived there in great comfort during her short married life. Like all her family, she was remarkably pretty. Certainly there is something extremely lovely in that clear delicacy of complexion, that sparkling brilliancy of eye, and that

* Bp. Jeremy Taylor.

changeful but always beautiful colour, which we usually see in consumptive patients. Within the first year of her marriage she became a mother, and from that time the sweet flower faded. The eye became more glittering, the blue veins more clearly defined on the pure temple and down the thin cheek; the colour was brighter but more changeful, and the delicate lips became yet more delicate and paler. We were sent over once with some little present to her, and young as we were—my dear companion will, I dare say, remember how much we were struck by the contrast which her beauty presented to that of her young neighbour, Honour, who chanced just then to bring her in a nosegay, such as country people make of marygolds and thyme, boy's love, gillyflower, and sweet peas. (Poor Honour! she must have missed that sunny garden of hers, when she went to live in the narrow close street in town.) Perhaps I have never seen two prettier women together since. Honour, a healthy, cheerful looking country girl, tall and well formed, with bright auburn hair, merry blue eyes, and a rosy colour; and the other so sadly, so touchingly beautiful : her dark hair braided back, as if, lest the weight of the heavy curls should increase the fever that swelled the veins and flushed the pale cheek. Her attenuated hands and her weak arms, sinking, as it were, from the weight of the small infant which yet they clasped so lovingly, and on which her bright melancholy eyes gazed with such unspeakable tenderness. And Honour stood looking on the form which was "wearing awa, like snaw wreath in thaw," with an expression of interest and compassion which added grace to her beauty. It was a sweet picture; I have not done it justice, but I think I shall never forget it. Poor Elizabeth! I hope and believe she never wanted sympathy or kindness; every one was interested for her; for her kind husband and her poor baby.

Death is always awful: we weep indeed, and tremble, even when the Lord's blessing rests on the righteous as he goes "to his grave in a full age, like a shock of corn in his season;" but when the green ear is blighted, when the young tree is felled, when the wind sweeps over the budding flower, and it is gone, and the place thereof knows it no more; then indeed, in the expressive language of holy writ, "our hearts faint, and our eyes are dim, and even all the merry-hearted do sigh."

Poor Elizabeth! many real mourners followed her to her grave, besides her husband, and her poor little girl, whose long white robe made a strange and sad contrast to the band of black love ribbon and the black rosette on her cap. It is a sad sight to see an infant in mourning for its mother, but it has been my lot to see it very often. And yet it is something more strange and sadder still, to see the bending and tottering form of the parent come, time after time, to the grave in which he longs to rest himself; but of which those whom he expected to be the strength of his age, take a premature possession. How the poor mother must have trembled when she saw once more the dreaded and now well-known symptoms appear in her only remaining son. She nursed him, and watched by him, but it was hopelessly, or only with "the hope that keeps alive despair." From the hour that the cough came, she knew George could not live, but she prayed that he might be made fit to die. We know whose promise runs thus—"Whilst they are yet speaking, I will hear." So I have good reason to believe there was hope in his end, and after a while his mother was comforted; and she had still one dear daughter left. This was her youngest, Susan, whom I remember seeing once, and only once. It was at the time of a contested election; and I recollect her blush and smile, as at her mother's bidding, she took off her bonnet to exhibit the shining blue ribbon, which one of our tory member's family had given her. All her relations, in common, I believe, with our parishioners in general, are attached—deservedly attached to that family, and to what we used to call the *high party*. Now, indeed, things are so strangely altered that we cannot exactly tell what to call ourselves. We *were* a very loyal parish, and so we *are*— "true blue" is our colour still—the colour of the gallant Falkland, and the colour of true faith, and of the unchanging sky. We may be in the minority, but we, who were born subjects to George the Third, cannot readily learn to speak evil of the rulers of our people. Oh! we feel ourselves "true blue" still; and truly our native member represented us at the last sessions.

We may yet see better times; there are right spirits

among us yet. How the people thronged to sign our petitions, surely with steady hearts, though by some unskilful hands. How we sent up parchment after parchment; and one man, who had chanced to miss the opportunity of signing, ran six miles, during the time allowed for rest at noon, and finding the throng so great that then he could not accomplish his purpose, took the same run the next day, and succeeded. There were true hearts among us. Poor things! their petitions deserved better treatment than they met with; but God give us right Protestant feelings, and we shall be able to bear whatever may come.

But women, you think, have little to do with politics and state affairs. An Englishwoman, however, may be forgiven for feeling an impassioned love to her own land—a deep grief when "any wrong her," that will sometimes express itself in words. Though I will own, untimely attention to high affairs may carry her away from the duties of her narrow sphere, as it has me from my story, for indeed I have gone a great way from pretty Susan and her blue ribbon. She married, and went to live in town; she was very happy, I believe, and it seemed that the warm situation agreed with her better than the air of our bleak hills; and for some time there appeared cause to hope that she might yet be spared to nurse and comfort her old father and mother, in their last hours. She was now older than either of her brothers or her sister had lived to be, and every year added to her poor mother's trembling hopes. She had a lovely baby too, and yet her strength returned, and she continued well. No wonder the poor mother flattered herself—no wonder she looked on this daughter as if all the love she had ever borne to all her children was centred in her. But Susan again became a mother, and then the family disease showed itself in her constitution. Her mother endeavoured to say "thy will be done," but though the heart consented, the voice refused, and her utmost effort only enabled her, like Aaron, to "hold her peace." All care was taken of poor Susan; every effort made to save her, but in vain. She wasted away as the rest had done; she died, and was buried in a city churchyard, with her husband's family. Then her parents felt that all was over: so the earth was filled up, and the grieving mother turned away from the grave of her last child.

To her, I doubt not, her heavy afflictions have been greatly blessed. She was humble and uncomplaining in her deportment, though indeed sometimes her heart appeared almost broken. She was very neat in her person, and to the last time I saw her, exhibited marks of having possessed that beauty which was so remarkable in her children.

I am sorry I know so little about her. It was my own fault, for I never went there without being welcomed; and never read her a chapter or a psalm, but that she listened with quiet tears, which showed how deeply she was interested. She was for her age, very infirm, who could wonder at it, when she had so long had to say with Naomi, "the Almighty hath dealt very bitterly with me." Yet weakly as she was, her death appears to me to have been almost sudden—at least I never heard of her being ill, until I also heard that no kindness and no attention from us could any more avail her. It is not the uncertainty of our own lives alone, but that also of others, which should make us remember, whilst we have time, "to do good unto all men." She died a few months since: her husband saw her laid here with her children; now the bell strikes out, and his own funeral is coming. There are a decent number of acquaintance and neighbours: they are grave and silent, but there is no expression of grief amongst them: there is no sorrowing brother or sister—no affectionate son—no weeping daughter there. And when the service is over, they will disperse quietly, mention him for a day or two, and then Philip's name will be forgotten: no one will trouble himself to see it engraven in its place on the tombstone: the freshly-heaped earth will soon sink down to a level with the path beside it. Many will not observe it; and a few, remembering who sleeps there, will feel that our clerk was right—"It is the grave of the last of the family."

*March* 5, 1830.

# THE DORCAS MEETING.

"Give wings to fancy, and among us come,
Tis near the hour, and we must soon attend;
I'll introduce you: 'Gentlemen! my friend!'"
CRABBE.

By this time I fear you are beginning to think me a very dull companion, and indeed when I review the scenes which I have exhibited to you, I am almost disposed to plead guilty. Come, then, I will introduce you to a little of the gaiety of our parish—to the "belle assemblée" of our Dorcas Association. It is just the right time too, for the moon is at the full, and we, like the fairies, choose that pleasant hour for our nightly meetings: not so much, however, for the romance, as for the safety and comfort of the thing. It is quite time to go, for it is long past four: show no city airs, if you please, at our early hours, and Thomas has been waiting and grumbling between the back door and the stable this quarter of an hour: and the little horse is harnessed, and the carriage is ready. You are astonished I see, but we do keep a carriage; only an open cart, but there is no time now for rude remarks, and we must make haste to clamber in: the easiest plan is to mount the leaping stock, against which the vehicle is drawn as closely as the horse will permit, and so step over the side into it. There are no seats but you will find yourself wonderfully comfortable on the bundles of straw which, to do him justice, Thomas takes great pains in arranging on these occasions. He covers the bottom of the cart with hay, so that our feet are in no danger of becoming cold, especially as by the time we are all in, we shall be pretty closely packed.

Having so convenient an equipage, we always consider it a point of politeness to offer a seat to our near neighbours, and now we are stopping for the purpose. "You are very full to night," says our friend; "Susan shall go another time." "O no, no," say half a dozen voices at once; "dear little Susan must not be disappointed." "I can put her into the pocket of my plaid," said one: "We can pack Susan in the hay at the bottom," said another. So the little girl, who was beginning to look rather grave, was lifted in amongst us, I cannot exactly tell where. We were crowded to be sure, but on these occasions "the more, the merrier." Thomas banged the tail-board into its place, and in answer to one, who, I shrewdly suspect, had no intention of exercising such self-denial, offered to walk, as the horse had so heavy a burden, replied in that deep sepulchral tone, seldom heard indeed, but which those who have heard can scarcely forget, and which others can hardly fancy, "the horse can go well enough;" and then, with a sort of sneer at our want of taste. "you may ride if you please; I'd rather walk by half myself." Then he got up in front, and away we drove over the new stones and through the old ruts, at a rate that shook us, closely packed as we were. Some kept their seats on the sloping sides of the cart, from which the bundles of straw soon slip down, pretty well. Others slid down after them, making vain and repeated efforts to settle it and themselves as they were before; and the wiser part, remembering that those who are on the ground can go no lower, fairly seated themselves on the hay at the bottom. All called to Thomas to go more slowly, but he made a slight mistake in the meaning of our entreaty, and went faster and faster: and we were every moment more and more shaken, and jolted, and tumbled.

But we are going to an evening party, and you are wondering how we manage with regard to our dress. I will tell you a secret; if you wear no finery, you have none to spoil; if you deck yourself in no jewelry, you can lose none; and if you carefully pin up your clean gown, and put a responsible cloak over it, you may ride in the rain a long way, in a jolting cart, and yet get it neither soiled nor torn. We were very merry, and rather noisy, I am afraid, when we first set out, but now, don't you observe, we are getting grave, and really, strange to say, almost silent. It is beginning to rain a little, so we wrap up more closely and sit more steadily, for I have observed ladies can, on most occasions, be more or less shaken as they please; and now we beg Thomas, whose horse has slackened his pace, to go faster, as just now we desired him to go more slowly, and we long to be set down. I can forgive our driver his apparent sullenness, for really he has very contradictory orders to obey, and a numerous and somewhat unreasonable set of requests to comply with; and the road is very heavy here, so the horse and his dissatisfied burden flounder on, from one rut to another, in singular style.

It rains faster, and begins to be dark and uncomfortable. I am glad we are at our journey's end; we shall find nothing dark or uncomfortable here. There is a hearty welcome, and our damp things are soon taken off, and we are settled in a room with a blazing fire, round a table on which are plenty of candles and the great basket of work. Some are already employed there, but kind eyes look up as we enter, and kind hands are extended, and we feel that we are amongst friends. Then we apply diligently to business, and I must say for the credit of our little party, it is not only nominally a working society. It is a point of courtesy to leave the flannel articles to be made by the elder ladies; I beg pardon, the ladies who wear spectacles: not that we doubt their ability to do the more delicate work as neatly as the most bright-eyed amongst us, but they profess to like this best; and of one thing I am sure, that if the younger members of our Association can in any way consult their comfort, it must be their pleasure to do so, for they know how highly they are honoured by the company of such elders, and they do indeed feel grateful for it. We are all settled quietly at work at a little after five, and though sometimes debates run rather high, and one could not help allowing that if we ladies talked only three at a time, we might be better understood, yet we were getting on with our various articles of dress, when the tea came in at half-past six.

We lose no time, because we do not remove our work, but go on with in between the acts, and there are very often pleasant private conversations carried on between those who happen to sit next each other; many kind feelings expressed, and sometimes words of consolation or advice exchanged. I hope we do, and I am sure we ought to feel something more than the regard of mere acquaintance to the members of our Dorcas Society; to me, certainly, that evening is one of the most agreeable week-day evenings in the whole month, and that party the pleasantest I ever attend. After tea, there is generally a proposal made for reading, and I always observe, the more interesting the book may be, the more rapidly the work goes on. In selecting books for reading on such occasions, it is well to remember that "the time is short," and that whilst the ostensible purpose of our meeting is to provide for the temporal wants of our poor neighbours, any opportunity for our own improvement is to be thankfully embraced. But the reading never lasts all the evening, and sometimes little Susan varies our amusement by repeating the beautiful hymns which she has learnt so perfectly and repeats with such wonderful propriety. Little dear! may she always have as deep a feeling of what is right as she now appears to possess, and may she always be as little ashamed of expressing it.

But you are glancing round at our circle, and you think that amongst so many young ladies there must be frequent changes. Not very frequent; though indeed the flower of our party left us soon after we first assembled. Now there are rumours of speedy changes, but we must not listen lightly to reports. To be sure we cannot help observing how, for a long time, one who is, as she well deserves to be, a general favourite, has been fetched home in the evening by some kind invisible. "*The person*"—how lucky that the word is common gender—always preferring to wait outside. It would be better, we thought to come in, but Cate never seemed to think at all about it, and, of course, it was no business of ours. She was never one moment putting on her things, and whilst others were folding up their work, or taking leave, she was dressed and gone. But the very last time, by some mischance or other—either because the dogs in the yard would not bear a stranger there, or that the servant was particularly stupid, or particularly determined—"*the person*" was prevailed upon to go into the little parlour, where we had left our bonnets. Our pretty friend rushed out of the room where we were sitting, perhaps to send him back again; but it was too late; we were all on the point of going. I thought it would have been kinder to have given her two minutes the start of us; and really it was not so much curiosity, as love of adventure, that made me run down with the rest. And there, in the farthest corner of the room, stood "the person,"—a hand-

E

some looking youth, wrapped in a picturesque furred cloak—the very person we might have expected to see, yet to whose name, when any one has been rude enough to question her about him, she has invariably answered with the most enviable self-possession. O poor Kate! how pretty and how ashamed she looked; what a very great hurry she was in, and how she trembled when one of the more staid of the party kindly detained her, to give her a pin for her shawl, and to advise her to tie her bonnet. She need not have been in such a fright; she was with friends: I am sure if they all felt as I did, they were glad to see her in such good company, and sincerely wished the young couple joy. But it is almost time to leave off work; the more nimble have accomplished theirs, and the others are tired, and must take their unfinished portions home; and here comes the neat servant maid, with refreshments. It is not printed in our reported rules, indeed, but one of our by-laws provides, that, in order to prevent any thing like emulation or extravagance in our entertainments, the wine and cake, &c. shall be home made, and the fruit such as in its season can be readily procured. There are but few who think it a duty to keep to the letter of this rule, though it is a useful one in its intention certainly. But the most part appear to feel that, on this occasion, they cannot possibly be too liberal: there is no emulation, I hope, but a great deal of hospitality amongst us, so that when we part, it is always with even kinder feelings than when we met, and I always go home believing the committee of our Dorcas Society the most agreeable in the known world. We need not be anxious about our charioteer, though it must be nearly nine o'clock. He will be punctual, as I dare say he is impatient to have done with us. Hark! there he comes lumbering down the lane. No rain; the clouds are flying away before the fresh wind, and the moon, the beautiful silver moon, is at her highest.

But when seven or eight people pack into a cart, to be jolted along a very rough road, there is neither time nor silence for romantic admiration of the moon, though I should observe for the credit of the party, we do generally endeavour to be quiet and orderly on the king's highway. We drop one after another of our party on our way home, and by the time the horse gives himself and his master a shake of congratulation at our own door, it is nearly a quarter past nine. There is, you see, even in this age of civilization, one out-of-the-way place in the world, where such hours are still kept. They are the most natural, however, the most reasonable, the most healthy, and certainly the most agreeable; and we are at home in proper time, and, I trust, in no improper temper, for that calm and holy assembling of ourselves together which, in sorrow and in joy, we have found to bring so great a blessing—which no business should ever be allowed to prevent, and which that cannot be really pleasure which would interrupt.

*March*, 1830.

# BLIND SARAH.

"Those eyes, that dazzled now and weak,
At glancing motes in sunshine wink,
Shall see the king's full glory break,
Nor from the blissful vision shrink.

Though scarcely now their lagged glance
Reach to an arrow's flight, that day
They shall behold, and not in trance,
The region 'very far away.' "
KEBLE'S CHRIST. YEAR, *4th Sunday in Adv.*

I HAD a pleasant walk after church last Sunday. I am very fond of quiet and fresh air, and they seem especially suitable to my feelings after evening service, after joining the earnest prayers, and listening to the solemn sermon. I am sorry to confess, that too often in the summer, the only quiet walk is to be found in our church-yard and our own sweet garden, for the bright weather sends out into our fields and lanes, groups of those of whom the utmost stretch of charity cannot prevent our feeling, "they are doing their own works, and speaking their own words, and taking their own pleasure on God's holy day." But it is yet too early in the year for any of these noisy parties, and this evening, though very soothing to my mind, was perhaps to some, more mirthful, cold, and grey, and gloomy. Indeed the mist, that threatened to become rain, as I stood hesitatingly in our home field, would perhaps have sent me back, if I had not made a promise to blind Sarah which I was anxious to fulfil. But I was glad I went on, for by the time the little white gate of the lane swung behind me, the cloud passed by, and the yellow sunshine streamed from the blue western downs through the leafless hedge, and across my path. The birds, grey linnets, I think they were, (the first songsters I have heard this year, except the robin) kept up an animated conversation on either side of me, in very sweet tones, and by short addresses to each other, which I doubt not, each well understood. Spring is really come, and I know it by the sign of our village children; you can set your foot on two daisies at once; so I should be quite sure, even if the vividly green leaves of the shining slippery dock, and the elegant wild parsley springing through the moss, whose seeds are nearly ripe, did not confirm the opinion. Then as I came near the ivied arch which leads to the farm, I was agreeably surprised by hearing a thrush singing its song of thanks, for the unripe berries which have been its chief supply through this long, hard winter. There were a few sheep, lying in a green pasture on my right hand; but few, indeed, yet on such an evening enough to remind me of the beautiful 23d Psalm, and "The Lord, my shepherd," &c.

Poor blind Sarah! if she could have had a glance at them, it could not have failed to remind her of that Psalm too, for it is a very favourite one with her, and when I have read the last verse, "Goodness and mercy have followed me all the days of my life," she generally assents with earnestness, saying, "They have followed me, my dear; they have followed me." And whilst I have listened to her story, I have assented too, and felt "so they have;" and the more I consider the ways of God in his providence, the more I am amazed at the wisdom and mercy, with which, according to a homely but expressive phrase, "he fits the back to the burden." It seems to me that, if some persons with whom I have conversed, possessing, nevertheless, the same high principle of action, and the same strong consolation, had had half to bear that poor Sarah has borne cheerfully, they must have fainted under it.

She was not born blind, yet she has no remembrance of material objects, as she became so during her infancy. Whether this is an alleviation of her loss or otherwise, is probably questionable. Rogers would consider it an addition to the evil, as of so many things she can have no "*Pleasures of memory.*" Her father and mother died, and left her as she said, and her lip quivered a moment, "to God and the wide world at twelve years old." She had brothers and sisters, but some went to service, and some to sea, and some married, and "it could not be expected," she adds, "that they having their own bread to get, would be burthened with me a blind girl." Indeed she seems to think that she was quite as well able to take care of herself, as they to take care of her. It is curious to hear her list of accomplishments. "I was strong and hearty," she says, "and I was afraid of nothing: I could clean furniture beautifully, and I could scrub a room, and nurse a child better than many who could see." Besides she has been used to brew and bake, and speaks of her attainments in those particulars with great satisfaction. She has been preserved from ever meeting with any accident by fire, and no child left with her met with any harm, though in her youth she was constantly entrusted by her neighbours with the care of theirs. She could nurse with quite as much ease, and, according to her own account, with more pleasure than hireling nurses generally feel: and I remark here, what appears singular, and yet what I believe inquiry will prove to be true, that blind women are often particularly pleased with the company of young children, and wonderfully expert in attending to them. There is a blind girl in our parish at present, who gains her livelihood as poor Sarah did, and is never better pleased than when she has one child in her arms, and another at her side. But blind Sarah was in her way, a milliner and mantua-maker. She can cut out any article of dress she wants, taking the pattern in paper first, and can make and mend, in a way, which would put most of the *seeing* women of our parish to shame.

As long as she can remember, she says, she was particular about her appearance; and when she was young, the neighbours would look after her, and wonder who kept her so nice, and whether she could possibly dress *herself* with so much exactness: and that she observes, "was great encouragement, I could not be untidy after that." When I reached her house after my walk, I found her sitting alone in her neat kitchen, the floor sanded and the fire-irons polished: every cup and glass, each exactly in its own place; her neat dark gown pinned quite evenly, and her cap, handkerchief, and apron, as stiff and clean and clear as they could have been on her wedding day. On her wedding day? Yes! blind Sarah was married. You are not more astonished than she was, when the proposal was made her. She was very grateful, but expressed great wonder at her intended husband's rashness. "It was not likely," she says with great simplicity, "that I should be able to give satisfaction—I could clean my room to please myself—so I told him, but how could he be so foolish as to think of such a poor creature as I, when there were so many who could see."

But when all the objections in such a case, arise from a woman's sense of her own unworthiness for the honour intended, there is no great fear but that they may be overruled, and so it was now. "God had promised to be a father to the fatherless," was Geoffrey's answer, and God would make good his word by fitting him as long as he lived to be a kind guardian to the blind orphan. So they married, and he kept his promise to the utmost. I have heard of true love, and I have seen it; but truer I never expect to see, than that which existed between this singular couple. Geoffrey was a collier, and like most of that portion of those men who work under ground, he was grave and thoughtful. His affection to his wife, however, was so uncommon, as to carry in it something of a romantic character; and his religion was as enthusiastic, as sincere religion can be. He was many years older than Sarah, and he possessed some property, two houses and their little bit of garden ground, which he settled on her. In one of these they lived, and to hear poor Sarah describe it, you would really believe she was speaking of some green spot in fairy land, or some dwelling in Arcadia. "My home was so beautiful," she says, "that strangers used to stand and look at it, and I used to hear them wonder how the blind woman could keep it so—and we had all kinds of flowers, and my husband made me a beautiful arbour to sit in, of roses, and yellow and white jessamine, and honeysuckle, and it was very pleasant!" Poor thing! I should like to see that bower in my mind's eye as she sees it. Who knows? Fancy is more gorgeous than reality; perhaps her view of a pleasant and beautiful bower, is more lovely than any I can ever have, because where real roses are, I must see blight, and where there are earth's flowers, I must see dust, and drooping, and withering.—Her husband was in the habit of reading to her in the word of God, but his bible was small and old, and she determined to make him a present of one.

At this time she went out every day to wash, and unknown to him laid by a small portion of her weekly earnings for the purpose. It was a long time before the pence and sixpences amounted to the requisite sum, for she intended to give him a large handsome bible; but she kept her secret; and the day on which she and a neighbour went to pay the money and fetch home the book, and the evening when she gave it to her husband, are still remembered as among the most joyful of her life. She has been for many years a thankful and cheerful christian—but the days of her married life were really days of joy. "They were ten of the happiest years," she says, "that I think any one ever could spend on earth." The bond of affection must be strengthened by other than merely earthly ties, or it will decay like all that is of earth; and Geoffrey and Sarah learnt to love each other more and more, because they were companions to the house of God, and because month after month found them kneeling with thankful hearts at his table.

And here, perhaps, it may not be out of place to mention the delight, with which she speaks of that holy ordinance, and of one particular circumstance connected with it. All other things she *fancies*, but when the sun shines through the chestnut leaves, that shade the eastern window, on the spotless table, the gleam of the fair linen and the sheen of the plate and chalice, are *really* presented to her dim eye. Then and then only she knows what it is to see. As "the gentle footstep" is "gliding round," it is not by her ear alone that she is sensible when the precious memorials are about to be presented to her. "The light shineth in a dark place." "It is a bright speck," she says, "but I am ravished." This was her strong expression, "I am ravished with thinking how much broader the light of heaven will be."

Sarah is never weary of talking of her husband, or of telling how very kind he was to her. How he thought every thing she did was well done, and always said no one ever made his clothes, or mended them to please him half so well as his blind wife. And she takes great pleasure in showing the handsome clock which he gave her, teaching her how to feel the hour and how to wind it up. "Did you never break it?" I asked. "O no, my dear," was the answer, "I never break any thing, my thoughts always go with what I am doing, ('it would be well,' think the grave mistresses of families, 'if all giddy young people understood the secret') and I set about every thing very slowly, and I don't break any thing once in seven years."

But ten years is a long time for happiness to last on earth, and Sarah's time of trouble was come. Her kind husband was taken ill, and after six weeks died. He died many years before I can recollect; and I cannot tell you much on the subject, because pleased as she is to talk of him generally, and cheerfully as she tells the rest of her story; when she comes to mention his death, it is with such agonized remembrance, and such deep feeling, that I should be hard-hearted indeed if I allowed her to proceed. Of this much, however, I have been assured; the God who knoweth whereof we are made, raised up friends for his servants in this time of trial. The best medical advice was freely procured for the one, and the most comforting kindness was shown to the other; and "He who never leaveth nor forsaketh," guided his departing servant through the valley of the shadow of death, giving him not only a peaceful but a triumphant departure. It is more than two and twenty years since Sarah pressed her husband's hand for the last time; yet still, she says, she dreads the day to come round, and at that time she always prays very much for strength that she may not sink under the remembrance, and "when I go to my bed at night," she says, "I always pray that I may not think so much of my dead husband as of my living Lord; besides I am getting very old now, and in heaven my husband and his blind wife will see each other." But if the loss of a friend is at any time a very, very great affliction, it certainly may be aggravated when the loss of the means of life is consequent upon it; and poor Sarah has known in the latter years of her life much pecuniary distress. She was obliged to rent a house nearer the place where she worked, and to let her own two houses she soon found would presently ruin her. She generally had tenants to be sure, but she had almost insurmountable difficulties in getting her rent; and when they did pay her, her outgoings for repairs would always nearly equal her income. And then her unprincipled tenants were always taking advantage of her, leaving without giving notice, and breaking windows wholesale, and pulling down walls, as if for the very amusement of the thing. Still whilst she had health she could work, and though sometimes she must have lived very hardly, she never complained.

At last, after an illness, it was thought reasonable to make her some allowance from the parish, and for some time no objection was made. But then we had a new overseer, a "little industrious man," as he calls himself, very energetic and always busy, who came into office with full purpose of rectifying all abuses, and full confidence in his power to do so. He resolved that Sarah should have no more "parish pay," as it is called in these days, until she gave up her houses. I do not blame him as much as he is generally blamed,—right, I doubt not, was on his side; but for poor Sarah to part with the houses which her husband had thanked God that he had to leave her; oh! it went near to break her heart. For a long time she would not yield, and during the many weeks in which no allowance was made her, she was reduced to great distress. At last want of bread made it necessary for her to give way. She sold her houses, and has been living on the price of them now, nearly two years; but now the money is waxing very low, and when it is all gone, I suppose she must apply again to the parish, but they can give her very little, and her working days are over. I cannot tell how she will contrive to keep out of the work-house, and to go in there would be indeed a very great sorrow; for now she can receive her visiters, and smile when they admire the order of her little establishment; she can pack up her tea, sugar, &c. in her "ridicule," as she calls her old covered basket, and go to spend every afternoon with her crippled neighbour, the sailor's widow, and she can listen with pleased attention to the tracts which on such occasions, Mary reads to her; and she can take a turn in the fresh air or the sunshine, whenever she pleases. Oh! what a charm there is in that—to go out or come in when one will, no man making one afraid. Not that I have a word to say against the keeper of our poor-house. But a poor-house is only one remove from a prison, so the poor think at least, and so they hate it. Oh! I hope poor Sarah will not be obliged to go there. But why should I trouble myself about it, she is not so anxious. "I will surely do thee good," was the promise of her covenant God to her, and "good will be the word of the Lord." I am sure none ever trusted in him and was confounded. The God of the Gospel dispensation is the God of nature also, and that sweet Sunday evening's walk declared his truth to me, for according to his unfailing promise, the spring-time was coming back again.

The moon which he set for certain seasons, hung like a dim silver lamp in the eastern heaven before me, and the sun, which he taught to know his going down, cast the lengthening shadows across the ancient hills as he did six thousand years ago. I stopped at an open gate, and looked toward the long line of southern downs, and could plainly distinguish the outline of the grey Cairn on the summit. Man passes away, I thought, and his monument remains only to bids us ask, "who lies here?" But God says, "I am the same, I change not,"—and in whom is it that the Christian thus puts trust? In the Great Spirit of the American woods, or the being that Socinianism proposes to itself as an object of worship? O, no, we feel whose "Spirit rules universal nature." "His who wore the platted thorns with bleeding brows."\* And, oh! thou God and man, it is because thou, Jesus Christ, art the same yesterday, to-day, and for-ever, that we feel as David did, that we shall never see the righteous forsaken.

So it was with pleasant thoughts that I came quietly through the lanes and up the silent home fields, and my remembrances of my friend Sarah, further arranged themselves in the following verses, which by way of variety, I here offer to you:—

### THE BLIND COMMUNICANT.

    The mother led her sightless child
      Forth, in the fields to play;
    And cheered with voice of kindness mild,
      Along her shadow'd way:
And gave her flowers of varied hue,
Which the blind child might never view.

    But she grew up, and loved the song
      Of the glad birds to hear;
    And roam'd the scented heath along,
      In spring-time of the year.
But knew not how those flowers were fair,
Nor how the bright moths flutter there.

\* Cowper.

To childhood's voice as still she grew,
  That woman's heart would swell;
Yet the bright face she might not view,
  Nor the young features tell;
But to her heart, the form would strain,
And love the clasp that press'd again.

But most she lov'd the one kind voice
  That bade her glad heart bound
One step, that made her soul rejoice
  With its so well-known sound.
She fancied what that form might be,
And lov'd the smile, she could not see.

She never saw—nor sparkling day
  Rainbow, nor morning's grace,
Nor brighter than Eve's brightest ray,
  Affection's beaming face.
But yet to her, one gleam was given,
In earth's dim walk, a glance at Heaven.

For when the noon-day's glory bright,
  Shone on the chalice fair
On priestly vestment pure and white,
  And she was kneeling there;
One moment on the quivering eye,
The holy light shone tremblingly.

O! blest through this dim world of ours,
  To follow calmly still—
The star that shines on Zion's towers,
  And lights up Judah's hill.
Undazzled by earth's meteor-gleams,
Or bursting flowers, or sparkling streams.

O blest! with faith's unchanging gaze
  That star alone to see—
And so, through this life's varied maze,
  Press forward stedfastly.
Until, upon the strengthen'd sight
Bursts forth in Heaven, the Lamb! the Light!

*March,* 1830.

# THE STRAWBERRY FEAST.

"And still the green is bright with flowers,
And dancing through the sunny hours
Like blossoms from enchanted boughs—
 On a sudden wafted by.
Obedient to the changeful air,
And proudly feeling they are fair,
 Sport bird and butterfly.
But where is the tiny hunter rout,
That revel'd on with dance and shout
 Amid their airy prey?"
                        WILSON.

You have given me a subject, on which to write, my dear friend, and I will not refuse it, though there are reasons why it is not a favourable one for me, and why remembrances must arise to my mind, little suited to my joyous title. Anniversary days have been sometimes likened to the stones erected along the path of our journey, and whilst they remind us that we are come another mile nearer the end of it, they also make us sigh at the observation, that some, who commenced our way with us, have ceased to travel in our company; but such an anniversary as our Strawberry Feast was, planned early in childhood, is more like the pole, erected in joy and glee in the sunshine of May morning, but from which as we gaze at it, even in the following summer, the garland flowers are fallen off, and the dancers are gone.

Yet why should I begin in a melancholy strain? When the May-pole is lifted into its place, it is with a shout of rejoicing; and bright wild flowers are hung about it; and glad faces look up at it; and there was nothing but joy in the first celebration of the Strawberry Feast.

I do not remember the first time, nor I suppose can you, for we were very little children when it was proposed by one, always anxious and able to give pleasure, that once in every summer, we should make an excursion to the cottage of an old woman at the other end of our parish, to drink tea,—the materials for our meal being carried by ourselves; and to enjoy the particularly fine fruit, with which her hilly and sunny garden would supply us. But in many ensuing summers you will recollect the joy expressed, when the day was really fixed. On the preceding evening, how anxiously we watched the sunset, and foretold fine weather, however it threatened rain,—or feared rain, however glowing and glorious the setting sun might be. How contradictory children are! Some of us are not very different now. And when the day really came, how suspiciously we questioned every gentle and well-intentioned cloud that ventured within our ken; and with what dismay we noticed even the cooling and glittering shower, that but for a minute dimmed the bright sunshine. Ah! so we did! So we do! for we are human beings still. Still we tremble when the dark cloud hangs on our horizon, though mercy's covenant rainbow be painted on it; and still we shrink from the storm, though we know that it comes from heaven, and will descend in showers of blessing.

At last, the morning passed, and the lessons were ended. Children now, I understand, such is the "march of intellect," delight in their tasks, and tell their parents in the letters they send them, that "they are absorbed in their studies." So I hear, at least, but in my day it was not so. You will candidly own with me, that to us, as Pollok says, "Tasks *were heavy*," but the labour for that day was over, and the trouble for that day past; and we, at any rate, had wisdom enough then, not to add to our grievances by looking forward. Then came the pleasant business of watching those who were really busy, pack up the tea, and sugar, and cream, &c. &c., and happy, and a person of great consequence, was the one who was sent over to the shop for the new loaf of baker's bread. "Adulterated," says Accum, but infinitely preferable, we thought, to the stale and more wholesome home-baked, which served for ordinary occasions. At last, it was four o'clock, and we set out. Once or twice, I think we went in the cart, and were driven by the old farmer.

He was a specimen of what one expects to see in a gentleman's servant; in many respects far superior to our present chaperon. Grave and neat in his dress, and though rather peevish, perhaps, with troublesome children, very respectful to his superiors. Poor old man! I saw him the other day, and he wears well. His hair is scarcely thinner, or more hoary than when he lived with us; and when I met him, his blue eyes looked up with a kinder expression than I used to think it in their power to bestow. Yet I always liked him, and was quite glad to see him look so cheerful; for he has had troubles lately, such as go near to break a man's heart, and yet such a man would rather his dearest friend did not know. Poor old farmer! perhaps that was the reason we met so kindly; we had both sorrowed since we parted last. But in those days things were different; for though you and I fully agree that children have troubles, yet we did not then muse upon them when they were not actually troubling us; and as we went up one hill and down another, and up and down again, before we stopped at the bottom of the shaded lane, that led to old Betty's cottage,—we felt so very joyous, that had the king passed in his chariot and eight, (oh! what an adventure that would have been,) he might have moved our admiration certainly, but I believe not our envy. We went to the same place, I think, for several years; and the old woman used to receive us in her neatly sanded kitchen, all her furniture in its holiday polish, and herself in her Sunday dress; we used greatly to admire the gaiety of her tea-service and the flavour of her fruit; and once in particular, I remember we found great pleasure in the discovery of a bank, joining the wall of the cottage on one side, down which we could scramble, and find our way round the house to a little window at the back, where sat the old woman's son, a cobbler, at work. That was certainly considered a wonderful discovery, and a great amusement; but, I think, it was not till old Betty became too infirm to receive us, and the meeting was adjourned to the house below the hanging gardens, beside the river, that we found out all the pleasures of that evening. We could not ride there to be sure, but you know how lovely the walk is, down the fields on a summer's evening, and through that deep and stony lane, "the most extraordinary path," your friend W—— said, "that he had ever heard called passable."

Even now, though the tasteless hand of a waywarden has been there, and smoothed it in some degree; and though three or four very ugly houses,—I will not call them cottages,—have been perched on the banks, as is the fashion of the people here, wherever they find waste ground, and whenever they can collect stones and lime sufficient, without asking leave or license of the lord of the manor, much less of poet or painter: still the lane has many beauties, steep and broken banks, and pieces of rock, in some parts bare, and in others wreathed with ivy and woodbine, and tufted with dwarf oaks and hazels; and still in the time of the winter rains, the stream, which has been forced on one side and covered over, asserts its ancient right to the middle of the way, and gushes free, and clear, and sparkling, rejoicing down, down, making again uneven and rough, the path, which a vestry meeting had ordered to be smooth, and dancing and dashing in defiance even of a waywarden. The scene of our festivities was a large lofty room, in an awkwardly built house, designed originally for the agent of a certain concern which failed, as many other concerns have done; so that for years the extensive works connected with it have lain void; offering irresistible, or rather, unresisted temptation to some of our lawless people for breaking windows, carrying away tiles, and stealing old iron: but the great house was let to a poor but very respectable family, who thankfully allowed us the use of their large room on these occasions. It was a curious old place altogether; but its chief charm was the garden, built according to the taste of the times, sixty years ago. Perhaps, I should have said laid out, but there were so many flights of stone steps leading through brick arches, to broad straight walks one above another; and so many square summer-houses with stone walls, and square doors and windows, that your first thought was of the buildings: and stiff and formal enough it must have looked when it was first planned. But now that the brick arches were falling to decay, and ornamented with faithful wall-flower, and wreathed and half covered with ivy, that the summer-houses have lost many of their straight lines, and that old trees shaded, and jessamine and wild climatis concealed the rest; and the steps were so broken, that we were obliged to be careful how we ascended them;—it had become interesting from its appearance of antiquity, and it offered wild and strange scenery to those who were old enough to love the picturesque,—and danger and difficulty enough for those who were so young as to delight in adventure. For when we reached the top of the last flight of tottering steps, we found ourselves in a wilderness, where, up the steep side of the hill, grew untrimmed bushes of red and white roses, tangled with the wild bramble, and overtopped by stately old pear-trees; and there were overgrown branches of all sorts of luxuriant lilac, and the beautiful jessamine, untrimmed for years and years, threw itself on the long grass at the foot of the moss-grown trees, as if in despair of finding support, and hopelessly longing for sunshine. Then, when we had pushed our way through these, we came amongst the underwood hazel bushes, scarcely taller than the giant docks and nettles that grew amongst them; and many a frock was torn, and many a tumble we met with, before we reached the arched summer-house, with the bath in the middle, at the very top of the hill. And, oh! what a view we had then. The steep and singular garden up which we had just climbed; the old buildings and tall chimneys clustered together so very far below us; the barren and quarried hill, with its yellow spots of gorse and broom, and its purple shade of heath, raising itself above the dark heaps of dross on our own side; and then the river, the beautiful, soft, flowing river that we have all loved so well, laving as kindly our rough and barren banks, and holding its pure mirror to us, as truly as to the embellished and fertile scenery on the other side; and how clearly we saw every reversed image of the trees in the little copse-wood beyond, —the thriving willow, the silver stem of the beech, and the red seed of the maple; and how very pretty we always thought the little farm-house looked, that stands amongst the poplar trees; and we liked it all the better, because it was a porter's lodge once, to the monastery which in old time stood a little to the west of it; and of which we can still trace two or three ruined buttresses in the next field to that, where those aged elms grow, which formed part of the avenue to the gateway.

We could not look on such green fields and such pleasant lanes, and not long to be there, so we used to hurry our tea, that we might have time for a walk before the strawberries were ready. Not a brisk half hour's walk, such as we were obliged to take for exercise every day, but one, long, and rambling, and loitering. On the other side of the river too, where we went so seldom, and we might load ourselves with blue-bells, and red maple seeds, and crooked pieces of sticks, and moss, and snail shells; and we might run out of the way after the moths and butterflies, and we might stop to watch and wonder at the shining beetles, with their quivering and jointed antennæ, like lordly crests,—for they are the knights in black armour of the insect world. Oh! the wonders we saw. The delight of those walks to us when we were children, and even when we ceased to be children, you know how very pleasant they used to be to us. For she whose company is at all times a pleasure, was accustomed to join us then, and any others for whom we had particular esteem or value; generally F———, and more than once your kind friends W——— and N———.

You know how we enjoyed those evenings. You remember the sloping and silent field, where the pear-trees grow, and where we sat so long by the side of the sparkling mill-stream. You know the narrow road where the limes are planted; and the wide pasture where the quiet cattle are; and you can see in your mind's eye, the stile and the low wall on which we have all rested so often, at the top of the steep wood where we used to gather the pensile flowers of sorrel and wood anemone, and where the stately fox-gloves grow in such wonderful and gorgeous luxuriance. But you recollect also the elastic foot, that bounded down that path, and must never bound there again. You remember the light form that climbed the top-most trees' highest bough, and gloried in the danger. You can hear, even now, the shout of the clear sweet voice that is hushed for ever. You shudder at the remembrance of the daring, with which that light-hearted and dauntless one rocked our boat, as it glided over the calm and deceitful water. Oh! the glory of our party is gone! We shall have no more Strawberry Feasts; no more such meetings of rejoicing! Oh, my dear friend! you should not have given me this subject, and I should not have attempted to write on it.

*March* 30, 1830.

# THE LAYING OF THE FOUNDATION STONE.

"Consider now from this day and upward,—from the day that the foundation of the Lord's temple was laid, consider it,—from this day will I bless you."—HAGGAI, ii. part of the 18th and 19th.

It is Easter, beautiful Easter. The time in all the year when nature's types most clearly shadow forth the realities of the Christian dispensation. For the first butterfly has burst from its grave clothes, and is gone up toward heaven in the light of this season; and look! a thousand blossoms hang on branches that were to all appearance dead last week—nay! that but a fortnight ago, (so changeful is our climate,) were bending beneath a heavy mass of snow; and see how the chestnut buds wrapped up as they were by God's own hand with "inimitable art," fold within fold, the blossoms carefully concealed between the delicate closed leaves, and those again covered in a substance softer than the finest wool, and then altogether sealed up in a "case russet and rude," but varnished with odoriferous gum. See! they have heard the voice of God in the garden in the cool of this day; now, alas! man too often hears it not, but they have heard, and they burst their cerements and spring forth in beauty, exulting in the life He has renewed to them; and the primroses are up, round the foot of the old cross; and the daisies and cuckoo flowers are awake too, and rising out of their graves under every hedge, tell each other and man a tale of hope and the resurrection.

It has been altogether a fine Easter, from the time when the last storm drifted away on Sunday morning, just as we set out for the distant church to which we were unexpectedly summoned. The sunshine burst through the clouds, and lit up many an east window, and shone on many a white linen vestment, and table cloth; and gleamed on many a plate and chalice, meetly arranged that day, for our church's highest festival; and streamed, like "faith touching all things with hues of heaven" on many a group of communicants, and on us, as we knelt on the grey stones worn by the worshippers of centuries; beneath one of which rudely sculptured with the figure of his staunch hound and his cross-bow, rests the last forester of the king's wood. It was a pleasant Easter Sunday, for in the afternoon we worshipped again with those most dear to us, and in the place hallowed to us by thoughts of the living and of the dead; and the sun set brilliantly, and the following days were bright too, clear sunshine and fresh air; but in the middle of the week it was not so fair; and towards yesterday evening the old weather-cock, who I beg leave to observe in vindication of his character, which is generally much traduced, unlike others who are carried about by every wind, he always faces the storm. The old weather-cock who is a particular friend of mine, for besides that we once had an interview on *terra firma*, when he came down to be gilded, he stands where he can always amuse me with his motions as I sit in my place at dinner. He, I observed yesterday, was gravely and gradually turning himself, to consider certain indications of rain in the south-west; and I noticed them also, for they came between me, and a scheme of pleasure which we had formed, and they gathered and darkened, and when night came, not a star was to be seen; and when I rose this morning, the very day I had hoped to see so fresh and shining,—oh! how mild, and misty, and quiet, and drizzling it was.

We were sorry, but the laying of a foundation stone for a new chapel within our own boundary, is a sight not to be seen every day; and a sermon is to be preached in the old-fashioned gothic church at the most distant part of the forest, which we have never seen; and if it would clear up, what a pleasant expedition it might be. And it did look likely enough to be clear at one time, and "it has ceased raining" we said, as we stood on the step at the front door. No, there are heavy drops falling still. Only from the eves though, or from the old cherry boughs, as the blue titmouse, or the gay chaffinch springs from one spray to another, in search of the minute insects which nature has hidden there for their provision. Really, I do not think there will be much rain; there is a light behind the dark fir trees, almost like sunshine; we will take umbrellas and set out, white gowns and white stockings can be washed, luckily.

So I suppose the kind-hearted market women thought, as I crossed the green by the leaping stock, where they were resting with their baskets; for as I passed and wished them good morning, one of them looked compassionately at my white clothes and then at the mud, and said civilly, "most a wonder you don't wear pattens, ma'am." But I am soon tired in pattens, and we were setting out for a very long walk, over many a stile, and up and down many a steep, and many a heavy-ploughed field. Our path lay first down the lane to which I introduced my reader, when I told old Samuel's story; and the hedges are looking beautifully green now, and the primroses in the willow bed are in blossom, but we have no time to stay and look at them. We get over the first stile and straight across to the coal mines. O, those great steam engines, how they disfigure our landscapes. What frightful volumes of smoke, and what an unnatural stream of steaming water, and what a deafening noise! Oh! a tasteless man he must have been, who first polluted the green fields, and the fresh air, and the quiet of the country, with a steam engine. Never mind, we are passed in safety, and the great boiler did not burst, though for the din it made, it seemed likely enough to do so. Now we have a different view before us. Through this little narrow lane, and here we are at the top of a steep field. A great variety of trees all along the bottom, mark the course of a little rill which is the northern division of our parish; as clear, as sparkling, decked with as fresh primroses, and hidden from the summer sun, by as green branches of ivy and eglantine, as when four hundred years ago, the stately herd of gallant wild deer came down by moonlight, to drink its crystal water. Come on! there are no wild deer now, and we have a long way before us, up the hill and across the ploughed fields leading to the road. It was very dirty, along what the people here call the black causeway, and my companion was fain to mount the wall, and walk along the top of it to escape some of the mud: and then as we were crossing a very wet and dirty gate, as carefully as we could, by passed a grand dowager in her chariot, and she, as well as her laced footmen, seemed much amused at our condition; but they did not offer us a seat, so we travelled on. Two miles and more of very uninteresting road; and yet perhaps it was so, as indeed, I believe upon consideration we shall find that most things are, only because we were ignorant. Every tree has wonders to show; every cottage a history, often of deep and touching interest, if we did but stop to inquire into it. There, perhaps, where we saw an old woman look up hastily from her labour, as a tall lad in a sailor's jacket, passed—lives a mother, whose son is buried in the wide waters, and yet she trims the fire for him, and keeps the place for him night after night, vainly expecting his return. In that neat cottage, which looks as if it had lately been repaired, lives, probably, a newly-married couple: in what order their little garden is, and what a beautiful blossom they have on their old pear tree.—Ah? there is the pretty mistress of it, with her little infant in her arms. But come on! don't let her see us looking at her; she is pale, and looks very, very sad, and her clean cap has a close, deep, mourning border. How very young she looks, poor thing can she be a widow already? Oh, wherever a human dwelling is, there must be some feeling with which human hearts should be able to sympathize; some tale to which a human ear should listen with deep attention.

But now we are come to a beautiful descent of the road. The sloping fields on our right, and the aged trees stretching over our heads, with all their lovely variety of budding foliage,—chestnut and lime, scented poplar and lofty elm, green weeping willow and silver birch; who can pass on and fail to admire them. And, hark! up the soft wind comes another sound mingled with that of the rustling branches,—a merry peal of bells. Ignorant I am of other music, but I know how I love that sound. The time may come, as Keble says, when

"Strange to our ears the church bells of our home"—

it may; but I think I must be very deaf, or very mad, before that sound can lose its interest to me.

We were weary with our long walk, but our steps sprung more lightly as they moved to that music, and we soon came in sight of the flag floating round the low spire; and then into the church-yard, which was thronged with people waiting for the expected procession. We took refuge out of the bustle in the quiet church, and had much pleasure in looking round on the grey arches and the gothic windows. The one opposite my seat was quite hidden by mingling sprays of dark ivy, and the light, young leaves of a dwarf elder, which grew outside; and I was glad to see the church, as all places dedicated to the worship of God should be, in good repair and neat order. Then came the procession, flags, and music; the workman looking very important with their blue cockades, and the school-boys displaying their "peeled willow wands," and all the paraphernalia usual on such grand occasions.

But we had no longer time for looking on. The service began to remind us that we were in the house, and before the face of "Almighty God our heavenly Father;" and that our fellow-men were for a while to be forgotten; that we were sinners who had pardon to crave,—work to do with Heaven, of importance to make us pause even in earth's noblest business. The first lesson for the day was appropriately the twenty-ninth of the first of Chronicles, recording the cheerfulness with which Israel once gave for the erection of a temple to her God, when "the people rejoiced for that they offered willingly, and David the king also, rejoiced with great joy." Oh! for such a spirit under a better dispensation than that of Moses. After the second lesson, according to the beautiful provision of the rubric, admonishing the people, that "it is most convenient for baptism to be administered, when the most number of people come together, for that the congregation may testify the receiving of the newly-baptized into the number of Christ's church; and that every man present may be put in remembrance of his own profession made to God in his baptism;" "the priest coming to the font, then filled with pure water, and the sponsors and the people with the children being ready,"—I saw to my great delight, that there was to be a public baptism. All the services of our church are scriptural in their origin, and soothing and strengthening in their tendency. This is one of the most deep interest; for they who have had the smoothest passage, must know something of the tossing waves of this troublesome world; they who have seen least of the tempest, yet know that deep answereth to deep, "and lifteth up her hands on high;" and that there is safety only for those who have been received into the ark of Christ's church. And listen! we are commanded not to doubt, but earnestly to believe that He will favourably receive these present infants; we do not,—the promise is made by one, who, for His part, will most surely keep and perform. So we looked on with thankful hearts, as the clear water glistened on the calm brow, and the cross was signed, and "the young soldiers duly sworn." Blessed children! to be laid so early in their kind Saviour's arms. Blessed church! that so faithfully brings them to Him. The country choristers, who, from their number, and from my observing amongst them, certain grave faces which I have seen elsewhere, I think were strengthened by the assistance of all their musical brethren from the villages round, sung the one hundred and twenty-second psalm beginning,

"O 'twas a joyful sound to hear
Our tribes devoutly say," &c.

in what appeared to my uninitiated ears, very good style for a country band. A little allowance needs always be made for the strong accent, and the determined loudness of voice; for they think it beneath their dignity to sing low, but on this occasion, only a *little* allowance was necessary. "It *was* a joyful sound," and I enjoyed it. The sermon too,—and thanks to the neat matron who acted as pew-opener on the occasion, we were placed near the pulpit, and so that we could hear well,—was one which I had better not attempt to describe, because I have here neither time, nor ability to say how scriptural and how appropriate it was. But we were so interested by it, and it so completely took up our attention, that not until it was quite over, we observed how the clouds had darkened, and the mist thickened, and was descending in a soft, steady rain.

"How very unfortunate!" said every body. The people who formed the procession, which was here to be joined by many clergymen and gentlemen, had more than a mile across the country to walk; and then it was so wet for the women and children in their best clothes, and the umbrellas, under every one of which two or three were crowded, soon got so completely wet, that they really did more harm than good. "How very unfortunate!" thought the smart lad promoted that day to carry one of the flags, as he looked first at one hand, and then at the other, and saw to his dismay, that as the rain streamed down the blue flag-staff, it had left a deep green on the palm and fingers of his smart new yellow gloves. How very unfortunate! perhaps they were a "*gage d'amour*" from the dark-eyed servant maid, who, though trembling for her gay best bonnet, as she heard one heavy drop plash down after another, yet stood waiting under the fourth of an umbrella to see the standards and the standard-bearers. How very unfortunate! thought the trim gentlemen from the city, who had come in carriages to church, and were now obliged to walk two and two, through the middle of the mud,—country mud, of which some of them had little idea. "It will be long enough before you find any of them walking in a Kingswood procession again, I should think;" and yet that is not the case, there is many a one there of whom I have reason to know well, if there was any duty to be done, one good work to forward, or one friend to serve, they would willingly submit to more inconvenience than to-day's, and come through heavier roads than these to do it.

You will think that considering how far we were from home, we must have thought it rather unfortunate also. But I know not how it is, my parties of pleasure always turn out well. In this unkind world, it has always been my lot hitherto to meet with kindness; and so, during all the rain that day, I found myself comfortably seated in a carriage, amongst strangers, yet treated almost as a friend. My companion had joined the procession, which as it came through the trees, and across the ground to the appointed spot, really looked extremely pretty; and when the rain passed off, which it did presently, wanted nothing but a gleam of sunshine to make it a most glad and joyous spectacle. But that gleam, I must confess, was wanted. The red cross flags streamed out, and the gorgeous lions ramped in gold; and the lion and the unicorn in their bower of rose, shamrock, and thistle, quarrelled for the king's shield, and held up their gilded fists at each other, and grinned, and showed their golden teeth, as usual; but the sun disdained to look at them; however, we did very well without him.

I do not understand exactly the mechanism employed on these occasions, it is very simple, I believe; but the crowd is at such times so great, that one cannot expect then, to take a lesson on the powers of the lever and pulley; but I saw the little glass in which were enclosed the coins

G

of the present reign, and the names of the principal persons concerned, and I looked at it, wondering who shall see them next. When the temple about to be erected shall have fallen at length by slow decay, and the plough of the husbandman, forgetful that it ever stood there, shall find itself impeded by the mouldering foundation; these coins, perhaps, as those of the Roman emperors have sometimes been, may again be cast forth to light. Who shall decipher then, their image and superscription? Will the truth of God, and his ordinances be then continued to our country; or will God before that time, being "weary of a race like ours," have removed the candlestick out of its place? Who can tell? And this great multitude, one eye after another shall be closed in death; one voice after another shall be hushed, and every one be quiet in his grave; and the little children who were brought to lay their hands on the stone, that they might tell their sons, and their sons' sons that they had done so; they, and all their generations shall have passed away, and their names shall be forgotten. O, changeable world! what an unspeakable blessing is that gospel which lifts our hopes and our hearts above thee.—As soon as the company had established themselves on the platform, and quiet could be obtained; the hymn, the words of which were beautiful, and which sounded very sweetly in the open air, rose; and the voice of prayer was heard, entreating God's blessing for his Son's sake, on the work begun, and his presence in his temple, when it should be accomplished. The stone descended to its place, and when the money which was collected toward defraying the expenses of the intended building was laid on it to be counted; the band was desired to play the national air: but a valued friend of ours, very characteristically requested them to "praise God first, and the king afterwards;" so in a moment, many voices joined in the old doxology,

"Praise God, from whom all blessings flow,"—

and the sweet and well-known music rose clearly on the soft fresh wind. Nothing remained, but to "bless God and to take courage." As the company began slowly to disperse, the band struck up the air, without which a loyal

English assembly, met together for a good purpose, never ought to separate; and even in times like these, we felt our pulses quicken to the words, "God save the king."

The workmen then joined the procession, to return to a dinner which was provided for them; and the gentlemen who had come from a distance, returned also for the same purpose; and we, as soon as we could find each other, set forth on our pilgrimage home. Happily, we had no more rain, so that our journey was—to me it could not be otherwise—very pleasant; and we compared notes of our adventures during the short time we had been parted; admired the words of the hymn; and joined in hoping that as the foundation has been laid in prayer, the top-stone may, ere any very long time, be put on with shouting.

*April* 17, 1830.

# THE VESTRY.

———" Thank the God who placed thy state
Above the lowly, but beneath the great;
And still his name with gratitude revere,
Who blest the Sabbath of thy leisure here."
REV. W. L. BOWLES.

THERE are few places that I like better than our little Vestry-Room, perhaps because there are few with which I am so well acquainted. Certainly, it has not antiquity to make it interesting; no particular beauty of proportion, nor architectural ornament; and excepting the Oxford Almanacs, which are preserved year after year for the sake of their prints, no embellishments of any kind. Yet to my eye, it has many beauties, and to my heart many interesting associations. Come with me, a country parson's daughter, of course, has a right to the key, and we will go in there together. The oaken floor is clean, and sanded; and the walls and ceiling neatly white-washed. The little fireplace is built of freestone; and displays round the grate, scripture stories painted in a blue colour on Dutch tiles, in a manner more calculated to excite a smile, than, I hope, the artist intended: and as the season for fire is past, our sexton very tastily decorates the hearth with long sprays of sweet briar, and budding lilac fresh every Sunday morning through the summer. The old oak table also, whose surface is so unpolished, and marked with so many ink stains: (you cannot think how much it looks like king Arthur's, when it is unfolded to the full amplitude of its dimensions, and drawn into the middle of the room;) and then too, we can take its place in the south window, and look on the fair extent of prospect; and on a sunny April morning, I much doubt whether it is possible to find a more soothing scene, than the one before us. More glorious landscapes there may be. Riven rocks, and lofty alps; unfathomed, and mighty waters to speak of the power and majesty of God; or glittering towers, and gorgeous palaces to tell of the pride of man. But this tranquil scenery breathes only of the love, and mercy of its Creator; and is, therefore, in better keeping with the spot immediately before us,—the quiet churchyard where the Christian is laid to rest, his face looking toward the east, as watching till the light come. For the soft, green fields that join the burial-place, are full of wild flowers, which though they cry, as of old time, "All flesh is grass!" add also, "Awake and sing ye that sleep in dust!" It is a lovely prospect; look over the white gate at the end of the avenue; the woods on the other side of the river are tinted with all the hues which spring employs; almost equalling her sister Autumn, in variety, and far exceeding her in freshess. The pear-trees, even at this distance, are very evident; shining as the shadow of a cloud passes from them, like a fall of snow. The green hills rise softly one above another, each crested by its varied copsewood; until where the most distant is traced on the horizon, we lose the dim line against the pale, blue sky. Beautiful scenery! we know that earth's flowers are fading; that her blossoms fall, and that clouds dim her sunshine, and yet we cannot look on such a view without being thankful, that pilgrims, wayworn pilgrims, as we oftentimes feel ourselves to be, we are permitted to pass through so fair a world as this, on our way, we humbly trust, to one which has never fallen from its first high estate; never been cursed for the sin of its inhabitant.

But this is distant scenery; look through the arched door towards the east. Our garden door,—I am sorry to tell you, that once we had a low, white hatch, looking much more countryfied than that; but the boys used to get over it to steal our apples. I really am ashamed of the lawless manners of my countrymen;—and we were obliged to substitute that close door; but I left it open as we came in, that I might show you the home view. Look up the narrow, winding walk, leading under the blossoming apple-trees; and by the white rose bush, into the paved court, at the back of the house. There are a variety of rose-bushes, honey-suckles, and laurustinus covering the low wall which runs round that pavement; and at the higher end, grows a huge bush of berried ivy, which shall not be cut, because the blackbird, whose nest is in the hawthorn hedge at the bottom of the garden, is so tame as to come there for food, all through the winter, and late in the spring. Indeed, last winter was so very severe, that the birds eat the very buds of the laurustinus flowers. Against that side of the house, is a large, and in summer, a most luxuriant jessamine; under the wall is a narrow border of common flowers; primroses grow very well there, and the iris with its long rushy leaves, and polyanthuses which love the shade; and there also grows a wild flower, which was found once during a summer evening's ramble, and brought home, and planted there as a pledge of true love. I well remember the night; the friends, he who planted it, and she who held the lantern for him, whilst it was being planted, are far away now; but the little flower springs up every year to remind us of them. Carry your eye across to the left, up the green slope, to the noble variegated holly, and the two sycamores; round whose honeyed blossoms, the bees and butterflies revel by day, and the cockchafers and moths swarm at night: and admire, you cannot help admiring, the singular beauty of the pensile birch-tree, which towers above a laburnum and mountain-ash, whose streaming yellow wreaths, and whose scented white flowers are just ready to disclose themselves. Beyond that group of trees is a straight walk, most pleasant on a May evening, when the white lilies stand there in their unblemished beauty, reminding one, as they spread their pure and gleaming blossoms in the twilight, of the angel forms,—could they be freer from earth's stain,—that shone once in a sepulchre.

Ah! there passes on its glittering wings, a swallow, and another, and another, sweeping by, and glancing to and fro, like lightning. Beautiful! wonderful creatures! whence do they come? and how do they so clearly understand the exact time of their return? What unseen hand traces a path for them, through the trackless air? Ah! this is one of nature's secrets; kind she is, and gentle; amply rewarding her faithful admirers, with here and there an explanation of some word or line of her wonderful book; but on one broad page after another, though it lies for ever open before us, we "only cast a wishful look." Well, no matter if the God of nature will but reveal *himself* to us; we can thankfully wait until we reach another world, for an explanation of his miracles in this. So I thought in verse; will the lines give you any amusement, my gentle reader? Here they are:—

## THE VESTRY.

A watcher I, by bush and stream,
  A loiterer by the field and fold;
A lover of tradition's dream.
  And peasant tales of days of old.

A gazer on each flower that springs,
  And bud that grows on heath, and wild:
A questioner of hidden things,
  Nature's unwise, but loving child.

A follower of the bee and bird,
  As to their secret homes they hie;
A listener when the voice is heard,
  That wakes the shrouded butterfly.

God of the wonders that I love,
  Let me each day know more of Thee;
Till in Thine unfallen world above.
  Through no dark glass Thy face I see.

Give unto one, who nothing knows,
  Through this dim earth thy steps to trace.
Thy might, O Lord, each atom shows,
  And every flower displays Thy grace.

If nought I know, Thy wisdom more,
  May, through Thy grace, beam forth in me;
Sun! shine, whilst I the page explore,
  Of Thine own nature's mystery.

But our little vestry has yet another view. Open the opposite door gently; it leads into the church, by the chancel. We have, you see, no altar-piece; but the broad uncoloured window is pleasantly shadowed by the thick leaves of the tree, which from the outside conceals it entirely, "casting a dim, religious light;" not exactly such a one as Milton intended, yet no less suitable to the place, I think, nor to the feelings of the worshippers. The morning sun is shining on the white stone which covers little Mary's grave; and on the marble monument above it. What a quiet scene! No stir of human life; nothing heard, but the clear song of the bird, whose nest, I suppose, is amongst those rustling branches; his note is so like the nightingale's, that if we were not aware of the deception, we might mistake it. But we have seen the silvery grey of the shining wings, and the velvet black head, and know the stranger,[*] for he arrived only last month very well.

[*] *Motacilla Atricapilla,*—Black Cap.

He has flown away, and it is deeply silent; and when we speak, echo returns to us, as if fearful of disturbing so solemn a spot. Oh! what thronging thoughts come into our minds,

> "All round us memory, at our feet the proof
> How deep the grave holds all we treasure here."

Yes, and what comfort there is, in thinking of those who knelt at that holiest place with us, in faith and hope.

Truly it is a meeting of but short duration; and we rise and part, and some never return again. Blind Samuel's kinsman led him, as for many years he had been accustomed to do, up to the place, where they knelt side by side at the altar rails, on the Sunday before the old man laid down on his bed to die; and in three weeks after he was buried, his aged kinsman was laid in his grave too. But, thank God! I have seen the young come there also; in all the vigour of health, in the morning of what seemed likely to be a long, glorious day. I have seen young hands stretched forth to receive the cup of blessing, and bright heads bent in prayer; thank God! I have seen it. And what if the eye that hath seen, sees it no more? Then, the next time we come, we bless God, for all His servants departed this life in His faith and fear; and we press on, in sure and certain hope.

But I am never in this vestry, without thinking of two ladies, whom I once saw here: the younger of whom was come to return thanks for her recovery after her confinement. I remember looking at them, as they stood by the little fire-place, when we passed through from church. They were two very lovely women,—a mother and daughter: the elder one had been, as I have heard from those who knew her in her youth, remarkable as well for her vivacity and intelligence, as for her singular beauty; and even then, though she had known perils by land and by water, for she had crossed the Atlantic three times; and though she had been early left a widow with a young family, her cheerfulness and easy manner, still added much to the grace of her person.

Her daughter was extremely like her, yet more like Dominichino's St. Cecilia. The eyes as large, and dark, and bright, were shaded and softened by just such long silken eye-lashes; her cheek was, that day at least, as purely pale. I never saw the painting, only a print from it; but Dominichino would not, I should think, give his St. Cecilia much colour;—a dweller on earth, listening to the harmony of heaven; ecstacy might be expressed in the lifted eyes and the parted lips; and inspiration too powerful for the weak earthborn frame, and she would be pale. And Mary, oh! who could look at her that day, and wonder if the bloom of her youth was gone! Yet you will think it was a joyous occasion. Her infant—and a lovelier was never laid in its mother's arms,—grew and improved daily; and her health, though she had been very, very ill, was nearly restored to her; yet no wonder her lip quivered, when kind friends addressed her; no wonder her eyes were dim with weeping; she might well be pale.

Her husband, to whom she had been married in a distant part of the globe, and to whom she was much attached, had brought her here, a few months since, to place her under her mother's care, at the critical period when such care is most needed. During the preceding years, since her marriage, her kind sisters had more than once provided for her,—as sisters love well to provide; and we had been shown the delicately wrought robes, which were to be sent so far, as tokens of love to one so very dear. Time after time, however, we had been told, that their care had proved unavailing; the child so fondly expected, was dead. But at this time, her husband's business called him to England, and Mary gladly accompanied him. Her mother and sisters looked forward with unmixed delight, to receiving her. She came: I remember the first time I saw her, on a clear winter day; the fresh wind had given her a bright colour; health, and hope, and youth shone in her clear eyes, and spoke in her cheerful tone. The delight of visiting her family, after so long a separation, was no doubt very great; and then also, what a pleasure it must have been to her, to introduce to her old friends,—for she was a native of our parish,—such a man as her husband; so lively, so intelligent, possessed of such a fund of information, and such a talent for conversation. Every one valued his acquaintance, and was sorry that he was only a visiter. Time passed on, and it was necessary for him to make a journey into the north: it was business which could not be delayed; and though he left unwilling to leave his wife just then, yet he did leave her. Her health and spirits were good, and her mother's care, and her sister's attention unwearied. His journey was to be but short, and they parted cheerfully. Only two or three days, and the long-desired child was born; and Mary's first thought, as she looked on it, was, "oh, the delight of showing her to her father!" Her strength returned rapidly, and her infant gave more than usual promise of health and beauty. "Dress her in her best robe and cap, to-day," she said one morning to her nurse, "for I am sure her father will come." But he came not. "Should not you think he must certainly be here soon, mother?" she asked the next morning, and the next; but her mother sometimes was silent, as if she did not hear; and at others, answered her anxious question in some vague and indefinite manner. At length she insisted on writing to her husband. It was in vain that her sisters told her she was too weak, in vain that though she had scarcely strength to guide her pen, she yet struggled with her feelings, and with a trembling hand inscribed one line after another, expressive of deep affection; that letter was never to be sent; she was a widow. News of her husband's sudden death had reached her family, but they kept it from her as long as possible; and whilst she wondered at the length of his journey, they knew that he was still in his grave; and when she chose the delicate colour of the dress, in which, when her husband came home, she intended to appear at church with her infant, as one arrayed for a festival of joy and thanksgiving,—they were secretly getting their mourning ready, and preparing for her that deepest of all mourning—a widow's weeds. There are scenes on which a stranger's eye may not look. I know not who told her the news, nor in what manner she received it; whether with the "great, and exceeding bitter cry" of agonized feeling, or the silence of a despair too deep for tears: but I know how she must have doubted the reality of the tidings. How impossible she must, for a long time, have found it, to separate the thought of her child, from the intention of showing it to its father; from what a dream of hope she awakened, and what a blank this busy world must have been to her; and then too, how her dreams, when at last she slept, were filled with the strange and distorted representations of the same images which distressed her mind by day; and how sometimes in her sleep, she fancied him alive and conversing with her, and yet even then, knew that she must awake to find sorrow the only reality, and happiness a dream. But her frame, as might be supposed, sunk under the trial. She had a very long and alarming illness, so that although her child was born early in spring, it was, I believe, verging toward the close of summer, when we met her here in the vestry in her new mourning. Oh! no wonder that her cheek was pale, and her eye dim with weeping; or that notwithstanding the long weeks of illness she had experienced, she answered the inquiries of friends by saying, that she "knew of no pain now, but the heartache!"

But you will connect the idea of our vestry, with none but gloomy associations, I am afraid. You would not have done so, if you could have run down with me the other morning, so desire our sexton's wife, to fetch some green boughs for the grate, though it was not Sunday; and to place on the old table, a basket of tulips, lilies of the valley, scarlet anemone, and sweet briar. You would not have thought so, if you had stood with me in the gallery, as the gay bridal train passed up the aisle into it. It has been many a long day, indeed, since it was graced by so joyous a party.

It was a bright sunny morning, and I was glad; for says the old line,

"Happy is the bride that the sun shines on;"

and the white dresses of the bride and bridemaids: (I admire the taste which prescribes white as the wedding dress; it seems to me one of the few occasions to which white is suitable:

"Dust will soil, and thorns will tear,
Is it fit for this world's wear?")

The white robes, by turns, looked either like snow or sunshine, as they waved under the changeful shade of the trees. I scarcely ever saw a prettier sight; nor it appeared to me,—as I looked at the faithful, young couple, and thought of all the troubles they may have to struggle with together; the changes and chances of this mortal life, which they must see; sickness or health, riches or poverty, good or evil,—one more interesting. May the God of Isaac and Rebekah keep them! I believe the solemn voice which pronounced the prescribed blessing, as they knelt hand in hand at the altar, was responded by many a heart; I am sure it was by mine. Have I not introduced you to them before, my dear reader, and have you not before heard me wish them joy?

But who are these grave and consequential personages coming up the avenue; and why has Martha been so long dusting the table, and setting the chairs in order? She is too civil to say so, but I believe she is marvelling, in her own mind, why I stay here, and half wishes me out of the way. And her father, the sexton, himself has peeped in two or three times, to see how things stand; and casts a half glance of wonder at me: he can drive away the boys, and the school children who trouble him; but I suppose he considers me beyond his jurisdiction; for though he evidently thinks me out of my place, he says nothing; though he appears exactly, in what people call a fidget. But there comes the clerk, in something between his Sunday and his working-day dress; and he and I being on terms of greater intimacy, he presently gives me to understand very politely, that my absence is requested; that there is going to be a parish meeting, and the gentlemen of the vestry are even now in the church-yard.

Oh! I beg their pardon, I am sure, I would not hinder their important business a moment. One look round the little vestry. I wish they may admire it, as much as I do; and that its quiet may never be disturbed by noisy debate; and that their recollections of this place may be as pleasant and peaceable as mine have been.

*April* 30, 1830.

# WHIT-MONDAY.

> How oft, when Memory's pensive eyes
> Gaze down the vale of years,
> Must sorrow's clouding mists arise;
> How oft, descend in tears.

"WHAT a morning!" I said to myself, as the first sound I heard, was the pattering rain against my shaking casement; and the heavy drops danced, and bubbled on the leads at the top of the house, and ran in a noisy stream through the gutter, into the shoot which crosses my little attic. "What a sad morning for Whit-Monday; the school children will not be able to walk,-that's certain; and the young visiters whom we expected to join the festivities of to-day, how they will all be disappointed!" I did not own how much I should be so myself, but as I sat looking at the heavy grey clouds, I began to think of Whit-Mondays in general; and of one or two that I recollected in particular.

I thought of the pleasure the words conveyed to us, when we were children; with what delight we looked forward to it for weeks together, when the clubs were in prosperity; and used to parade with flags and drums through the parish, to the number of four or five. How very handsome we thought the orange and blue, and spangled cockades in the men's hats; and how we admired the huge nosegays, pionies and double stocks, which most of them displayed at their button holes; and how we ran from one window to another, from the front door to the slope, and from the slope to the church-yard, as the sound of the music told us, that the procession was on its way down the road, and toward the church. Since that time, however, most of the clubs have broken up, and of the two,—I believe there are only two remaining,—the one finds the public exhibition of itself, too expensive; and for the other,—O tempora! O mores!—the church service is too long, so we see nothing of them; and if it were not for the school children, Whit-Monday would pass to us, as quietly as all the other Mondays in the year.

From the time our school-room was built,—1785, says

the date on the front,—it has been the custom for the children to walk with the master and mistress round a part of the parish, to ¡be back in time to attend divine service at church; and after singing a hymn in the vicarage garden, to receive a cake each, as they pass under the sycamore trees into the road, and are dismissed for their three days' holiday. Now the meeting of all the children in their best clothes, and in high spirits, so early in the morning, is really a pleasant sight; the sound of their singing very sweet,— (Ah! I am not afraid to say so now: we have been told this very day, by the only person capable of judging,—for he has been to hear them all,—that our school sings better than any in the neighbourhood; there's an unexpected triumph for us!) and their shout at setting out very joyous.

And then there are children of another class.—Are there not little William and Edward? to whom we can give pleasure, by asking them for that day; young acquaintance to whom living all the year in the city, the happiness of one long summer day in the green country is very great. Are you curious to see the style of our invitation cards? It ran something like this:—

### AN INVITATION FOR WHIT-MONDAY.

Come ye, come ye, from town and tower,
The feast is spread in our sylvan bower;
The chestnut sconces are lighted on high,
And her new robes waveth the butterfly,
And fair are her holiday robes to see,
Wrought in their velvet embroidery;
And the heart's-ease blossoms are shining in mirth,
On the glittering hour of the rose's birth;
And our woodland choristers wake a song,
That unpaid, they shall warble the whole day long.
And, oh, the soft and the dewy glade
Is varied by long streams of light and shade;
By turns, 'tis all sunlight, then shadow all,
As the wind bids the branches arise or fall.
'Tis now all a scene for calm and sweet
Deep musing; then glitter for light hearts meet;
Still mid such changes our joys must be,
To our varying bower, O hasten ye!
The gueldre rose, hath her white globes filled
With nectar, from sunshine and dew distilled;
And bright wreaths wave from laburnum's bough,
Which the next wind may scatter.—Come now! Come now!

Oh! haste ye now! for although they are bright,
Laughing and dancing in sunshine light;
Though the dew is pure, and the flowers are gay,
A garland, how meet for the brow of May!
Ye know how the fairest buds bloom to die;
O'er the youngest flowers how the frost winds sigh,
Though the sun shines at rising, in giant might,
Ye know how he sinks in the wave at night!
Yet come ye, come! for around our cell,
Hope whispers from every hyacinth-bell;
And even in fading their message give,
"We wait for our rising, from death we live!"
And the beams that fade through our chestnut bowers,
Closing the eyes of their thousand flowers,
Leave on our hearts no trace of sorrow,
For they tell of a glorious rising to-morrow;
And to us, o'er the graves of earth's fairest things,
Sure hopes are waving their sunny wings.
Have ye known grief in this world of sadness?
Come! we have balm in our bower of gladness;
Haste from your labours in tower and town,
From your chambers of study,—oh, hasten down.
From lofty roof, and from crowded hall,
Come at the spell of our charmed call!
For the feast is spread in our sylvan bower,
Come ye! oh, come ye! from town and tower.

"No great inducement for them in our wet garden, to-day," I thought again; it will be just such weather, as it was on this day two or three years ago, when I remember I saw some of the school girls, startled by the first drop of rain, as they were loitering down the road; but though they put their handkerchiefs over their heads, and ran for it, the storm came on so fast, that many a new ribbon was stained, and many a best bonnet was damaged, before they got into the school; and there, poor things, they sat, one disappointed and gloomy comrade after another, coming in with dripping clothes; for they would not give up the hope and chance of going, till, at last, at ten o'clock, having waited nearly three weary hours, in the vain hope of drier weather, the master came in despair to order them all home.

It was in vain, that the maker of the great flag had worked to get it ready, so diligently. The red and white cross was inserted in its place on the deep blue ground; and the last letter of the motto, wrought in white wool, "Fear God and the king" was filled up, and the initials and the date were there; but the flag belied the private motto of the worker, which was marked in small letters, in the middle of the cross, "Through all weathers," on this the first day of its completion. Oh! that was a gloomy day. How one heavy storm gathered and poured down, before the other was over; and to-day, I said, will be just like that. How different from that bright sunny morning, which had been so long expected; and which came yet brighter and more sunny, than our expectations promised it should be. How pleasant the lanes looked with their wild geranium and blue veronica, and hawthorn, as we returned home through them; and though there was, I remember, a slight shower at noon, how sweetly it cleared off toward evening, and

"'The yellow light stream'd from the western heaven"

through the damp branches, making every dewy green leaf shine with the light of a glow-worm; and shooting its long level rays through the ivy that hung in festoons round the trunks of the old trees, and smiling on the low blue flowers, that creep down to the very edge of the quiet stream, to look at themselves in the silver mirror. Ah! that was a pleasant day and a pleasant walk; and yet, then, I do not think, I enjoyed it half as much as I might have done: I really believe there is a time in some people's lives, when they think it wise to be melancholy; perhaps, trouble is generally necessary to teach us, that it is the part of real wisdom thankfully to receive and enjoy present blessings. It may sound very sentimental to say, as I well remember I did on that pleasant day,

" I can ne'er behold the summer blue,
But I look sadly for the dark clouds too ;
Or see the bright wreath's glow beneath June's sky
But my first thought is,—they are come to die."

But in indulging such a frame of mind, must we not plead guilty to St. Paul's accusation of the heathen of old, " Neither were thankful." Let us desire now, in whatsoever state we are, to be therewith content; to bear patiently storms and clouds when they do come ; but to bless God, and rejoice in the sunshine.

"Really," I said, as I looked up when I finished the last sentence, "it is not raining now ;" and I rose up quickly, "they will surely set off without me." So I ran down-stairs in as much haste, as if some very important consequence was to be the result of my speed; and I looked into one room after another, but the unoccupied chairs, and the unopened work-boxes, and desks were all in their respective places, my companions were gone on, and nothing was left but for me to follow. How often, in this busy world, one may muse away half the time, in which the active set about their work and do it.

I found it very muddy in the road, and although it did not actually rain, the willow trees which, to our sorrow, were so much cut up in the spring, because they incommoded the travellers on the top of the mail, the only genteel conveyance which statedly passes this ungenteel road,—were still dripping from every leaf, as I passed down. Yet damp and gloomy as it was, when I entered the school, (newly white-washed and painted for the occasion,) I found it nearly full. All the girls had arranged themselves in their separate classes; and were too happy, in too good temper, not to be well-behaved. One group was standing every foot, in exactly its proper place, round the newly-chalked half circle. Every hand lifted into precisely the same position; and every tongue gravely repeating the same hymn. Another class, in nearly as great order, stood quietly listening; and a third, at the further end of the room, were sitting in a long row, opposite the door, probably tired of being still, and longing for the signal to move. It was given and we all went into the boy's room; and though it appeared to me, that I saw something more than usual of the distress of the times, in the bare feet, and scanty and shabby clothes of some, both girls and boys; yet altogether it was a pleasant and interesting sight: at least, our little visiters, who were there waiting for us, looked as if they thought so. The children knelt down, to the number of two hundred and sixty; and the loved voice, which offered up the simple and impressive prayer for them,—God grant that it may long be heard amongst them, was disturbed by no sound; all were attentive and still. No sound, did I say? Oh! there was a dear little one present, too young to know what prayer means; though many a prayer is daily offered up for her, and her voice was heard when the other voices were hushed, and her little foot moved up and down the long lines of quiet children, when every other

foot was still. They rose up and sung, and the little creature sung too for joy; and the boys shouted as they stood in their order of procession, bearing their blue sticks, and their "streamers long and gay," and the baby waved her hands and shouted too in the excess of her delight...
——"It is a very pleasant sight," said dear nurse, as she stood by me watching the many-coloured train, as it wound down the road; "yes," I turned round to answer her; but the remembrance of past days, and of her long past, but unforgotten service, came associated with her form to my mind; and I thought "it is indeed pleasant to see you." Her delicately-white mob cap, her neat black satin bonnet, and her dark chintz gown, each and every article of her dress was in exact keeping with her station in society; she looked like a young clergyman's foster-mother. The frill which she had on,—she never wore any thing so gay before,—was worked for her, by her other foster-child, and new yesterday, when, for the first time, she came to hear her son preach. What a pleasure it must have been to her; and what a pleasure it was to me to walk round the garden with her afterwards, and listen to the interesting story, which I have often heard, and yet always hear with fresh interest. "I could not help recollecting," she said, "when I saw him stand up in his pulpit, the first time I ever saw him; what a dying thing he looked then, poor dear!" and she went on to tell me how sorry she was, that she had been sent for, to nurse him, because she felt sure he must die. How her heart ached to hear his cries, which weak as they were, yet seemed as if they would end only in the silence of death; and then, having watched by him for many days, and he appeared somewhat the better for her care; and as she could nurse him only on condition of taking him to her own fire-side, because her family much needed her presence, she carried him to her cottage, in the comb under the high hill, stopping many times by the way, to listen to his almost imperceptible breathing, and more than once doubting whether she held a living or a dead infant to her bosom. But the God of the child Moses—blessed be His holy name!—watched over the little sickly one. His foster-mother's care was day by day rewarded with some token of improvement. "Yet," said she, as she concluded her story, "I never thought he would live to preach,

or I to hearken to him." Surely the duty enjoined in the fifth commandment, extends to such a person as this. I confess I have sometimes been astonished, that young people, in general, do not show more affection to their nurses. In early times, we know they were considered persons of great consequence; and I should think, in proportion as the kindly affections are allowed to exert their natural influence, and we keep out of the chilling atmosphere of a selfish world, the more tender and faithful nurses will be; and the more grateful and affectionate their children. It is a pity, that in a day which professes to be one of so much improvement; masters and servants should appear to understand less than they used to do, of their respective duties; such, from the complaints we hear on every side, seems, at least, to be the case: but let us look all well to ourselves; the Abrahams of society, I believe, will most often be blessed with Eliezers; and it is Philemon's runaway servant, who will most frequently become the penitent Onisephorus.

Eleven, was the hour appointed for service, and the children were all quietly in their places before that time. There were quite as many of the parents present, as I expected to see; and I trust the service of the day, and the very faithful and affectionate sermon, to which they afterwards listened, had its due effect on them; it appeared so, certainly, for many a tear was shed, and the manner and the countenances of many evinced deep attention. There was simple Isaac, who for that day, laid aside his black working dress; and arrayed in his Sunday suit, with a sprig of thyme, and two or three double daisies in his button-hole,—looked really as clean from head to foot, as if he had never seen the inside of a coal-pit in his life. He has a pale mild face; with rather handsome, but singularly inexpressive features, and sometimes, when he has attempted to do errands for us,—to be sure, that is quite out of his line,—we have had reason to think his intellect none of the brightest: but never mind, Isaac! "The fear of the Lord is the beginning of wisdom;" and the attention and interest with which you heard to-day, of him who "shall feed his flock like a shepherd, and gather the lambs with his arm," proved plainly that the mysteries of religion may be revealed, and the poetry of the gospel felt by the illiterate and the simple.

But there is no want of expression in the countenance of the old man, who sits at the top of the aisle. I observed him when first I came into church: his face was turned toward the children, his hands were lifted up, and his eyes closed. You saw at a glance that his whole heart was engaged; he was praying for them. One tear after another streamed quietly down the thin cheek, but God's peace which passeth all understanding, shone on the placid brow. The exhortation began, and the expression of his features altered, with every alteration in the touching service: there was still attention, deep humiliation, exulting hope: and then again the children sung, and again the old man wept and prayed for them. Our service has, with him, its full value; for by the help of his large, old-fashioned prayer book, he keeps word by word with the minister throughout it. But the preacher may be eloquent or pathetic, it is all lost upon him; he does not know the words beforehand, and he never hears one syllable of the sermon. He hands his bible over our pew door, that we may find him the text; and he likes well, he says, to meditate on it; but he has entirely lost his hearing for many years:—

> "But patience! there may come a time,
> When these dull ears shall scan aright,
> Strains, that outring earth's drowsy chime,
> As heaven outshines the taper's light."
> KEBLE.

Happy, good, old man; one would think it must be only a short time, before that world of brightness, and that burst of music shall break upon him. He has been an aged man as long as I can recollect; and the thought of him comes to my mind, connected with some affecting remembrances. I never can look at him now, without thinking of one day in particular, when a beautiful little boy was brought into the church, before the congregation assembled, on purpose that good old John might see him. The child raised his dark wondering eyes to the old man's face; as taking one little delicate hand in his, he laid his other on the clustering curls of shining hair, and prayed "the God that had fed him all his life long,—the Angel that had redeemed him from all evil, to bless the lad!" And surely, there the blessing rested: the child grew: how green an olive-tree in the house of his God, why should I pause now to tell you. I saw that old man lift up his eyes in prayer for him, when thirteen years after, he knelt for the first time, to receive the emblems of his Saviour's redeeming love: again, the holy feast was spread; and again came the aged man and the youth. A few weeks,—a very few past, the old man knelt at his Lord's table, in his accustomed place; but as he came, he had paused, to look upon that light-hearted boy's grave.

Hark! there is a shout of joy from our garden; there is the bounding of glad steps, and the song of rejoicing hearts. I cannot go amongst them now. Come quietly away with me; and we will walk up and down the narrow path, by the sweet-briar hedge; and we will listen to the low song of the black-bird, and the fresh air will cool our aching brows, and we shall find comfort. To these things, fresh air, and the bird's song, and the fragrance of the lowly flowers, God has given a blessing; like sleep they are his medicines,—" Balm of hurt minds." We will walk to and fro, under the shade of these elms, and we will be calm; bitter recollections shall be made sweet, by the thought of his mercies; and in the midst of the sorrows we have in our hearts, his comforts shall refresh our souls; and our minds shall be stored with many pleasant thoughts, sweet, like the perfume of these flowers;

> "Like the memory of well-spent time,
> Of things that are holy and dear;
> Of friends departed this life,
> In the Lord's faith and fear."

And so shall end our Whit-Monday: and it is well for us, that our very days of rejoicing should end even so; with a sigh for that land, where joy is in its own country; where there is no more sorrow, nor any more crying, because God wipes away the tears from all eyes.

# A DAY OF GLOOM.

"Although the day be never so long,
At last it ringeth to even-song!"

THERE are days in our lives in which without any visible reason why it should be so, the tide of our spirit sinks far below its usual level; all our evils real, or fancied, swarm about us at once, and we fully assent to the divinely-inspired sentence, which says, "Man is born to trouble."

It is not at all necessary to feel the pushing, and thronging of a rude world, to know how many inconveniences are found in life. If his fellows do not vex him, "man disquieteth himself;" yet, "What should you know of the trouble and misery of the world, in this retirement," has been often said to me; but it has been vainly said; "the whole creation groaneth," and the groan is heard as deeply in the shade of the forest, as in the heart of the city.

Now it happened, that I sat down to write, on one of these—the spirit's *ember* days. I had been wearied with the sound of the melancholy bell, which had been tolling muffled all day;* and as night came on, and the lowered flags drooping heavily from the distant towers, could no more be distinguished, and the minute guns fired hour after hour, in answer to the deep knell; I became very gloomy indeed, and I lay awake listening; and when at last I slept, the solemn sounds mingled with my dreams. I thought, as I suppose most other people in the kingdom did that night, of the worthlessness of earth's treasure, and the changeableness of earth's certainty; and the impression continued strongly on my mind many days. The pomp and circumstance of the procession was different, certainly, I thought; there was the monarch of a mighty land himself, and nobles and princes as mourners; and banners and escutcheons, to show how mighty he had been, whom the purple pall covered; and partially displayed in the torch-light, were the white robes of priests, and the re-

* This chapter was begun about the time of the late king's funeral.

versed arms of soldiers: but now the royal corpse is left as valueless a thing, as unattended, in as deep gloom, as that of the peasant child; which half a dozen country girls, and its sorrowing father and mother, laid to rest, on that same stormy evening in our bleak church-yard.

O Lord! in thy sight, what is man, with all his pomp and pageantry? What are we? Altogether vanity. A high estate cannot defend, a low estate cannot shelter us from the hand of death; any more than from the miseries of life. And then,—for it was a day of gloom—I went on to consider how fully it had been my lot to know what that word misery means. Nay, my gentle reader, do not smile so incredulously. One need not be grey-headed; one need not have accompanied Howard to Turkey, or even Mrs. Fry to the prisons of the metropolis, to understand that word. Sit down with me amongst the beautiful purple heath, visited by the wild bees, and the blue butterflies; and breathe the fresh air of our rugged hill, and look on the fairly-extended prospect; and know that man, the sinner, carries that within him, which, unpurified by God's grace can defile the fairest scene. The fertile source of all woe springs forth in his heart; and as I have read,—I forget where—the cross is the tree of healing virtue, which alone can make the bitter waters sweet: oh! would to God the secret were generally known; would to God, all the broken in heart knew to whom to apply, as the healer of the wound. But so, it is not. Many despair, as Hagar did, when she cast down her child under the shrubs that she might not see his death; who will not open their eyes with Hagar, though the angel of the Lord points them to the gushing water. Oh! it is a melancholy world; there the sick unto death, lie along the road, obstinately refusing to be healed, though there is balm in Gilead, and a physician there.

Then I remembered a story, which I heard when I was a child,—and what we hear as children, we seldom forget, —of one of those broken hearts which would not be bound up: it was of a suicide; and when the coroner assembled his jury, and the oath was to be administered, there was found no book in the house, which they could acknowledge as the word of God. What! not one copy of the good news brought from heaven to sinners; not one New Testament of Him who longs to be our Lord and Saviour Jesus Christ? No word of consolation? Oh! what a commentary on that unhappy being's miserable life, and yet more miserable death. No! on that awful occasion the men shuddered as they sent out to borrow a bible; and as they turned a hasty and terrified glance on the pale and bloody corpse before them; the most careless could scarcely fail to feel a wish too deep, too hopeless for utterance,—"That thou hadst known in thy day, the things that belonged to thy peace!" Have I vainly trifled with your feelings; uselessly lifted the veil from so awful a scene? The world in which you live, abounds with such; and my purpose in writing, is to charge *you* to lay hold on the hope set before *you* in the gospel. The wind and the tide may be in your favour now; but you know not in how short a time you may have to say, "All thy billows and thy storms are gone over me;" "Deep answereth to deep." It may, therefore, not be unprofitable, having gazed for a moment on the miserable wreck, to turn from it with softened and humbled hearts, and inquire how the bark passes the waves of this troublesome world; when

"Hope, as an anchor firm and sure, holds fast
The Christian vessel, and defies the blast."

Do you see those five very tall poplar-trees near to the water's edge? A little way behind them, but concealed from us by the rugged side of the stone quarry, is a row of miserable houses,—I will not honour them by the name of cottages,—the wretchedness of whose outward appearance is but too faithful an indication of the misery, and I fear I might add in most instances, the guilt which dwells within. It is truly the worst part of the parish; yet bad as they all are, one at the further end, lower and narrower than the rest, is the most wretched of the dwellings: and there, bearing for many years, a wasting and painful disease; enduring neglect, cold, and hunger, and one trouble greater than all the rest, with uncomplaining patience; with a fortitude unadmired by man, but not unseen by angels, nor unapproved by God; lived and died at the early age of twenty-seven years, poor Esther. "The world has its objects of admiration," says Cowper, in one of the sweetest letters, perhaps, ever written, "and God has his objects of love; those make a noise and perish, but these weep silently for a short season, and live for ever." Such, I surely believe, has been Esther's enviable lot. She, I doubt not, through much tribulation, has entered into the kingdom of God. Shall I tell you what I can recollect of her story? Her distresses began early, for her mother died; and her father's family presently became the scene of all the confusion and discord which vice and misrule create. She appears to have been naturally of a gentle temper; and to escape from the daily scenes of violence, which she was obliged to witness, she married very imprudently, when scarcely eighteen years of age. I did not know her until long after this; but all my inquiries respecting her conduct at that time, lead me to believe, that although the full power of God's grace, as revealed in the gospel, was not then manifested to her; there was yet in her, as in the young Abijah, some good thing towards the Lord her God. Her neighbours speak of her, as having been peaceable, industrious, and honest; and with regard to her husband,— if deep affection and true faith deserve return,—her husband was heavily indebted to her, and a fearful recompense may be required of him. I will not linger over this part of my story, it is one of every day's occurrence: at first they were happy together, but after a few years, and the birth of several children, Esther fell into an ill state of health, and her husband became weary of her and neglected her; two of her little ones died, and this distress, added to her former troubles, brought on a violent fever. She had no medical attendant, and if her constitution had not been naturally strong, surely she could not have struggled through what she then endured. For five weeks she kept her bed, and was, for many days, entirely insensible; and when she recovered her reason, it was perceived that her arm was dislocated: she was carried to the Infirmary, but so long a time had elapsed since the dislocation took place, that it was pronounced irremediable. She was, however, received into the house; and her cruel husband immediately sold every article of the furniture which her care had hitherto saved from his wretched habits of waste; and leaving their only remaining child, a remarkably handsome boy of about two or three years, to the unwilling charge of strangers, he went away.

It is well indeed for miserable man, that in his hour of deep distress, he has one to whom to apply, more pitying than his fellow-sinner. "My heart was almost broken, when I heard of it," said poor Esther, "but the Lord does all things well." It was within an evening or two after her admission into the hospital, and while she lay thinking, I suppose, of her forlorn and hopeless condition, in the loss of all earthly comfort, and having then but vain and unfounded hopes for heaven; that the chaplain having read prayers in the next ward, stopped at the stranger's bed. He was one well used to instruct the ignorant, and to comfort those who mourn; yet from Esther's account, I fancy he must have found more than usual difficulty in his first introduction to her. "I thought it very strange and very unkind of him," she said, "so to insist upon it, that I was a sinner; I did not then know with how what a holy God I had to do; and I recollect I hoped he would never come again. But he was very patient with me, he came day after day,—blessed be God for it; and I learnt, little by little, how I was born in sin, and had sinned in thought, word, and deed; and I saw that there could be only one Saviour, but, thank God, I saw that he was mighty to save! And then, oh, how I used to long for the gentleman's coming; and if he could have talked to me all day, I am sure I could have listened: I shall never see him again on earth, but, oh, dear me! if ever I get to heaven—" And she would stop abruptly and weep, as if the greatness of the hope had overcome her.

She had been in the Infirmary many weeks, when some one who visited her there, told her that her step-mother was about to place the child in the work-house, as she could not be troubled with him any longer. "And he is the only one I have left, my beautiful child!" she said, "and I shall never, never see him again;" and she burst into a passionate fit of weeping, which those about her strove in vain to quell. The physicians were kindly anxious to have her under their care yet a little longer; but she would not be detained. They told her she needed constant attention, and her only *chance* of recovery was her patiently remaining under their care. But the mother felt that she had rather die with her child, than live away from him; so she was carried home to the miserable hovel which I have pointed out to you. She left the conveniences and comforts of the well-aired and neatly-arranged ward for the most wretched of beds, and the scantiest and coarsest of food; but happily for Esther she had found, and she carried with her to her sordid home, "the pearl of great price;" and to the uneasy bed on which she was laid, when she arrived there, and from which she never rose again for the three remaining years of her life, her Lord's comfort while she lay sick on her bed, " Thou, Lord, didst make all her bed in her sickness." Her change of character was remarked, though the reason of that change was not duly appreciated, by the ignorant and careless people amongst whom she resided. She was a new creature, possessed of new motives and new actions; new sorrows and new comforts: a new support through the accumulated woes of life; and an entirely new hope in the prospect of death. Without any outward means of grace, the work of the Spirit of God silently, but rapidly advanced:

"Stillest streams oft water fairest meadows."

"It is wonderful," said one, "to see how she bore her illness; how very patient she was, it was unaccountable to see." Perhaps, few Christians ever were called to a longer exercise of that one grace of patience. For Esther's troubles multiplied, whilst all her earthly comforts seemed reduced to one single blessing; all that life had of joy to her, centred in her little child. He was a child worth his mother's affection, and he loved his poor sick mother dearly; he was gentle and affectionate, in no common degree; and his beauty resembled what his mother's had been, and she had once been very fair. It needed years of suffering, to mar the form which God had made so perfect; but disease effects fearful ravages in the brightest face; and poverty and want trace the brow even of youth with untimely furrows. The winter came on with great severity; and though fuel is so cheap here, Esther had often to bear cold in addition to her other miseries; often for days together, no one came in to kindle her scanty fire. If there was bread in the room, the child would reach it for her and divide it with her; and when there was none,—" I have often been very hungry," said Esther, "but I thought my Lord would never suffer me to starve, and I believe he never will." No, I think it is well to take God's promises literally when we may; and the rich in this world's goods cannot, perhaps, fully enter into the preciousness of that promise when literally taken, "Bread shall be given thee." "Nothing is more easy," says the venerable Bishop Hall, "than to trust God, when our barns and coffers are full; and to say, 'Give us our daily bread,' when we have it in our cupboard; but when we have nothing, when we know not how or whence to get any thing, then to depend upon an invisible bounty, this is a true and noble act of faith." Our poor Esther lived in the daily practice of such faith.

It was on one of the coldest days of that fearfully cold weather, when the ground was frozen like iron, and one could not breathe the freezing air for a minute, without remembering the text, "Who shall abide his cold;" when the icicles hung glittering from the low roof of her miserable dwelling, making a strange contrast to all that was dark and gloomy around them; that a neighbour charitably came in to light her fire; and putting the small apartment in better order than usual, left it. It was set in order for a funeral. The child had not stood by the fire a minute, before his thin night dress was in flames: "O Richard, Richard! my son, my son!" shrieked the unhappy mother. She made a convulsive effort to rise, but instantly fell backward; and feeling her utter inability to assist him in his agony, buried her face in the bed-clothes, and lay senseless. The poor infant's cries presently alarmed the neighbours; they put out the fire, but it is needless to record the state to which those few moments had reduced him: he was immediately carried to the nearest hospital. "That night," said Esther,—the ignorant, you know, are always superstitious,—"that night, just as the clock struck three, I was lying here all in the dark, crying about my poor child; I felt something pass, and step softly on the bed just as he used to do; and I looked up and saw him, and he looked so beautiful, and I was just going to say, 'Is it you, my son?' and he was gone!" "Ah!" said I, "when we dream of friends that are dead, they often do appear to us very beautiful." But Esther evidently did not think it a dream. "I did not know then," she said, "that he was dead; but when my step-mother went in to see him the next day, the doctor told her that he had died just at three o'clock,—just when I saw him;" and she raised her dark, melancholy eyes to mine, with an expression which seemed intended to ask, "You do not think that it was only a dream?" But I was sure that a controversy on that incomprehensible subject, the possibility and the probability of apparitions, would be worse than useless; so I generally ended that part of the conversation, by reminding her, that he who had said, "Suffer the little children to come unto me," would certainly not leave her comfortless, though he had taken her last earthly comfort away from her; and that I doubted not her little Richard would look very beautiful when she saw him in heaven: "And I think I shall see him," she would answer calmly, "and my Lord has not left me comfortless."

It was a few months after this heavy affliction, I well remember the day, when we were fully repaid the labour of a tiresome walk, by discovering in poor Esther,— accidentally as it seemed to us,—one of those so exactly pointed out by our Master;—"Sick, and ye visited me,"—"Inasmuch as ye did it unto one of the least of these, ye did it unto me." I well recollect how shocked we were, not so much at her extreme poverty, as at her solitary and deserted condition. Her husband, as if he had one, and only one human feeling left, had come to look at the child as he lay in his coffin, but utterly neglected the dying mother. Her only support, the pittance which the parish compelled him to allow her, was grudgingly and irregularly paid; yet I never heard her mention him, but with pity, and in a spirit of kindness. The sister who slept with her, left her early in the morning, and returned very late at night; so that, except when a neighbour came in at uncertain intervals, Esther might hunger and none give her bread,—be thirsty and none give her drink. I have several times found her faint, for want of a morsel of food: generally there was none in the room, but sometimes she has said, "There is bread there, but I cannot reach it." It is sad that such things should be in a Christian country, but I have not exaggerated.

My gentle reader, I fancy you young, healthy, blest with a competent supply of this world's goods; and perhaps

with what is much more valuable, good sense and leisure.
I charge you, as you will answer it at the day of judgment,
use these things, for they are "talents." Let there be in
your neighbourhood no forsaken Esther to whom you
might have ministered. I do not advise you to look for
your reward, in the gratitude of those for whom you may
exert yourself. I would say,—I believe it is a sentence of
the excellent Fenelon,—"Sanctifiez toutes vos actions, en
leur donnant pour motif, l'envie de plaire a Dieu;" but I
can assure you, that I have found amongst the poor of this
place, uncivilized and disorderly as our genteeler neighbours are pleased to account us, an affection which has reproved my coldness towards my greater Benefactor; and
gratitude which has made me blush for my unthankfulness.
So it was remarkably in Esther's case: "all good things,"
she has often said, "came to me in that day, I often think
of it, when you and that young lady came in first." And
really it was astonishing, how many friends we met with
for her; one procured her a blanket, another some needful
articles of dress; others supplied food; and after much
consultation,—for ours is a very poor parish, and we are
often obliged to manage in a way which would create a
smile in richer neighbourhoods,—we procured her a new
bed. The tick was bought by subscription; then doubts
arose as to the filling; millpuff was too expensive, and oat
chaff not to be procured here; but ."necessity," said our
old neighbour at the shop, "is the mother of invention;" we begged worn-out pieces of carpet from various
persons, delighted the younger children at the school, by
employing them to pick it entirely thread from thread; and
you would have been surprised to see what very respectable filling it made: and Esther's joy and gratitude for this
unexpected, but most necessary gift, was such as she could
not express, and I cannot describe. "Bless the name of
the Lord!" "He has done all things well," were the
phrases constantly in her heart, and on her lips. I believe
I never, during the two years I knew her, heard her express any thing like dissatisfaction in God's dealings
towards her. I never remember her complaining, though,
indeed, there was cause of complaint of the carelessness
with which her relations treated her. Those who approached her low door were more than once astonished at

hearing within a weak, but not unmelodious voice of joy; for often when alone, she strove to amuse herself by singing the few verses of hymns which she knew; thus beginning in the dark valley of the shadow of death, that song of praise and triumph, which I believe she is singing now, in a very different tone, and under far other circumstances.

But you are getting weary: you think I have forgotten my motto,

> "Although the day be never so long,
> At last it ringeth to even-song."

O, no! Esther's day of gloom closed at length. Her daily bread was provided to her to the very day on which she died. I saw her on a Saturday; she was wasted to a state that it was melancholy and humiliating to see. Some such form, perhaps, presented itself to Milton's mind's eye, when he described the place,

> "Sad, noisome, dark, a lazar house it seemed;"

but no pen but Milton's should attempt to describe such a sight. Oh! blessed are they, who bearing about with them such a body of sin and death; yet cling with sure and certain hope to that promise, "It is sown in corruption, it is raised in power." I recollect nothing particular in our last interview; she was patiently waiting until her Lord was ready for her; and though in great pain and very weak, she smiled affectionately, and even cheerfully when she saw me. I had been entrusted with a small sum of money, on her account; and as I knew some days would elapse before I came again, I went to the kind-hearted mistress of a little inn near, and engaged her to supply Esther with certain articles of food every day, whilst the money lasted. We reckoned it over together; it would provide her with that particular comfort she so much needed, until the Monday week following. "And whom shall I ask next?" I thought: nay take no thought for the morrow. Monday week came, and Esther had thanked God for her last meal. On Tuesday morning we heard the bell toll for her. She had been no worse; had suffered no more than usual: her Father's still, small voice had said, "Come!" and she was gone home. What matter if the traveller's scrip is empty, when the sunset shines on him, as he ends his toilsome journey, and enters his own father's house?

Ah! it is time for us to think of our walk home; for the sunset shone on us long ago, and the silver mist rises, tracing the long course of the river in the low grounds beneath us. Come through the corn-fields the rustling of whose ripening ears, once more reminds us of His faithfulness, who promised that seed-time and harvest should never fail;—down our own hilly ground, between the moist willows, and up the bank again into the home-field: and as we enter our silent garden, we cannot forget to take one look at the glorious jessamine. It is fifty, perhaps, sixty years old; and covers a great part of the south wall of the house. Just now it is in most luxuriant blossom, having lit up its ten thousand stars, and opened its stores of incense to greet us and the harvest moon; for the jessamine you know is a night flower. If we come to-morrow in the sunshine, we shall scarcely be able to gather one perfect spray. How gracefully it wreathes round the casement window; and hangs its light sprays about the low heavy door. No, you need not open it; we cannot go in to business, and candle-light yet: come through the little white gate; the moon shines on the polished laurel leaves, and on the white holly-oaks; the stately lilies are gone; but this high path is my favourite evening walk still: for see how beautifully the light and shade are thrown on that group of trees, behind which the church-tower rises. There are heavy clouds, but they are flying away before the clear night wind; and the few stars, and the full moon shine in their most perfect brightness. "How beautiful is night!" and yet this is the evening of what I called "A Day of Gloom." O, how mercifully God teaches us to seek peace in his word, and in the contemplation of his works; there, and there only it cannot but be found. Hush! listen! the wind is still at this moment; you may hear the distant chime of musical bells; they sound at this hour every evening. In one minute, our church clock will strike nine;—there it is, we must go in now: "it ringeth to even-song," and after prayers, I will show you some lines which though they are not exactly suitable to my subject, yet have occurred to me so often, when I have walked here at evening, that now I scarcely ever do so without thinking of them:—

### THE BLESSING AFTER SERVICE.

I was within a house of prayer,
And many a wounded heart was there;
And many an aching head was bowed,
Humbly amidst the kneeling crowd:
Nor marvel, where earth's children press,
There must be thought of bitterness.

Oh! in the change of human life,—
The anxious wish, the toil, the strife,—
How much we know of grief and pain,
Ere one short week comes round again.
Bend every knee, lift every heart;
We need God's blessing ere we part.

Then sweetly through the hallowed bound,
Woke the calm voice of solemn sound;
And gladly many a list'ning ear
Watched, that pure tone of love to hear;
And on each humbled heart, and true,
God's holy blessing fell like dew.

Like dew on summer's thirsty flowers;
On the mown grass, like softest showers;
On the parch'd earth like blessed rain,
That calls the spring-bloom back again :
Oh! to how many a varied sigh,
Did that sweet benison reply.

"The peace that God bestows,
  Through him who died and rose;
The peace the Father giveth, through the Son,
  Be known in every mind,
  The broken heart to bind;
And bless ye, travellers, as ye journey on!"

" Ye, who have known to weep
  Where your beloved sleep;
Ye, who have pour'd the deep, the bitter cry!
  God's blessing be as balm,
  The fever'd soul to calm,
And wondrous peace each troubled mind supply."

" Young man whose cheek is bright
  With nature's warmest light;
Whilst youth and health thy veins with pure blood swell;

  Let the remebrance be,
  Of thy God blest to thee,
Peace, passing understanding, guard thee well."

 "Parents, whose thoughts afar,
 Turn where your children are;
In their still graves, or beneath foreign skies;
 This hour God's blessing come,
 Cheer the deserted home,
And peace with dove-like wings around you rise."

 "Ere this week's strife begin;—
 The war, without, within:
The triune God, with spirit and with power,
 Now on each bended head,
 His wondrous blessing shed,
And keep you all, through every troubled hour."

And then within the holy place,
Was silence for a minute's space;
Such silence, that you seem'd to hear
The holy Dove's wings hovering near;
And the still blessing far and wide,
Fell like the dew at evening tide;
And ere we left the house of prayer,
We knew that peace descended there;
And through the week of strife and din,
We bore its wondrous seal within!

# A TALE OF LOW LIFE.

"Alas, in the depth of the human heart,
 What agonized thoughts are nurs'd;
What life-linked ties may be rent apart,
 Ere ever the full heart burst!

Then who shall tell in those few short hours,
 What anguish that true heart bore;
Till the frail form bent like a riven flower,
 And the broken heart bled no more."

I HAVE a story to tell you, and I know of exactly a fit spot in which to tell it. We have not been a long walk for some time; and the rain has laid the dust; and the heavy purple clouds hang about the sun, so as to cool and temper his rays—not to conceal—scarcely to dim them; for they stream through, edging the purple with the brightest silver; and lighting up every tower, and hill, and tree; and taking notice of every separate leaf, and burnishing every little wing in the gnats' unnumbered army, that rises and falls, and wheels forward and circles backward, with orderly, yet incomprehensible motions.

The wild roses are hanging in long garlands, the full-blown flowers pale, and the buds red; and the starry elder with its broad white blossoms, and its green of every-varied shade grows beside it, in the lanes through which we must pass. And there are wide grass meadows, where the old elms stretch their broad branches; and the aspen trembles in every lightly hung leaf; and the weeping ash, and the silver birch, those beautiful sisters, rise arm in arm, each bending to look at the other in the quiet stream. And there we shall find wild flowers in abundance: the medicinal comfrey with its rough leaf, and its little clusters of purple and white bell-shaped blossoms, of which the bees are so fond; and the yellow-hawk weed; and the vast variety of snap-dragons, from the bright crimson which loves the sunny wall, to that little delicate one with its purple brown leaf, and its purely white blossom, tipped with clear yellow; which we shall meet with, springing from the dewy moss in the freshest shade. The blue-bells are faded; but the *ragged robins*, as we used to call them when we were children,—and I know of no other name for them now—supply their place well; and there are the fox-gloves, the stately fox-gloves, six feet high, with more than a hundred bells; what a peal that must be, if they ring out altogether at midnight, when the fairy queen passes; and there clings the bright-eyed pink vetch, and the golden cinquefoil; and there, dearest and loveliest, close by the water's edge, that most popular of all flowers—the forget-me-not. Its form is elegant, and its colour, true faith's own; yet it is by pleasant association that we love it so well. And that is a charm which all field flowers have in some degree; and by which they are compensated for the want of that superior beauty and fragrance which their delicate sisters of the hot-house and green-house,—those fine ladies amongst the flowers,—possess:

> Mine be the flowers that freely blow
>   In each uncultur'd spot;
> Anemone, with leaves of snow,
>   And blue forget-me-not.
>
> Give me the wild thyme and the heath,
>   Because their blossoms wave
> On battle-fields, where rests beneath—
>   What true hearts! in their grave.
>
> Where Alfred fought, the same flowers bloom
>   On each embattled hill;
> There the wild furze and golden broom
>   Wave glittering banners still.
>
> And bring those lovely, gentle things
>   That deck our church-yard way;
> The soft grass, whence the violet springs,
>   And cuckoo flowers of May.
>
> There is a spell around those blooms,
>   Own'd by no rarer flowers;
> They blossom'd on our fathers' tombs,
>   And they shall grow on ours.
>
> To us, as to our sires, their tone
>   Breathes forth the same glad strain,—
> "We spring to life when winter's gone,
>   And ye shall rise again!"
>
> Uncultur'd, round our path they grow,
>   Start up before our tread;
> Perchance, as they did long ago,
>   Ere some dear friend was dead.

The fox-gloves in the sheltering wood,
  Say, "Here he used to hide."
And primrose whispers, "Thus we stood
  All blooming when he died!"

Thus every wild flower's simple leaf
  Breathes in its native vale,
To conscious hearts some record brief,
  Some true and touching tale.

Let the conservatory stand,
  I own their foreign claims;
Those glorious flowers from other lands,
  Rare plants with wondrous names.

Ye trembled in our martyr's field,
  Beneath the torches' glare;
Sprung from the turf where Falkland kneel'd,
  As now ye blossom there.

Ye in our childhood's garden grew,
  In our young brother's bowers;
My English heart beats high to you,
  My own wild English flowers!

So, having paid my respects to them, we will proceed; under these almost horizontal branches, where the banks rise so perpendicularly, that the roots of the trees are far above our heads; into the low field where the stream is crossed by one of the most picturesque of bridges. There is scarcely any charm wanted; for the buttresses show their grey stones, in some places, through the wreathing ivy; and finding nourishment enough for itself, in the loose earth between them, springs a small and very graceful yew-tree; and there also grows ash and alder; and the little antirhinum hangs there, its long festoons of tender green leaves and diminutive lilac flowers strung on its most slender stem. And there grows the wall-fern, ripening its innumerable seeds from their unseen blossoms on the under-side of the leaf; and there bright "with nature's varnish," the hart's-tongue: and not one leaf, nor one flower, nor one tinted stone in the small arches; but you see it reflected—so still, so pure, is the stream below.

But come, the sun has no very long journey to take; and I have a story to tell you, before we turn homewards: let us cross the bridge, and scramble—it is really a scramble,— over the bank, and up into the little copse on the opposite side the stream. We are not breaking bounds, for difficult as the path is, it is evidently in constant use; so our consciences may be easy on that score. Set your foot firmly on these contradictory brambles, and spring to that bank of soft, red, yielding mould, as steadily as you may; and now one effort more,—mind the briars,—and then down the bank, and here we are; and this is beautiful. Here is the softest velvet under our feet, and the greenest canopy over our heads; and we ascend a narrow and very winding path; sometimes passing round the fantastic roots of old trees, which had grown old and begun to decay before we were born, and which yet may weather many a winter storm after we are quiet in our graves; and from the fine mould in the crevices of the bark, grow the most minute and beautiful funguses and lichens: and sometimes our feet sink in the deepest moss; and then again, we have to climb over huge stones, tinted with many colours, which have at some time long ago, been precipitated from what was once a stone quarry above. Here is nature's home. The trees grow here, where she planted them; some rising up in stately and proud beauty, and others throwing themselves entirely across the stream, as if impatient of their separation from their opposite companions; and there is the wild climatis, wreathed as nature wreathes it; from one shady branch to another, till where it gains the free air and the sunlight, it shall shine with a crown of silver blossoms. And now look up, from the image of that proud rock in the silent water,—up through the young red leaves of this old oak tree; and the scented flowers of the woodbine which has clung to it in storm and sunshine so long, and so faithfully,—up through the living branches, to the pale blue sky, across which, the purple and grey clouds of evening are sailing so majestically; and own with me how beautiful is that scenery which God has made, and which man leaves alone.

But now,—for the mind may become luxurious, as well as the body,—I am doubting whether the sad tale of low life, which I have to tell, is in exact unison with the quiet, the purity of this scene. It is not pleasant to turn, in such a place as this, to the consideration of common misery and vulgar distress; and yet, alas! when we draw from the life, such things must constantly present themselves. It is not pleasant,—yet a heathen poet having discovered that he, being a man, could think nothing belonging to man uninteresting,—it is not surely for Christians to turn with a disgusted ear, from the "natural sorrow" incident to their fallen human nature ; not for Christians, since their divine Master dwelling in the perfection of unapproachable light and beauty, condescended for their sakes to become acquainted with the details of a life of poverty, and the pangs of an ignominious death. With these considerations, then, sit patiently down by me, on this moss-grown branch, and listen to my true story.

It is almost two years since, that the secretary of our little Society was applied to, for relief, by a young woman, whose appearance certainly spoke of any thing but want. She was dressed more smartly than most servant-maids, even in these days. The tasty straw bonnet, gaily lined and trimmed, displayed under its spreading front, a double row of edging, and yet gayer ribbons on the cap; and the long ear-rings—whether they were gold or not I cannot tell,—danced and glittered as she moved, as brilliantly as if they had belonged to a titled lady: her shawl, green and red shaded silk, was pinned so as to display to advantage, a stately and finely-made form ; and she moved as one who was conscious of her superiority. Yet if the gaiety of her dress, (very unfit, truly, for her station) and a certain haughtiness of look made an unfavourable impression ; it was done away in the moment in which you heard her speak. Her voice was clear and sweet ; and her bright hazel eyes looked down upon one with an expression of humility, when she asked her favour, which, though her appearance altogether led you to suppose they had little used, yet became them well. She was not a native of our parish ; the propriety of her mode of expression, even more than her slight Welsh accent, forbade our thinking so for a moment. Her face as well as her figure, brought to mind some of Westall's beautiful and majestic Jewesses: the strong outline of regular features, the arched and dark eyebrow, the quick eye, the proud curve of the upper lip, the rosy colour of the clear brown complexion; forming altogether a style of beauty, which in a woman, we are, perhaps, more apt to see with admiration than love. "How very handsome she would be thought, if she were a lady," we said, "and Sir Thomas Lawrence had painted her portrait; and Heath or Danforth had engraved it for one of the Annuals." It was strange that such a one should need the homely assistance we could supply; and our secretary paused a moment, as she looked at the recommendatory ticket, sent by a liberal subscriber. "Had she many children?" "She had lost some, but had only one living." "But her appearance,—really the secretary doubted, was afraid it was a very poor society; and what it could afford, would be scarcely worth her acceptance." "She would very thankfully accept the smallest gift: times were not with her, what they had been." Again the secretary glanced at her dress: "Had her husband employment at present." "Her husband"—the poor young woman's voice failed her, and she burst into tears,—"he was very good to her, very kind; he had always been so, but now—" Our kind-hearted secretary was moved: "Times were bad," she observed; and though in her heart she had quarrelled with the long ear-rings, this burst of natural tenderness had overcome her feeling of disapproval; and she promised all the Society could supply, as soon as it should be needed.

I cannot tell how long it was after this, that we heard Martha was very ill. From the description, we were sure it was the same young woman, whose appearance we had thought so striking. She was at lodgings at the bottom of the fields, and there we went to seek her. "Your lodger is ill," I said to the mistress of the house, a very untidy woman, who sat idly by the ashes of a grate, at which three or four unruly children were lighting shavings. "Your lodger is ill, I understand;" but I stopped as I looked at the shattered window, the dirty floor, and the miserable furniture; it is not surely possible that noble looking young woman should live here. "Martha has my up-stairs room," said the woman, as I hesitated,—"I'll show you up, if you please:" she did so, and I was glad to find that Martha's apartment was in far better order, than that of her hostess. Yet it was only by contrast that it bore any appearance of comfort. The grinding of the sand, with which the floor was strewed under our feet, was a sad sound for a sick person's ear; and the low fire had an appearance, mournful rather than cheering, as the cloud of smoke issued into the room, in answer to the draft from the door. Besides Martha had been taken ill so immediately on her coming, that there had been no time to unpack or arrange her few articles of furniture, which for the most part stood piled against the wall. And there was no one on whom she could rely for help; she was far away from all her kindred: oh! there is a charm in that word; others may be charitable, strangers may oblige us, but in the hour of distress, it is to a mother's voice that we would unhesitatingly listen for comfort, and on a sister's arm that we would rest with confidence.

I looked towards the bed; was it possible that such a change could have taken place in so short a time? Could sickness have done it? Not sickness alone. Grief and care make fearful ravages, even when health and ease of circumstances struggle against their effects; but when they come in the hour of nature's trial, what wonder if the faint heart sinks under them? Such a wreck, so sudden, so entire, I never saw before; I trust never to see such again. Terror and sorrow had done in one fortnight, the work of years. The bright eyes were sunk and dim; the lips were parched, and the finely-formed cheek was pale and hollow. Oh! how those expressive words of the Psalmist were whispered in our ears, with a fearful repetition, "When Thou with rebukes dost chasten man for sin, Thou makest his beauty to consume away. Man in his best estate is altogether vanity." Poor Martha evidently remembered us as we drew near the bed; but she could not speak without an effort which it seemed almost death to her to make. With a trembling hand, however, she lifted up the coverlid, that we might see her infant; but when we made the customary remarks on its healthy appearance, and expressed the usual good wishes that it might live to be a comfort to her, she did not smile. From her, all earthly hope seemed to have passed for ever. Her husband, so I learnt from the neighbours, had, as she said, always been kind to her; and she took pains to deserve and to keep his affection. But I fear neither of them knew that "except the Lord build the house, their labour is but lost that build it." The fairest fabric of earthly happiness, unless founded in the fear and love of God, is but a house built on the sand, which the first storm of temptation will cause to fall. A time of distress, such as our young people had never before known, came on; labour was scarce, and provisions were dear; and it was said that Thomas made use of dishonourable means for supplying their necessities. It was said so, yet there were those who had known him a long time, and who still expressed entire dependence on him: and perhaps, I can scarcely judge; yet I fear the suspicions entertained against him, were but too-well founded. This much I know, no man's morals, be his rank in life high or low, are to be depended on, in a time of trial, except so far as the grace of God upholds him: and Thomas knew nothing of that only refuge in the day of trouble. Are any disposed to say that they are "not as other men are?" At any rate, let them add with the pharisee, "God I thank *thee;*" and those who only hope to plead "God be merciful!" will at least feel compassion toward a fellow-sinner. The poor wife heard the news that her husband was thrown into jail suddenly; and the effect of that news was fatal to her. She made an effort to visit the prison, and when there, she was almost happy, for she was with him; and it was not till she was sternly ordered to leave him, and she returned to her lonely room, that she felt the extent of her misery. Her illness came on, but her only exclamation during her hour of agony, related to her "poor husband!" Her infant was laid beside her, but no smile of welcome beamed upon it; and when the nurse told her it was a fair child, her only answer was, "fairer, if her poor father could see her!" Her strength failed, for she lay awake hour after hour, and night after night; and when, at last, nature was completely exhausted and she slept, her dreams seemed to be full of fearful and mournful images, for she started often, and often wept. "You have been asleep a long time," said one who stood by her when she awoke: "Yes," she answered, "I have been dreaming all night long of my burying, and that Thomas might not come to it;" and she burst into tears, and wept again. "If any one ever died of a broken heart," said the doctor, "she will." Oh! it was a melancholy sight to see,—a fine, healthy, beautiful creature, thus in the very pride and prime of life, brought down to the brink of the grave; not by a sudden stroke,—for the young tree that is felled, falls with all its graceful foliage and all its thousand blossoms, and in all its beauty,—but like one shivered by the lightning; in one moment, indeed, and yet every leaf seared, every spray withered, and every flower fallen, before the axe of the woodman cuts down the towering forester.

But with her bitter tears, other thoughts came. She was a sinner, a dying sinner, she said; oh! who would come and show her the way to heaven. She listened to the beautiful fifty-third chapter of Isaiah, and seemed to feel that He, of whom the Prophet spake, was bruised for her iniquities; and she responded with a fervent assent, to the Psalmist's expression of humiliation, contained in the fifty-first Psalm. She accepted gratefully, though with a dull and dying ear, and with exhausted attention, the kind instruction administered to her, by one able and willing to give comfort and advice. Ah! why had she not sought it before? Why had she not listened in the hour of her health? Nay, that is no question for us. Have we not ourselves "pulled away the shoulder, and stopped the ear, and refused to hearken?" It becomes us thankfully to take our station, *now*, in the vineyard; but to bless His mercy, who calls even at the eleventh hour.

It was the evening of an October Sunday. The red leaves yet danced, rejoicing in the mild air; and the yellow sunshine smiled on the last flowers of the year: the daisies sprung amongst the long grass on the graves, as freshly as they had done in May; and the last degenerate crop of golden-cups and starwort glittered as if to show how fair their predecessors had been. The congregation was dismissed, for the afternoon service was ended, and the parting blessing had been given; but there still remained two or three scattered groups. There were mothers who came to return thanks for their deliverance from their "great pain and peril." Little children brought to be washed in the water of baptism, and presented in faith and hope, to their merciful Saviour. Grave fathers thinking, perhaps, of new exertions to be made in answer to the calls of an increased family; and young sponsors, serious, yet evidently pleased with their interesting office. I left my accustomed seat, and went, as I sometimes do on such occasions, into the gallery behind the font. I was alone. The christening parties went into the vestry, and I sat looking on the empty seats and the silent aisles, which, as the evening closed, became every moment more and more dim.

The rising wind in the tossing chestnut branches, was, for a short time, the only sound I heard; and then a light was placed on the communion table, and an orderly party knelt at the rails, and there arose a sweet, clear voice of praise and thanksgiving. It ceased, and the train moved down toward the font. There was the priest, in his simple dress of "linen, clean and white." Long may such a dress be a meet emblem that thy priests, my country's church! are "clothed with righteousness!" And when he had taken his station at the font, the light which was needed, and yet which struggled imperfectly with the fading gleam of evening, shone on a varied and pleasing group. The elder women's scarlet cloaks formed a bright contrast to the long white robes in which the infants were arrayed; and the mothers, and the young female sponsors wearing their best,—light cotton gowns, silk shawls, and new straw bonnets, formed, for a poor country parish, a very gay assembly. Do not quarrel with my word,

"The innocent are gay,—the lark is gay."

I assure you, that as the service began, there was a silence which spoke of the mind's attention, and of the heart's prayer.

The priest took one fair child after another in his arms, "received him into the congregation of Christ's flock, and did sign him with the sign of the cross;" and one mother after another stepped tremblingly forward, and took her own precious one, and folded it to her heart; feeling more than she had ever done before, all the depth of a mother's love, and pouring on its young head all the fervency of a mother's blessing. There was a pause, and two or three persons dressed in shabby mourning, which had evidently been worn for many a relation, and many an acquaintance before,—brought to the font, an infant, whose sickly form, and weak, moaning cry, told more than the narrow band of crape round its cap, or the rusty black shawl in which they had wrapped it, a tale of "father and mother's forsaking." It might be fancy, but I thought the tone of tenderness, in which the minister had addressed each unconscious child, as it lay in his arms, was yet more tender, when he looked on this one. The mothers, I thought, gazed with deeper love on their own happy children, as the cry of this little motherless one reached their ears. The fathers looked graver, and there were tears in the young women's eyes :

> And well the gathering tears might start,
> As they nam'd the infant's name ;
> Whose mother had died of a broken heart,
> From mourning its father's shame.

Poor little thing! it was come into a troublesome world, to be sure; it was tossing on rough waves, but the frail bark was soon to be in port, where no storms come. The woman whom the parish officers engaged to nurse the child, proved extremely careless of it; and the next thing we heard, was, that in consequence of her neglect, it had met with a frightful accident; and the overseers removed it to another nurse. Having heard thus much, I could not of course be surprised, when passing one winter's day through the church-yard, I saw a little, narrow grave, dug in the part called the poor's ground; and heard upon inquiry that it was for Martha's child. It was buried that evening. No knell had tolled for it when it died, no mourner stood by the grave; the nurse brought the unornamented and nameless coffin under her cloak, and there was no pall to cover it. It was of little moment; the grass and the spring violets grow there, in token that being "sown in weakness, it shall be raised in power;" and the spirit so forsaken, so lonely on earth, found, doubtless, a bright and innumerable company to welcome it at the gates of heaven.

# A PARTY OF PLEASURE.

"Les plaisirs sont les fleurs que notre divin maitre,
Dans les ronces du monde, autour de nous fait naitre,
Chacun a sa saison."———

I DID not mean to have written another page; but I am afraid you will accuse me of melancholy, and indeed, that has unavoidably been the character of my two last chapters. I should be sorry to leave you with this impression. There is enough to make us sad in this world, to be sure. We know it is a wilderness; yet even in a wilderness are some wild flowers, some touches of beauty, such as only the hand of a divine artist could leave there; some bursts of sunlight streaming from heaven, through the brambles, and across the waste, lighting up the rough stones, and painting even the heavy drops of the last storm with the colours of hope's rainbow.

Peace is always offered to our acceptance; happiness, I believe, generally is so; but for pleasure, there is only a little time. That little time, for once, we found yesterday. We put into execution a plan which had been long in agitation; though our scheme was simple enough, one would have thought, to have been accomplished on the same day in which it was first thought of. But half the pleasure of these country adventures consists in overcoming difficulties; and inconveniences not to be borne at other times, become then, but fertile sources of amusement.

In the spring, we talked of making a party to the woods and the mill; but the spring passed, and the showery summer was stealing away, and I thought, "we shall not go this year." At last, however, the day was fixed; but then, in a climate like this, who is certain of the weather, one hour before another; "Certainly," we said, as the clouds gathered, and the hail beat down on the days previous to that of our appointment, "we shall not go on Tuesday." But the moment the sun shone again, we observed how much more beautiful the country appeared under such circumstances, than in any other, and remarked how much we enjoyed

"That beautiful, uncertain weather,
When gloom and glory meet together."

But then, let the weather be what it might, some of the party could not walk so far; and where in the world, (in this parish, I mean,) should we look for a conveyance. There is our own little open cart, indeed; but though we do travel in it to the Dorcas meetings, on a dark winter night, that is no reason why we should choose to ride in it at noon-day, especially through so very genteel a village as that to which we are bound. There is no vehicle in the parish at all suitable, to be had for love or money: to be sure Haynes the cobbler has a curious *shandridan*, sometimes open and sometimes covered, but it is a chance if that is at home. It was at home, and willingly lent on the occasion. Yet when it stood at the door with its flapping sail-cloth covering; when we saw how low it was, and considered how crowded the inmates must necessarily be,—the only two seats where either air or light were to be obtained, being those for the driver and his companion; and they, with all their advantages, could not hold up their heads, because the tilt was so low; I really thought the whole party would be disposed to walk: nothing, however, was farther from their intention. Four of them, besides shawls and provisions, and the pretty fair-haired lass who was to act as driver, were already stowed in; and assured me, when I came to the door, that two or three more might find ample room. But sunshine, light, and free air; oh! how well they are worth having, so I joined the walking party. They drove down the steep, stony lane, that we pass at first setting out, steadily enough; the horse wondering, I suppose, at his unaccustomed load, and feeling his way most circumspectly, having, said one of the party, " a doubt on his mind which side he ought to take." Afterwards, however, when we lost sight of them, I fancy they drove on, more triumphantly: for when, having crossed the fields, we met them at the stile; they were going on at a gallant rate, the two in front looking exceedingly merry; and little William peeping out at us from under the covering behind,—(the fastening of which had been jolted out of its place,)—and laughing with all his might.

It was a sweet afternoon for the scenery of those quiet

fields. A narrow stream runs through them, shaded on either side by varied and picturesque foliage of many trees. Among them are some particularly fine silver-leaved willows, contrast well with the darker hue of other branches; I have admired them often before, but I never thought them so lovely as then. We went to the very spot from whence Danby's interesting view was taken: Oh! he forgot nothing, there were the same wild flowers, the very leaves of that water-plant, nay, the same lichens on the same stones. It is by entering into the minutiæ of things; by condescending to detail, that descriptions either in writing or painting touch the heart. Man's life—woman's life, at least, is made up of trifles; the fount of feeling lies deep, yet it is usually one simple recollection, one household word, that, as with a magic spell, will send the bright and clear waters forth from the hidden fountain. So I thought, I recollect, as I looked at that exact picture, and so I felt again as I traced the original scenery; and remembered the many pleasant hours I had spent there, in days that are gone. It cannot be helped, it must be so in this fallen world; the shadow of the grave passes us in our brightest moments; in our gayest and loveliest circles, are vacant places for the dead and the absent; and when we listen to the sweetest and most beloved voices, there is often a still whisper in the sinking heart, reminding us of some voice to which we may not listen. So it was even then. We are content that it should be so; here is not our rest!

Our companions had left their carriage at the inn, and were waiting for us at the bridge. We followed the course of the quiet stream through many pleasant fields, and met with some new wonder at every turn: here we stopped to admire the purple eyes on the pinions of the peacock butterfly: there were wreaths of wild convolvulus, bearing a greater profusion of its spotless blossoms, than we had ever noticed before; I fancy they like these stormy summers as well as I do: and as we were looking at the reflection of some tall purple flowers in the clear water, the large dragon-fly, glistening with its green and gold, diverted our attention; reminding us of Mrs. Hemans's beautifully descriptive lines;

>——"Brightly free
> On filmy wings, the purple dragon-fly
> Shot glancing like a fairy javelin by—"

Further on, were a group of snow-white ducks, and purple-headed drakes, as happy, as full of life and glee, as Southey's\* mountain geese, and wanting nothing but such a description, to make them as interesting. Many a quiet green nook we passed, where a poet might muse away the long summer's day; and many a spot was pointed out to us, on seeing which, an artist might well thank God, for the ability to pursue his delightful employ. Presently, we passed the ruins of a house which, some time since, had been burnt; and we could not but remark the beauty of the gay Indica roses, which clustered round the discoloured door, and over the shattered windows. "There's a subject for you," said some of the company, and I versified it accordingly.

> See, where around yon ruin grey,
> In beauty mantling its decay,
> With glossy leaf and fragrant flower,
> Bright as if wreathed round festal bower,
> The faithful rose springs forth to tell
> "How firm her heart, who loveth well!"

> 'Twas night, and flaring up the sky,
> The fearful fire blazed wild and high;
> And before morn, the dwelling lay
> A ruin, desolate and grey;
> Then did the rose her flowers renew,
> To weep its fall with tears of dew.

> No careful hands support her stem
> Ever, so rear'd so nursed till then;
> No maiden comes from out her bower,
> To tend and watch the favourite flower;
> Or in the summer's drought to cheer
> With sprinkled waters pure and clear.

> Yet there, neglected and alone,
> Still wreathes the rose, that ruin's stone;
> And ever, as the breezes sigh,
> Passes the faithful mourner by.
> The listener hears affection's vow,
> "I lov'd thee once—I love thee now."

\* See Southey's Colloquies, vol. i. p. 146.

"Thy walls deserted and decay'd,
Still from the noon-day heat I shade;
And still in earliest hour of spring,
Round thee my fairest boughs shall cling;
Still bear I to thy shatter'd door
Flowers, as in happier days I bore;
And to the winter winds I tell,
How firm her heart, who loveth well!"

But we have no longer light and sun-shine, until almost nine o'clock. There is an autumnal freshness in the evenings now; and if we intend to drink tea in the open air, it is high time to settle where it shall be. It was of little consequence where; all had brought with them a disposition to be pleased. Yet when we arrived at the spot which was, at last, appointed, we could not but feel that where God had made things so lovely, man must, indeed, be ungrateful not to enjoy and to admire. It was a strangely beautiful spot which we had chosen; the wood rose almost perpendicularly in front of us; and from a fantastic rock garlanded with ivy, and decorated with long leaves of ladyfern and hart's-tongue—which graceful themselves, always delight in wild and uncultured scenery,—sprung forth, drop by drop, a little stream of the coolest and purest water, dripping down into a natural basin, worn in the rock beneath it. It was a spot on which you could not look without longing to know what was the old legendary record respecting it: connected with so fair a mountain, there must surely be some tradition. Was it dedicated to the holy mother herself, or to some inferior saint? And were not these grey stones worn in old time, by the feet of the pilgrim who came hither to pay his vows, or to be healed of his malady? Were there ever such beings as fairies? Hush! don't speak so loud, unless you are sure there are none such now; for if there are, here is the very place, on this mossy bank, when the glow-worm's lamps are lit, that they hold their moonlight revellings. I cannot tell how that may be; but certainly, I thought, as I turned again to look at the clear water, here the wounded doe fled, when the hunter's shaft had reached her; and here, perhaps, in after days, paused some loyal cavalier, when hot and weary, he withdrew from the field, where he had fought so gallantly, and with so little success; and unbinding the heavy helmet from his aching head, blessed the coolness of this welcome stream, and the shadow of this quiet wood.

Happily those times are past; yet the fountain has very constant visitors still, and we are even now standing in the way of one of them. "Come, little Anne, fill your pitcher, and get tea for us as soon as you can; and bring the table and chairs out here on the green bank; we are quite ready, we shall only cross the light foot bridge, and stay down there until you call us, listening to the waterfall." With that sound, another and a sweeter mingled. It was a clear voice of song; the words were beautiful, and the music, I believe, quite equal to them; of that, perhaps, I cannot judge. You who were my companions in that pleasant excursion,—and it is chiefly for your amusement that I have written these pages,—know how much we enjoyed that strain; and how well it accorded with the scenery, and with our feelings. You know also how kindly the minstrel repeated his song after our merry tea-drinking was ended: and you will acknowledge that when people are disposed to be amused, it is wonderful what strange sources of amusement they discover. We wanted more butter, had not brought enough bread, and our knife was blunt; and we were unweariedly watched by a great quiet dog, who begged us with a most touching expression of countenance, for what we were so ill disposed to spare. You know with what regret we turned, at last, from the beautiful scenery, and set out on our journey homeward; taking in our way, the silent path through the woods, and climbing the steep, from whence we had a view of the grand and castellated mansion of the noble owner. You who rode, can, I dare say, tell how commodious you found your well-appointed equipage; and I can answer for the pleasure of the quiet twilight walk; the beauty of the dark outlines of trees and hedges which we passed; and the pleasure with which we trod the last stony and steep path, because we knew it led homeward; and how, above all, we enjoyed the stillness of our own sweet garden, as the door opened to the touch of the accustomed latch-key;—our garden perfumed, as it was that night, with the scent of autumn flowers, and its old trees wreathed with woodbine and climatis, amongst whose yet unblossomed, but tenderly green sprays, the last roses are clustering. It was a pleasant scene, and combined, with the remembrance of that which we had been visiting, to prove that unworthy as we are, we are dwelling, like the Israelites of old, in "a land which the Lord our God careth for; the eyes of the Lord our God are always upon it, from the beginning of the year, even unto the end of the year."*

*August* 25, 1830.

\* Deut. xi. 12.

# CONCLUSION.

Ah! dearest mother, since too oft
 The world yet wins some Demas frail,
Even from thine arms, so kind and soft,
 May thy tried comforts never fail!

When faithless ones forsake thy wing,
 Be it vouchsaf'd thee, still to see
Thy true, fond nurselings closer cling;
 Cling closer to their Lord and thee.
    KEBLE'S CHRISTIAN YEAR.—*St. Luke's Day.*

It is time now for us to part; yet before we do so, let us take one more turn round our pleasant garden, down the steep trelliced walk, and along the path on that side the house, which the grafted pear-tree nearly covers. The busy day is done, we hear no sound, but the hum of the beetles as they pass us; no other living thing is stirring. I beg your pardon, old grey tabby, you are there, are you? You always walk up and down with me in the still twilight, and I own I am very ungrateful to forget you. The last ray of evening sunshine has faded away; and the last light rests on the young and polished leaves of the laurels, and on the stately blossoms of the fleur-de-lis. Do you not admire that princely flower? And was it not very fit for the purpose to which it was applied, in the days when the elected king of old France was chosen with the shout of a hundred clear voices; and the waving of a hundred good swords, the weakest of which was "strong to turn the flight," raised amidst his nobles on no other throne but his father's broad shield; and no other sceptre for his hand, but his country's native flag-flower?

Let us cross the grass, and pass by the graceful Persian lilac,—stoop under the hanging boughs of the quince-tree; and seat ourselves for a few minutes, on the step of the old cross: and you will ask me, perhaps, what is the age of this grey stone, and who raised it? And wherefore was it raised in what was once the depth of a forest? Tradition tells of a knight who dying far from home, begged to be buried in his father's grave; so those who stood round his bed, when his confessor had received his last sigh, closed his eyes, and straightened his limbs, and wrapped him in his winding-sheet; and set off in dark and sad procession, bearing him over hills, and up steep and stony valleys, a long and weary way, till they came at night thus far through the forest, and here they halted; and the requiem was sung: and where the corpse had rested, there, next morning, they built a low cross for his soul's health; and the stone on which you are seated, is the only one remaining. Such is tradition's story. I cannot tell who was watching the gallant knight's return to his distant home: I know not how long his mother had waited, looking out at her window, and chiding the delay of his chariot wheels; or whether his dark-eyed sisters, and his young bride had finished the broidery which described his conquests, and which they were so soon to lay aside, or to spread as a pall over the cold corpse. I cannot tell—but of this I am sure, if he, at whose desire that cross was built, really feeling himself a sinner, had grace given him to look through the countless forms and errors of his imperfect religion; and to turn for safety to that cross in which St. Paul glorified; it is all well with him. We have been brought up to a purer worship; let us consider how we have improved our privileges. It is an interesting story. How would it tell in verse?—

> What is there in that shapeless stone,
> With lichens and with moss o'ergrown,
>   That bids thee, traveller, stay?
> No sculptor's art, with choicest care
> Has traced Corinthian beauty there,—
>   Why tarry on thy way?
>
> The sun, that wakes our primrose flowers,
> Has seen as gay a race as ours,
>   Now to their graves gone by;
> And yon rude stone bids memory tell
> How, from the bower of Isabel,
>   The Spaniard came to die!
>
> She stood at his side, in her pleasant bower,
>   The Lady Isabel;
> The iris gleamed in the sunbeam shower,
> She looked pale, yet bright as that trembling flower,
>   As he bade her a last farewell.

## CONCLUSION.

"Lady! farewell! the evening breeze is sighing
  Along this cool and willow-fringed shore,
The nightingale her hymn to eve is trying,
  Together we may hear that sound no more!

"Lady! farewell! the blessed summer eve
  Wakes with its gentle breath our orange flowers,
Those flowers shall fade and flourish, but I leave—
  For ever leave—my native Spain's fair bowers!

The Lady gaz'd on his shining eye,
  The Lady Isabel;
On his noble forehead, pale and high,
But his sunk cheek flush'd, and told silently,
  That he bade her a last farewell!

Paler his cheek in our chilly air,
  His brilliant eye waxed dim;
And strangers smoothed the damp dark hair,
  And composed the weary limb.

And vainly the learned leech had striven
  To lengthen his life's short day;
But the priest the weary soul had shriven,
  And it longed to fly away.

And "Thanks," he said, "for the kindly tear,
  And thanks for the gentle tone,
Yet I would not rest amidst strangers here,
  But with Isabel my own!

"As ye would rest with your fathers brave,
  Would sleep where your mothers lie;
For His sake who only our souls can save,
  Bear me home to Spain,—to die!

"It may not be, this fluttering heart—
  This trembling—this faintness tell—
Father! pray for the soul, that so soon must part,
  And the corpse bear to Isabel."

That eve he died; and at early morn,
  Whilst the dawning was still and grey,
Forth was the worn-out body borne,
  And the long train moved away.

They moved along over plain and steep,
  Through valley, and moor, and fell;
Till they came to the forest's dark shadows deep,
  In the King's Wood where hunters dwell.

> On the damp, dark boughs shone the moonbeams pale
> As they waved in the midnight wind,
> And the priest's psalm rose on the chilly gale,
> And the corpse was borne behind.
>
> Just on this spot, by a dark oak's shade,
> (A lone wild place was here,)
> The requiem they sung, and the prayer they pray'd,
> At the side of Don Juan's bier.
>
> And next morning this rude stone cross they built,
> On the spot where the body lay;
> That the traveller might think how Christ's blood was spilt,
> And tarry awhile to pray.
>
> A purer worship hast thou been taught;
> But yet, from this ruined stone
> Turn not, until thou hast raised thy thought
> To the Cross as thy trust alone.

And here, as I am on the point of taking leave of you, allow me to advert to the principles which I have expressed during our interviews. If there has been any pride in the spirit with which I have expressed myself; any bitterness towards those who differ from me;—I am sincerely sorry, such a feeling should have been apparent to you; by me, certainly, it was not intended. Such a feeling, I am well aware, is utterly unlike the spirit of the Master whom I profess to serve; and hers, through whose ministry, I was brought to Him. But whilst my prayer, with regard to my country's church, is only

> "Not drought on others, but much dew on thee;"

whilst I recollect that she bore me, a senseless and helpless thing, in her kind arms to my Saviour, at my baptism; that the hand of her blessing has been laid on me, and on the heads of those most dear to me, in the holiest hour of their lives; that month after month, I come, a faint and weary pilgrim, to receive from her the cup of her Lord's blessing, and his broken bread, to strengthen me in my journey; that the voice of her consolation has sounded to me, from the graves of my well-beloved; and that she cheers me with the belief, that I, at last, shall rest in Christ, as my hope is, that my brethren do:—when I think of all this, can I feel coldly towards her? No, God forbid! And you, whoever you may be,—whatever your principles are, you would not in times like these, respect me for shrinking back; you cannot but feel that through good report and evil report, a daughter's heart must cling to her mother.

But the dew is falling, let us rise and walk on. The blackbirds have finished their evening hymn; and the redbreast, who has been so busy, attending on his nestlings ever since the dawn of day, is, at last, resting on the ivy spray above his nest. It is all quiet; the beautiful yellow moths pass us with an uneven motion, like the leaf of a blossom, carried by a soft wind to sleep on the moss; and the whirring of the beetles' wings, only serves to remind us of Cowper's line—

> "Stillness, accompanied with sounds like these,
> Charms more than silence."———

So I often find it here: but you must go back into the busy, rude world again: back to the crowd and the press of life, to the labour of business, perhaps, or the struggle of ambition, or the whirl of pleasure. Beware, lest you seek the living among the dead: and when disappointment comes,— as surely it must, if you do so,—think of this quiet garden, and the shadow of the chestnut over our low altar; and come and learn where peace dwells. But it is duty which calls you to the strife, and the din; then go and prosper! Carry the charm of peace about with you "In the world," says He, whose word is truth, " ye shall have tribulation:" so you would, if you staid here; "but in *Me*,"—there is the unfailing spell,—" in *Me* ye shall have peace!"

> "There are, in this loud, stunning tide
> Of human care and crime,
> With whom the melodies abide,
> Of the everlasting chime."

Such be your lot, my kind and patient companion: we may perhaps, meet again. If not, assure yourself that you bear with you my thanks, and my best wishes.—Good night.

SECOND SERIES.

TO

ALL WHO HAVE BEEN KINDLY INTERESTED IN

THE FIRST,

THIS SECOND SERIES

OF

SCENES IN OUR PARISH,

IS RESPECTFULLY AND GRATEFULLY INSCRIBED.

# INTRODUCTION

## TO THE SECOND SERIES.

> Loves, friendships, hopes, and dear remembrances,
> The kind embracings of the heart, and hours
> Of happy thought, and smiles coming to tears—
> These are the rays that wander through the gloom
> Of mortal life; wells of the wilderness.
> POLLOK.

I AM come to introduce myself to you again, gentle friend, but not now as a stranger. You have been interested in the scenes through which I have already led you—and you are willing to look upon them once more. Our society will not be more polished, nor our walks more romantic than they were before; but you were pleased because you saw nature, and nature you shall see still. During the year that has passed since we were last together, some events have occurred in my little circle worth my relating to you. I have met with new proofs of the wakefulness of God's Providence—new reasons for knowing that blessed are they that trust in him—firmer assurance of their wisdom who set their affection on things above, and unexpected and tremendous evidence of the perishing nature of all trust in this unstable world.

Allow me also to renew my expressions of deep attachment to the church—I will say the persecuted church—at present established in my country.

If I see her attacked on every side, her rights threatened, her clergy insulted, her property destroyed, is it a time even for a woman's faint heart to shrink from her? O, no! If in addition to all my former reasons for loving her, I see her patiently and humbly bearing this her time of trial, looking to Him who is able to save—if I hear, as I have lately done, her voice of prayer lifted up in intercession for some of her *deadliest enemies, can I but recognize her allegiance to her Master, and therefore acknowledge her right to my fealty? I am sure you will answer, No! and therefore if we proceed together, it must be with the same understanding in which we set out at first. I am a Church of England Christian, and claim a right, when occasion offers, to express feelings with which my very life seems bound up. I have been blamed more than once for the melancholy colouring generally observable in my pictures. I will confess the truth. I am living in a sinful, and therefore a sad world: where I really see cloud and storm, how should my picture be a very sunny one? Yet I have endeavoured never to be unnecessarily gloomy. I have earnestly desired to show, what my heart believes, that all trials—and, O, there are tremendous ones, at which flesh and heart may well fail!—all trials are bearable to him whom God teaches how to bear them.

When we write from nature we need scarcely say that we do so—because such writing bears with it an internal evidence of stronger power to convince, than any mere protestation can be. Therefore I should not now say—all the portraits I will show you are from life, and all the scenes which I describe are real; but that one of the following papers, "The Extract from a Letter," I have been requested to insert, though it is a fancy sketch. I hope its admission will not discredit the truth of the rest.

And now, I cannot allow a Second Edition, and a Second Series, to go out into the world without expressing my gratitude for the many and unexpected marks of approbation which I have received from those whom it is indeed an

---

* I refer to the prayers of the congregations in several churches being desired for the unhappy criminals condemned for the part they took in the riots.

honour to have pleased. I doubted long, as to whom I should dedicate my book. All my dearest relatives might consider themselves included in my first dedication. To my friends, would not have been explicit enough to have gratified any—and those whom I would have particularized know that I wish to please them. Then there are individuals, each alone a host, Dr. Southey or Mrs. More— but they must have had so many dedications from young writers in whose pages the most valuable words would be such names, that certainly they would not desire to add to the list.

There is the Bishop of our own diocese, to whom recent events have made all members of the Establishment look with more than common feelings of reverence and attachment—but it was a favour impossible to ask, and perhaps not to be obtained by asking.

My thoughts turned to others amongst the clergy. It was not that I was insensible to the honour it would have been to me and my book to have graced the title-page with their names—nor that if it would indeed be a mark of respect to them, it could be other than a pleasure to me to pay it: but I have prospered so well already—I have not known disappointment—that I shrink from making a request which perhaps might not be granted, or if granted, might in some degree fetter me. Then I thought of dedicating to the people of my father's parish. If only as a mark of interest and affection, I might well have done so; yet my conscience told me that if half of them could read and understand the dedication, I should not have made so free with some characters as I have done. So I came at last to the conclusion, that the compliment, if compliment it might be considered, was due to those who had kindly received the first nameless volume; and to them, and to you in particular, my dear reader, the following chapters are offered.

M*

Come then once more under the *chaperonage* of the Parson's Daughter, recollect the state of our roads, and array yourself accordingly. Two of the lanes were literally impassable last winter. Old Eleanor lost her shoe in a vain attempt to thread the one, and the constable stuck fast in the other. We have had a "partial reform," it is true, but pattens will still be necessary, and we will wear the old plaid—it is not now a time to slight old friends, especially such as are so much in keeping with the season and place. Besides here is an apology for its unfashionable appearance, which you cannot refuse to accept.

## AN APOLOGY FOR MY PLAID.

Those who live in courtly hall
Well may wear the regal pall—
Fur of price and costly gem,
Suit with lordly diadem—
Yet I doubt if oft they shine
O'er a lighter heart than mine!
Stately belles who live at ease
China's graceful crape may please;
Theirs are forms not made to bear
Autumn sleet and winter air,
And, you know, they could not travel
Lanes all mud, and hills all gravel.

Shining at the altar's side
Snow-white robes beseem a bride;
At the font where sponsors stand,
White befits the maiden band—
But it suits me not at all,
Save at such high festival—
For it shows of every stain,
Rends with every careless strain;
Dust will soil and thorns will tear,
Is it meet for this world's wear!

Silken cloak with brilliant lining,
Suits in chariot to be shining;
I no carriage have, nor need,
Mine is health and strength and speed;
And together forth we go,
Bonny plaid, in wind and snow;
And when dark December lours
With his hail clouds and his showers,
O! a country girl like me
Joys, my ample plaid, in thee.

## INTRODUCTION.

> Think not I the fashion take,
> Loving it for Scotland's sake—
> England, fallen although she be,
> Is the dearest land to me,
> Though I know bold hearts beat true
> 'Neath the plaid at Waterloo!
> O, I love thee, though thou art rough—
> Thick! and warm! and wide enough!
> Glad am I, from evening's wind,
> Round me thy broad folds to bind,
> Friend! for storm and tempest made—
> Still be faithful, gorgeous plaid!

Come then, there is a gleam of sunshine, the first we have had for many a day. We take it as a good omen, and set out, hoping for pleasure and profit in our rambles.

# THE EVENING SCHOOL.

"It shall come to pass that at evening time it shall be light."

SHALL we go to-night to the adult school? It is Thursday evening—the last Thursday in the year. We will not mind the state of the roads, though bad as they generally are at this season, they are now worse than usual, owing to strange alterations, diggings down, and heapings up— and still more to the snow, and thaw, and frost of the last four and twenty hours. We will not regard it—hazy and misty as it is, it is yet moonlight, and we have but a little way to go. The school is near, and that is as it should be: the lambs of the flock should be folded near to their shepherd's dwelling. The room, for we use the children's school-room on these occasions, is prettily shaped, long, and not too low. It looks well now, as the dark shadows dance on the wall and floor, thrown by the bright fire from the heavy boughs of ivy and holly, with which the boys dressed the room before their Christmas examination.

The grate is so broad, and the fire is piled so high, that the blaze deadens the light of the half dozen slender candles that are ranged along the desk. Those candlesticks, by the way, are worth your seeing.

Hand us one of them, William; they are your making, I know, and do credit to your ingenuity. The fact was, you see, that when first our evening school was established, and for some time after, daylight continued until eight o'clock, and when the first autumn evening closed in suddenly, we were not prepared for it. Candles were to be bought at the shop below, but candlesticks we had none. "I can make some in one minute, sir," said our little pale friend yonder; so away he ran down to his father's workshop, chose in a minute four or five square bits of board, and stuck into the middle of each three large nails, between which we insert the slim candle. I was much amused when I saw them first; they struck me as being so entirely characteristic—displaying at once poverty and ready wit. But I think we have stayed here too long, the women in the girls' room are waiting for us. William has gone on before; he has lit our candles, and there he is ready with his bow and smile to do any service for either of us. I cannot help seeing that, with all the pains I take, I often fail to impress on the minds of my elegant neighbours the possibility that here in our forest may be found specimens of the best natural good breeding.

I wish I could introduce them to this little friend of mine: who, lame as he is, for he has always been a delicate boy, and is troubled with rheumatism, poor fellow! yet waits upon each of us with candles, snuffers, stools, and books, almost without our asking him. I wish they could see his constant readiness, and hear his gentle, pleasant voice. I think they must agree with me, that he is fully possessed of that, which, when we received it from those we choose to consider equals, we call "politeness;" but which we claim as a right, and only allow to be "civility," however gracefully it may be offered by those we deem inferiors.

But he returns to his companions, and we must set seriously to business. There is little to amuse during the next hour, for to confess the truth, in general our clever, (or to call them by their own apter term,) our '*cute* pupils are often inattentive, and our attentive as often stupid. We have no very regular plan, being, I believe, what a friend of ours calls "extempore teachers." Every one, except indeed she who is so happy as to hear the readers of the Testament, sits down with four or five pupils, and hears them stutter and stumble for a full hour over letters, or words, or sentences of one syllable. The description that a poor old woman here once gave us of her great-grandchild's improvement, often recurs to my mind as I listen to them, "She'll get the book," said she, "and she do *plunder*"—blunder perhaps she meant—"you would bless yourself to hear how she do plunder." In truth, so wearying is this hour, that I would on no account have brought you here as a visiter, but for the sake of introducing you to some interesting characters; and when the men come in, as they do with their good teacher at the end of the evening, to listen to his earnest and simple exposition, and to join in prayer, we will go a little apart, and I will give you a sketch of the history of some of them.

Amongst the men you will observe our old friend Isaac sitting at the top of the form, leaning over his Testament in deep attention to the passage which is to be the subject of explanation. He holds it close to the low candle, and nods his head as the verse is finished, with a smile of joy that tells how he also has arrived safely over all difficulties at its conclusion. Indeed Isaac is much improved, since the time, I believe, when he thought book-makers very unwise to trouble themselves and their readers with prosody, for he said to his kind master, who had been a long while trying to make him acquainted with the various intents and purposes of commas, colons, and full stops; and who, having repeated his patient instructions over and over again, at last said, "Now, do you think you understand me?" "Yes, sir, but the worst of it is, whenever I come to a long word I *must* make a full stop where I would or no." We used to think Isaac very simple, but I believe we were mistaken. At any rate, "Godliness is profitable for all things," and amongst the rest for improving the intellectual faculties. We used to think Isaac had a vacant look; but now, though there is a placid and calm expression of content, there is also a shade of thought on his brow—and truly poor Isaac has enough to think of. His wages in the most prosperous times never amount to more than ten shillings a week. This week he has earned only four, and probably next week may earn none, and he knows that though of his six children not one is able to help him, and the two youngest are, as his wife told me yesterday, the one not two years old, and the other little better than ten months, yet his diligent and active helpmate must soon have her earnings lessened by attendance on a yet younger baby. But I never hear a word of complaint from either Isaac or Nancy; there she sits, a picture of well managing poverty, close by her great market-basket, heavily filled with her richer neighbour's commissions, which she has brought safely thus far from town; and tired as she was, she made more haste than usual, that she might be in time for her Thursday evening lesson. She takes great pains, and as Isaac teaches her at home she improves, and is well satisfied with her improvement: for she told me when she could with difficulty put three letters together, that her husband said she could " read quite pretty." Well only one sort of learning is needful. Not many wise, according to this proud world's estimation, are called happy; and thankful shall we be if these ignorant ones, and their teachers, are made wise unto salvation.

And there sits poor Dinah, with her thin, flushed cheek, hollow cough, and sparkling eye. She has sinned, and it is not for us to desire, that sin, even repented sin, be made to appear interesting. She has been a wanderer, so I will say no more about her, or only this; there is now so much regularity in her behaviour, so much humility in her deportment, that her silence leaves us in hope, for she tells us very little, that he whose gracious voice once said, " Neither do I condemn thee!" has breathed the whisper of peace to her troubled conscience, and has impressed her heart with the sanctifying command, " Go, and sin no more."

The two poor girls who sit next are sisters, and seem much attached to each other. Poor Anna and Elizabeth! we saw them in deep distress this time twelve-month. It was a stormy day in January when little Marian was sent to ask for something for her mother.

The child's passionate grief alarmed us, and as soon as we had sent her away, we determined to follow. It is not an unpleasant walk generally, but there had been snow and rain, and the stream had overflowed the bank, and ran in many small channels over the frozen footpath. The hedges, and for this barren part of the world they are high and varied, were then quite bare of leaves, and so were the few shapely trees that grow thereabout.

We overtook little Marian, for her burst of feeling had spent itself; and she, pleased at the interest she excited by her account of her mother's illness—alas! it was not an exaggerated one—had stopped at many a door on her way to tell her melancholy tale.

" You should have made more haste, Marian," we said, "there is no time to be lost." No, there was no time, not even for the few minutes that the thoughtless child had loitered. There are sad varieties in grief. We saw it in the sudden paleness that chilled the poor child's cheek, as the sound of wailing reached us from the low door, and a younger one burst it open with the wild cry, "Marian, mother's dead!" O! I hear that shriek still. We saw it in the elder girl's agony of tears, and heard it in the poor father's low and often-repeated prayer for help and comfort, as he sat on the low stool by the fire, his face covered with his hands, his head never lifted as we entered, and his body bent forward and slowly swayed to and fro. We heard it in the low and agitated tone in which the nurse strove to give comfort, and in the vexed and complaining cry with which the frightened children repelled her; and most melancholy of all, in the wail of the new born-infant—the unwelcome one; a twin child, whose brother had forsaken it, at the portal of life, and had entered into eternity alone. O poor Amy! hers was a sad funeral. We stood to watch it as it wound its dark way down the churchyard. The snow lay heavily on the tomb-stones, and the poor little children cried the more bitterly as they stumbled over the hidden graves, and felt through their scanty clothing the chillness of that gloomy winter evening. There was the poor father, and his eldest son, come home from his work, in Wales on that melancholy occasion. Then came Elizabeth and Anna. Poor things! they showed feelings of strong affection then, that the rough usage of the world knows how to deaden. Both of them fainted that evening, and Anna's first question on her recovery was, "Poor father! how are you now?" Then there were the four younger girls, two and two—sorry, but more terrified than sorry. The pretty flaxen headed boy, that his mother had loved so dearly, was too delicate for the long rough walk, so he was left at home, and so was the new-born baby; but one more was there—the other infant, laid to rest in its dead mother's arms. Ah poor Amy! it was indeed a sad funeral. They were very poor before, but Amy was a diligent and frugal manager, and her authority kept the children in place. Now I fear, poor as they were, they are yet poorer; there is less regularity—less cleanliness—less subordination,—the loss of a mother, especially such a mother as Amy, is a sad thing. We are glad to be of what use we can to those two poor girls, for their mother's sake, and one at least of them well repays the interest we take in her.

And yonder is a genius. That pale, spare, mild looking man, whose appearance bespeaks such deep poverty; he is a singular compound of ability, and want of useful sense in the every-day affairs of life. I am glad he is here this evening; he does not often appear amongst us, but his absence would have prevented my describing to you one of the most remarkable households with which I was ever acquainted. Jaques—the melancholy Jaques, let us call him—can do every thing; but some how or other, he gains by nothing.

He is a common mason, and though he was never regularly initiated into the further mysteries of his trade, yet he never hesitates to undertake any part of a building, from

"Turret to foundation stone."

He can talk about the orders of architecture, and plan rooms and design fancy doors and windows. He makes curious grottoes of moss and shells, and arranges in them waxen figures, and birds neatly stuffed by himself. I have seen a bass viol, of which he has constructed every part, screws and all, himself; and at that very time he was so poor that he could only afford to purchase one string at a time; and I have heard him play on it music of his own composing. He can play on the flute too, and thinks he sings very well.

His wife, as warm-hearted a creature as ever lived, is in some respects a helpmeet for her husband. She sees and admires his talents, but cannot direct him how to turn them to any account.

She can sing to his music, and stand at the door of their cottage, on the top of the hill, admiring the beautiful scenery which spreads before them, but of making it clean and comfortable within, she has no idea. She will travel uncomplainly at his side through storm and mud for miles, to hear an eloquent preacher—for they are both great judges of fine preaching: but she cares not, and he has by this time learnt not to care, for the comfort of a neatly-ordered supper on their return home. There was bad management in the family in the first instance, and we need not refer to Butler's "Analogy" to know what evil effects proceed from bad causes.

Their unruly boys grew up rude and ragged to tease the untidy girl; you may see them sometimes driving her down the steep garden, and she, being light of foot, will climb a tree or scale a wall to be out of their way. O, they are a wild set!—in the mean time, probably, you would find the poor mother quite lifted above all terrestrial concerns, practising her husband's last new tune; and she would be as pleased to see you, and welcome you as kindly in the midst of her little kitchen, as if her room were as orderly and as respectable as it once might have been; and she would seem more sorry that the window is shattered, because possibly it may inconvenience you, during the few minutes of your stay, than because the wind and the rain often beat in; and neither she nor her husband, who live there always, are by any means strong enough to bear such hardships. But I should be ungrateful indeed if I stopped here, or failed to acknowledge the unvarying and earnest affection expressed toward us by these poor people. The readiness with which their services have been tendered to us—the interest they have taken in our concerns—their pleasure in our happiness, and their sympathy in our sorrow. There are others beside Lizzy, indeed, who send us their earliest ripe strawberries; more, who welcome us to the warmest seat by the hearth in winter, and to a rest in the shade in summer, and press us with an earnestness not always to be refused, to partake of their scanty fare. Many congratulate us when we prosper—none more sincerely than Lizzy; many prayers were offered for us when we were in trouble, but not one more fervent than hers: and if we went away, there is not one who would regret us more.

But the old man on the second form is quite a contrast in appearance to my man of genius. Is not old Jacob a very respectable looking personage? His neatly brushed coat is a little old-fashioned as to the cut to be sure, but whole and bright; and his dark green and brown striped waistcoat, looking so warm and comfortable, is open to show another of a lighter colour quite as good underneath, and to allow a glance at his large heart-shaped steel brooch, pinned on the clean neck-cloth to the clean shirt. He has a sensible, pleasant look; and with so many advantages of outward appearance, it would indeed be wonderful if old Jacob was not looked on as a person of some consequence —especially as he wears that crown of glory, "the hoary head found in the way of righteousness," for which even the levellers of this restless day must feel some natural respect. And he is a very good old man, worthy of regard, and really humble, I doubt not, yet I think he feels his importance. Did you observe the patronizing nod with which he greeted the lady teachers as he came in, and do you hear now, whilst every one else is listening in silent attention, his audible remarks—" True, very true!"—and his triumphant tone of exultation in whatever strikes him, as particularly sound reasoning, or ready speaking in his young pastor's exposition. Sound doctrine, happily, he rejoices to own it all.

But the little company are rising to depart, and you and I will depart too. If the glance we have had to night at the circumstances and characters of some of our pupils should have increased the desire we feel to benefit them, it will be well—we shall not then have to regret that for once, when others were listening, you and I were only looking on.

*Dec.* 30, 1830.

# A WALK ON A WET DAY.

> —How many a cause without a name,
> Will from our spirits hide the blame,
> When, thinking of ourselves, we cease
> To think upon another's peace!
> 
> WILSON.

"How much better to walk out than to stay at home, even on such a day as this!" said my dear companion, as we climbed the wet and slippery, hilly field on our way home. Much better! there we might have been sitting now chilly and comfortless over the fire, shivering whenever the door was opened, and thinking the day even more gloomy and stormy than it is.

But now we have paid two or three interesting visits, we have admired the irregularity of the broken ground on the steep sides of the lane, the wintry tints of the deep moss, and the withered oak leaves, and the evergreen broom and ivy. We have stopped at "the house that Jack built"—that low hut reared against the ruined glass-factory; by which contrivance Jack, saving himself the trouble of building a back and side wall to his mansion, soon reared up the other side and the low front, and laid on the rafters and tiles. I need not say how many of the latter, we may guess to have been gathered from the ruin. Jack, I suppose, thought that of little consequence, as their situation was but slightly altered, and they were of no use either to man or beast where they stood. The sin and shame he would have thought consisted in letting such good things be wasted. Well, I am not his conscience keeper—I make no inquiries —at any rate I admire his ingenuity.

"And did Jack do all this himself?" said I to his wife. "Jack and I," she answered, a little offended. "I did the work of a mason—I worked as hard as any horse." Whether all masons work as hard as horses, I leave those to settle who have had such gentlemen's long bills to pay: and I go on to the rest of their territories. Besides their own dwelling, he and his wife have built a stable of equally large dimensions for his steeds, those three poor asses that you see taking right of common on the broken and steep bank above their home. He has also fenced in two diminutive and oddly shaped pieces of garden, which he would willingly make larger at the expense of the public; but as this lane is a church path, he is not permitted. He has planted a vine against one side of his hut, and its long untrained branches hang straggling on the low roof, and contend with the small purple leaves of the ivy for its place on the ruin above. In the little garden also, there are beautiful double holly-oaks, delicate lemon colour, and pink, and deep purple, which every year excite our admiration; and there are rue, and peppermint, and thyme, and spearmint, and lavender, and "*featherfew*," as Joyce calls it, as fine an herb, she says, as any "*canny mile.*"

For Joyce is an herb woman. O, how different from the splendidly robed and sylph-like form, that one may fancy in connexion with that name—the high-born lady, whose honour is to move in the gorgeous procession, strewing the king's way on the day of his coronation with precious exotics. How very different Joyce looked to-day, as we saw her broad square figure seated on a low stool, just withinside the door of the hut, sorting the heaps of herbs, wild and cultivated, that she has been collecting for to-morrow's market. It was worth while to have taken the walk, if it had been only for the sake of learning the names of some hitherto unknown weeds; for it is under Joyce, and such as Joyce, that I study. It is amusing to hear her names; you can generally give a pretty fair guess at the real word, and consult the dictionary for the right orthography on your return home—then in a low mysterious tone she will add their medicinal uses, such as you may meet with in Culpepper's "Herbal," which by the way I once borrowed, when I was a child, from our clerk's wife. O! if half that Culpepper and Joyce say were true, it would be a ruinous day for the doctors. Jack and Joyce are a singular couple. Jack so gaunt and tall and spare, and Joyce so broad and square. Jack, certainly, has the advantage in person, and I think his wife is rather proud of him; for though when he is ill, and we ask after him, her reply is, that he is "Piteous ordinary," I do not think she intends the words to be taken in its literal meaning. I dare say she thinks us wanting in proper respect, in following the phraseology of the people round about and calling her lord and master, "Jack;" she always styles him, herself, "Our John!" and she is very fond of exhibiting her marriage certificate, which she keeps carefully rolled up in a nutmeg grater.

The hut is certainly high enough for Joyce, but I am almost sure that Jack cannot stand upright in it, except it may be at the furthest side, and that is almost entirely occupied by the bed. I never saw him make the attempt; his rules of politeness not rendering it at all necessary for him to rise when we enter. His deep, gruff, "Come in if you please," is the only welcome we ever expect; but after we have been there a little, and talked or read, I have observed that for the time he softens—then it is, "Now you make free at any time, if you please; you are welcome to my house any day." But by the time we pass next, the stern collier is his hard "self again." Yet the gruff "Come in!" is, I am sure, always intended as an invitation and an invitation he wishes to be accepted. Joyce is, on the contrary, always good-humoured, and in a bustle—always offers us her own chair, and presses us, hot or cold, to come "nigher the fire."

She is not half so attentive to the reading as her husband, yet loves the readers much better; and to-day there was real feeling in her tone, when, on our way back, we said, "we are going home, now;" she answered, "God bless ye, wherever you go!"

And now, stop a moment, dear reader, and notice the date of my chapter. It is January, 1831. Now I am copying this on the 16th January, 1832, and I have been to pay a visit to poor Jack to-day. And, O, how gradually, but how very much he is altered. I could not in justice leave you with the impression, that he is rough and stern. O! he is now so gentle—so very desirous of our visits. The tears stream down his pale cheeks when we read to him, or speak of the love of his dying Saviour, and yet more, when he himself speaks of his former sins. He is very ill —dying in a decline—but, O, what hope—what satisfaction we have in visiting him! "A broken and a contrite heart, O God, thou wilt not despise!"

One particular more I ought to mention. Jack and Joyce never ask for any thing. They have no hungry children, to be sure, but they know well what want is themselves. "The other day," said Jack, but he did not say it in a way of complaint, "we had not a bit of bread in the cupboard, nor a bit of coal for the fire, nor a mouthful of hay for the poor neddy, nor a penny piece to buy none!" They are ill often; now indeed Jack is always ill; and a little broth or a morsel of meat might be thought a necessary; but though they seldom have it, they never complain of wanting it. They are grateful beyond the expression of gratitude for the little that from time to time is done for them; but like a great many beside, I might say—indeed I think it the general character of our people, there is a patient, I had almost written—a magnanimous silence in the endurance of hardships which greatly commands my respect. You smile, my dear reader, and it seems to me an incredulous smile. You know something of my country people, for the surly collier who serves you with coal is from our hills; and he has been uncivilly earnest for his full price: or the market-woman, whom you employed to carry home your laden basket last Saturday, as she saw the well-selected luxuries taken out one after another, pressed you somewhat too importunately for an additional penny. Forgive them! they do endure hardships of which you little dream; for I am well assured, had the poor collier told you of his wife's long illness, and his children's want of bread, you would not have hesitated one moment to comply with his reasonable demand; and if your market-woman had not objected to complain, she would have told you, and you are much too kind, I am sure, not to have listened—that yours was the first payment she has received to-day—that her husband has done no work all this long frost—and that her poor little children, bare-footed and ill-clothed, were crying this morning for cold, and her heart ached to hear them. Forgive them! it is all true: to those who know little of them, they may appear over-reaching and discontented; we dwell among them, and know them to be enduring and grateful.

But the greatest pleasure of our walk was the visit to lame Myles.

There are some people born with amiable manners, and Myles is one of them. He could never have been other than civil or agreeable, but it is religion that has made him so gentle and so patient; religion that has quickened his perceptions, and exalted his ideas, and refined his feelings.

He was sitting by the fire in the same spot in which we always find him, his crutches in the corner at his side; and his bible, in which he is too weak to read for more than a few minutes at a time, lying on the table. We found him, as we too often do, paler than his natural paleness, and very faint from hunger; for his wife was not returned from town, and the children had taken the last bit of bread to school for their dinners.

The youngest boy was restlessly walking about the room, rummaging in the cupboard under the dresser, for a potato to roast, and cried because he could not find one. His father apologized for him: "I really am very sorry, ma'am," said he, "that he should be so troublesome; he is a good boy generally, but he must be hungry now; that is what makes him so restless: very hungry he is I am sure; he had but a little bit at seven this morning, and I have not any to give him till his mother comes home. I hope you'll please excuse him." Poor little boy! his peevishness was indeed excusable. He is a dear fine child, with mild, black eyes, and curling brown hair: it is wonderful, through what hardships (for "want can quench the eye's bright grace") some children maintain their claim to beauty. It is a worthless thing, we know—we are told so constantly—"a fading flower," that is written in every copybook—"vain," so even the word of God calls it; and yet what a lovely thing beauty is, and whether we own the weakness or not, how we all love it! All Myles's children are very pretty, most of them even prettier than this little one! yet I recollect he excited my admiration one day last summer, when I found him asleep on the sunny bank a few yards from the door. The daisies that he had gathered had fallen from his relaxed hold, as one hand was thrown over his head to shade his face from the light. One longed to see a sketch made of him, what a simple, graceful thing, it would have been! One would not have had him moved for the world. But the father had either more regard than I for his boy's safety, or less love of the picturesque. "He looks very pretty," said I, "asleep on the bank." "I dare say he does, ma'am," he answered quickly, "but I'd sooner he was lying on the bed;" and forthwith he sent Annie to waken her brother. I thought it was a great pity. Little Tom was not then the youngest. There was a baby—as sweet a little flower as ever blossomed amongst the thorns of poverty. Its young nurse, Annie, took great care of it, in the daily absence of its mother, and the infant did her credit. The poor sickly father might perhaps, sometimes, look with a sigh on the sixth helpless one, for the supply of whose wants he could make no exertion: but the mother joyed in her darling; and her weary pace quickened after her long day's toil, at thought of her baby. I was there one day, when the little one looked lovelier than ever. It had begun to take notice; I smiled at it, and it smiled at me again. We were there some time, and it was quiet all the time we were reading; and before we went, we praised little Annie for keeping it so neat. It was but on the fourth day afterwards, and we came again; the baby was yet quieter and cleaner. The little one was dead. She was dressed in her best cap and snowy robe, and laid on the table covered with a spotless white sheet. One blast, only one, had swept over the frail flower, and it was gone! Who weeps over such scattered blossoms?

> Like buds rent off before the blast
> On the cold ground they lie;
> They shall be flowers—in God's bright bowers,
> Where never storm sweeps by.

O! the mother grieved for her. She wept over her as if her heart would break. "I have known great trouble before," she said, "but, O! this is the greatest. It is so hard to lose a baby out of one's bosom." It was but natural passion. "Can a mother forget her sucking child?" "Yes!" answers the word of truth, "she may forget!" Then blessed are they who claim an interest in that love which adds, "yet I will not forget thee!" I comforted her with such common-place considerations as her extreme agitation gave me room to suggest. "You are sure that she is safe now;" said I, "if she had lived to grow up, you, don't know what trouble she might have caused you. Now you are sure the last trouble with her is over." "It will be," she answered sadly, "when we have laid her in her grave:" and then I understood that one part at least of their trouble arose from their extreme poverty. They had not one shilling towards buying the coffin, and she had been all the morning trying to make up her mind to take her Sunday's gown to pawn. It was the only thing she had worth taking, and she had never yet known the disgrace of pawning; besides she was very desirous to keep a decent dress in which to appear at church on Sundays; but must give it up now. Ah! she would have given more than that to have kept her darling with her. Are the poor sometimes accused of being hard-hearted?

It is not wonderful, that with so much to bear, their feelings should become callous. It is well, perhaps, if, in some measure it should be so; at any rate it does not become those to reproach them, who, when trouble comes almost faint under it, though they have nothing to do, but to close their windows, and sit down in the quiet gloom to nurse their grief. It would be better, perhaps, to consider what effect, strong, and painful, and unrequited exertion, made at such a time, would have on their own minds. But it was Anna's time of trouble, and she and her husband know well who is a present help at such a time. Such they proved him then. Friends unexpectedly provided for them, lent them the money so sadly needed; and in the midst of their succeeding poverty, it was regularly and faithfully paid. They are indeed very poor: Myles has been ill for six years, and since he broke his leg two years ago, has not earned one day's wages. His wife exerts herself beyond her strength. "The man that helped her up with her basket this morning," said Myles once to me, "said it was a shame a woman should carry such a burden!" Poor fellow! the blood rose to his cheek as he added, "It would not be so if I had strength to help it." But poor Anna's greatest distress with regard to her labour, except indeed when she has made herself really ill by violent exertion, is not that she does too much, but that she can find so little to do. They have a pretty little sunny garden on the hill side, above the house where I see the earliest primroses; but pretty as it looks, it is so parched and stony a spot, that with all their care, it produces no supply for the market. Anna is often obliged to borrow the money necessary to fill her basket, in the morning before she leaves home, and after having discharged her debt, her earnings, even on a prosperous day, when she has been up early, and travelled far, and that perhaps in inclement weather, seldom amount to more than eight-pence or nine-pence. Then there is the scanty parish allowance, and the low wages of the young boy; altogether so few shillings, that one can hardly help saying, " What are they among so many?" But the question brings its own answer with it, reminding one of Him who once had compassion on the multitude that had nothing to eat, and who, being the same yesterday, to-day, and for ever, will not now send his followers away fasting. There may be a great company, and "only five loaves, and those barley—two fishes, and those little ones." Yet if he take and bless the provision, they shall all eat and be satisfied. So I always think when I see Myles's decent children come into the schoolroom on a Sunday morning. The boy's pinafore is of the coarsest, and little Martha's blue gingham frock something of the shortest; and her nankeen spencer, faded almost white, is very scanty, and her small bonnet of the same material, bent out of shape; or rather into a variety of shapes, by so frequent washing, scarcely shades the handsome childish face.

But the straight auburn hair is so nicely cut, and brushed so neatly over the smooth brow, there is such a clean, wholesome, healthy look in all the children, such a gentle expression in the dark eyes, and their voices and tones are so sweet, and their words so proper; that if it were only fancy, it would be one worth nourishing,—there is a blessing on them. It is not fancy—the word of truth has promised, "the seed of the righteous shall be blessed!" In such belief, then, we cheerfully take leave of them, though this hard winter, in which we have seen so much want borne so patiently, is not yet over: and though since I begun my story, I find that the eldest son is come home from his place ill, and the two young boys have the measles, and that pleasant, civil child Annie, her mother's right hand, is very poorly too. It is a sad house indeed! Yet Myles's calm smile of peace is enough to set any one's heart at rest, and the humble and steady tone in which he expresses himself: " The Lord has kept me through many trials, and I am assured he will keep me, until I am fit to appear in his presence." And then with tears in his eyes, he adds, "and I have a hope and a firm trust that I shall be fit when he calls me out of time into eternity, not in my own righteousness, for I am a sinner; but clothed in the righteousness of Jesus Christ, my hope and my salvation!" In such belief and hope, then, we may cheerfully leave him in his troubles. Patience—and may the writer and the reader willingly apply the sentence to themselves—patience must have her perfect work! There is a land where none shall say, I am sick—to that land of health our feeble friend is hastening. A land where there shall be no more sorrow, nor crying; can we wish the entrance of this child of affliction should be long delayed? There they shall hunger no more—neither thirst any more! Happy Myles! not vainly did the Saviour say, "Blessed are ye poor, for yours is the kingdom of heaven!" Here are some lines written in remembrance of the pretty baby; perhaps they may amuse you after so much prose.

### THE COTTAGER'S CHILD.

From thy little cell of clay,
Spirit, rise, and fly away.
In this world of want and pain
Thou shalt ne'er know grief again!
Tears are in thy mother's eye,
Child! thy fount of tears is dry:
Sighs disturb thy father's breast,
Favour'd one, but thou shalt rest.
Long thy brother from his side
Thee shall miss at eventide!
Greeting him at set of sun
When his daily toil is done—
Vacant place and parting's woe,
Baby, thou shalt never know.

Taken in thy spring-tide charms
From thy little sister's arms—
She with memory sad and sweet,
Oft thy faded robes shall greet,
And renew at fancy's call
All thy sports, thy graces all;
Then whilst mingling thoughts shall crowd,
Bend the young head, and weep aloud.

They may weep; where thou shalt go
Passion's tempest dares not blow;
Sorrow's dark wings do not hover,
Death—no form of grace shall cover.
Steal, then, from thy mother's breast
To a home of deeper rest;
Cease around thy sire to cling—
To a mightier Father spring!

Thy young brothers ask thy stay,
Angels wait thee! soar away!
Since thy bless'd baptismal hour
They have watch'd in love and power—
Now in love they bid thee come!
And in power they guard thee home!

Flowers we will gather, as is meet,
For thy small grave, fresh and sweet.
Violets fair, and asphodel
Of spring's first coming feet that tell,
And cuckoo flowers, and daisies wild,
Fit emblems for the cotter's child;
Early, they like thee shall fade
On the turf where thou art laid,
And with spring's returning skies,
Beautiful, like thee shall rise.

Now with footstep soft and slow,
From the narrow grave we go:
Rest—thy pleasant journey's ended
Ere the morning's sun ascended—
Ere the toil of busy day,
Thee thy Master call'd away—
Giving thee just time to tell,
"Christ loves little children well."

*January*, 1831.

# ONE HALF HOUR TO POETRY.

*The pillar'd arches were over their head
And beneath their feet were the bones of the dead.*
                                        Sir W. Scott.

We had been all the morning long in the busy city, shopping and paying visits—pushed and pushing—and jostled and crowded; here forced off the pavement by men carrying heavy burdens; then drawing ourselves into the smallest possible compass, in fear of a chimney-sweep and his brushes; running over a crossing in peril of being ourselves run over by the prancing steeds of some chariot; and again hurrying away from the stunning of some dinning iron dray. I thought many times, that bustling morning, of the moss under our acacia tree. You turned through an iron gate down an entry into which I had never been before. But I knew if you summoned me to follow, it must be for some pleasant purpose—for from whom can I expect gratifications if not from you, who have always been so very kind? You, my childhood's earliest companion, with whom I used to play hide and seek, before either of us could speak plain—you with whom I have strung the fallen jessamine flowers on the fine blades of grass, and made daisy chains; and with whom in later times, I delighted in Saturday's long, pleasant walks, when that looked for day at last brought you home from school. Ol the tears come into my eyes when I think of all your kindness, your constant and steady kindness, both in happy and sad hours, and perhaps those remembrances helped to make the half hour of which I am about to write, one of so deep interest. There are strong ties in this world, but I doubt whether any much stronger than that which binds us together. As yet I have known few pleasures which you did not help to procure—certainly none which your presence did not heighten. I followed you down the silent entry, and through a low gothic door, and stood at your side in an antique and beautiful room—a room so beautiful, that I should vainly endeavour to describe it, and of antiquity whose deep interest I feel, but whose history I cannot trace. The records of old times doubtless have mentioned it, for the mightiest of their day laid its foundation stone, and hands of the most cunning workmen were employed in rearing it: but if my ignorance prevented my entering with the pleasure which an antiquary or an architect would have done into a consideration of its age and style, they could not have experienced a deeper or more delighted feeling than mine; the sudden change from the living, crowding, troublesome world to the stillness of that beautiful oratory. O, if one could live there!

From the coloured arch of the lofty window, and the curious coats of arms on the ceiling, to where the stained light streamed on the tessellated pavement, there was nothing we could wish altered—nothing but what suited the poetical tone of feeling which that sudden change had induced. Yet I knew not where we were—to some religious purpose doubtless the small and beautiful apartment had been consecrated—for the eastern side of the room was elevated as if an altar had been once erected there, for the celebration of the holiest rite of the Christian religion, and there was a small font for the reception of holy water, and the richly ornamented niches still showed where the guardian saints had stood. As Protestants we could not remember the anxiety with which the pious founders—and such charity may well suppose them—looked to those helpless beings for help in their last extremity, without a prayer that our purer faith, and our surer trust, may produce as evident, though not as splendid fruits in us. Was that hidden chamber a confessional? We could not look around us without a sigh of sympathy for the wounded hearts that had brought their burdens there. O, what whispered tales of agony and shame had been breathed there! What records of terror, and jealousy, and guilt, must the listener at that confessional have heard.

But "as in water face answereth to face, so the heart of man to man," and those who have most deeply studied their own hearts can most surely guess the confessions of the honest penitent. Happy days! in which we may turn with full confidence of being accepted, for the sake of our one Mediator, by Him who willeth not the death of a sinner, though from him, the dark secrets of no heart are hid. Happy penitents! who trust in the full, perfect, and sufficient sacrifice once offered for them, and bring all their load of guilt to the foot of the cross, well satisfied with his absolution who blotteth out transgression, and will not remember our sin.

But there was a place of yet nearer interest to us. We came on to a chapel dedicated to the worship of God according to the rites of our own simple and scriptural worship. It had been lately put into perfect repair. The new ornaments beautifully corresponded to the ancient decoration. "They that hewed timber afore out of the thick trees, have indeed known to bring it to an excellent work." I trust in God the time shall never come, though such threatenings have been heard, when we shall add, "Now they break down the carved work thereof with axes and hammers." There are those even now who "say in their hearts, Let us destroy them together those who long to burn up the houses of God in our land. O God, how long shall the adversary reproach? shall the enemy blaspheme thy name for ever!"

Ah! that touching 74th Psalm, how, with a little alteration, we may apply it to the troubled state of our own Jerusalem in these troublesome times! Yet it is a comfort to see beautiful new churches still daring to be built, and yet more beautiful old ones yet venturing to be repaired. We will take courage and believe that God in his mercy will permit us to see peace upon Israel in our days, and to find shelter in our time under the shadow of his altar. Such thoughts came to us with the silence and the sunshine of that holiest spot, as we stood looking at the ancient tracery which had been for many years concealed, and which accident had not very long since discovered. We were standing by the east window near the communion table. I do not envy their feelings to whom every place is alike. God is indeed every where present, and yet Peter and John, to whom a private chamber had been hallowed by the visible presence of their Lord, felt pleasure, we may believe, in entering together the beautiful gate of the temple where their fathers had worshipped. For my own part, setting the duty of public prayer out of the question, I know no more pleasure equal to that of being in a beautiful church. In going up the altar-steps there is to me a feeling like being nearer heaven: and then I could always long to be alone; as if, there, in the more immediate presence of God, I might the better renew all my sacramental vows, and come from there with a lighter heart, as if, like Christian in the Pilgrim's Progress, my burden of sin and sorrow had fallen from my shoulder at the foot of the cross. But I forget myself: what would the judicious writer of the natural history of enthusiasm say to all this? This much I think he would permit me to feel; if whilst we say, "How amiable are thy 'earthly' tabernacles, O Lord!" our souls are drawn with more ardent desire to add, "My soul longeth, yea, even panteth for the courts, the upper courts of my Lord; my heart and my flesh cry out for the living God!"

We went on to the twilight gloom of another aisle. The light was admitted through a dim window, and only partially discovered to us, that we stood in the midst of a mighty company. There they were, the warlike and the wise—the stoled priest, and the mailed warrior: "one event had happened to them all." There lay the gallant crusader on his stately altar tomb, arrayed in helmet and hauberk, and his hand on the crossed hilt of his good sword. There he was laid with chant and requiem, and the hand of decay did its work speedily on the mortal form beneath —but very slowly, though as surely, on the sculptured semblance above. For there the date and name perfect, and every small chain in the curious armour undefaced, is the reclining figure still. There, as if the solemn sound soothed him to his repose, he lay when matins were chanted every day for his soul's health—and yet, when the burning plague swept through the city, and, entering even into this consecrated sanctuary, carried off so many of the devoted dwellers here, that there was not one left of age to officiate as priest—there, in that silent hour of desolation, slept the knight well. Then came wars and tumults: other tombs were dismantled; other sculptured figures broken to pieces; edifices, as fair, razed to the dust, and the thunder of the cannon caused this quiet aisle to shake; but the chieftain lay still in his deep rest: and there, the curious eye has been bent on him; the careless hand has been rudely laid on him, but the mighty man has been reckless of the insult for these six hundred years. But our half hour was passing on. We stopped before another tomb that we should have called old, if we had not been so long pondering over one so much older. We might have been tempted to smile at the quaint and tasteless device of that monument, but the tale which it recorded was one that might well suppress a smile. There lies buried the son and heir—the last heir of his father's house. The young, the beautiful, perhaps, the cherished, the well-beloved, taken away, "being in the eleventh year of his age." Then, what a voice of joy was hushed in his father's halls—what a light foot passed from his mother's garden walks—how his little sisters missed him in their hours of play! But his favourite dog soon ceased to watch for him with almost human anxiety. His young sisters grew up with their own hopes and cares, which soon blotted out the remembrance of their playfellow. But his father and mother never, never forgot him. Their love caused the costly tomb to be erected, and that it is what we now consider tasteless, must be laid to the fault of the age in which it was reared. The simple inscription came warm from the heart, and therefore reaches the heart of the reader. No one can leave that aisle and forget, that there lies a young heir—the last heir of his father's house —cut down like a budding lily, "being in the eleventh year of his age." There were many more monuments, among which we would have gladly lingered, but only a few minutes, of our half hour remained. There was one to the "Ladye Margarite the Pearle," with its quaint verses and its extraordinary flattery. Surely it is very bad taste to load monuments to the dead with praise which makes you doubt how the living could have deserved it; and yet the lady might have been very lovely, and we will not doubt was so; and then, she died in the flower of her youth, just when her first child, perhaps, had learned to lisp her name, and needed all the care that only mothers know how to bestow. They were sincere mourners, doubtless, who stood round the grave where we are now standing; but the tears are long since dry—the throbbing of those wounded hearts is still. Her lord was laid beside her two hundred years ago. We turned to go away. Yet once more, as we looked on that mighty company, a strange overpowering feeling of awe impressed us. We stood amongst the silent dead indeed—but "all live unto God"—and we felt that there was nothing wanting but one blast of the archangel's trumpet,

"To call the sleepers around us to rise!"

And even now, how much nearer the spirits of these departed may be to us, than we know! It was an awful feeling! It seemed irreverent to speak aloud. I can well understand how stories of visions and apparitions may have arisen amongst the dwellers in monasteries, in some cases, without any intention to deceive. Myself not at all superstitious, I can well understand to what a feverish state of excitement the imagination may be quickened in such scenes. There is something in them, to me, beyond expression impressive; and that perhaps is the reason why, though I have seen so few of them, such are so very often presented to me in my dreams.

Then, only suppose one to fall asleep—as we read old Wulstan, the last Saxon Bishop, was accustomed to do—in such a place as this; what solemn feelings of terror, and awe, and devotion—what visions would attend one's awaking! I recollect my own impression once after a dream—a dream so striking, that I put it into verse, and as it may serve to illustrate my meaning, I introduce it here.

> I dream'd I was alone—through the fair aisle
> No lingering worshipper remained to pray—
> And lightening up the lofty Gothic pile,
> The western sunlight cast his reddest ray,
> In gorgeous colours sunk the summer day.
> Hushed was the hallowed tone of praise and prayer—
> More lovely grew the quiet evening's smile,
> And all in heaven was bright—on earth was fair,
> Gay life was all without—the dead and I were there.
>
> I linger'd till the trembling twilight shed
> Her doubtful shadows o'er the altar's pale—
> From the bright pane the deep reflection fled,
> The fretted banners flapp'd in the chill gale—
> The night-bird pass'd the tower, on flagging sail,
> I laid me down on an old tomb to rest,
> A tomb with quaint device, and 'scutcheon spread;
> Sunk with the scenes of varied day opprest—
> Fearless 'neath that high roof the only living guest!
>
> Then, in the visions of the silent night,
> Just, as when deep sleep falleth upon men
> I saw a form of majesty and might
> (And yet I cannot tell thee, where nor when,
> But my eye fix'd, and my heart panted then)
> In mist above me—yet I felt not fear—
> All indistinct, by its " excess of light:"

I may not outline how it did appear,
One thought was on my heart—that God was near!

Though as I gaz'd, by its own brightness dim—
All undefined—though altogether fair;
Yet, by the hand, I knew it to be Him,
The Crucified! the God who answereth prayer—
And I rejoiced to feel that he was there:
His look was love: I knew not if he spoke;
But with Him, my heart held deep communing:
O'er my own grief his love like sunshine broke—
I knew his right-hand held me—and I woke!

Our half hour was gone. We looked one moment more on the shadowed monuments. We passed under the richly ornamented gateway, into the sunshine that streamed down the brilliant windows of the beautified chapel. We paused a moment in the silent confessional, spoke not as we left the narrow entry—the iron gate closed behind us, and we were in the busy, living world again.

# THE LADYE ELIZABETH.

> Come! linger in our garden bower
> A little while with me,
> As closes the gum-cistus flower,
> And homeward flies the bee.
> I have a true, sad tale to tell
> And you shall pause and listen well!

I HAVE been reading Clarendon's History of the rebellion, and my mind has been naturally led, from the distresses of a royal household, to consider the blessing of living in quiet, though ever so lowly retirement. I have turned from the misguided faction of those times, and from the people's wild shout, "Justice! Justice! Execution! Execution!" thankful that the insignificance of our parish —I hardly dare hope it is any thing better—prevents us from troubling ourselves to join to-day's eager cry for a reform, which, after all, may prove no reformation. And here, I must express my gratitude to that God who has preserved us all through this fearful winter—and really it has been such in many parts of the kingdom—from every appearance of disaffection and outrage. I can only express my gratitude and my wonder. Why our poor have been so peaceable, I cannot tell, except as I know who "stilleth the madness of the people." They have wanted bread as others have done, and as yet have used no lawless means, blessed be God! to procure it. Masters, through the pressure of the times, have dismissed some of their workmen, and have delayed the payment of others, and they have borne it patiently. "How could he pay my husband?" said a poor sickly creature to me, whose every look expressed exceeding want; "how could he pay my husband, when his customers did not pay him?" It has happened very often that those who receive parish pay, have been sent away without it, because of the impossibility of collecting it from one week to another, to meet the increasingly heavy demand; and the consequence has been, that many have not known at all where to seek their next week's living.

"We can't find fault," said a widow, one of the sufferers, the master would be glad to pay us if he could; and how can we blame the poor things that used to pay their rates, times are so hard for us all?" "Thank God!" said another, "we never trouble the parish; my husband always has work," (he earns ten shillings a week, and maintains six out of seven children) "and when we have a herring with our potatoes, we ought to bless God: how many poor creatures there are who have none!"

The only expression of disloyalty—that is, disloyalty as it used to be—and complaint against the powers that be, that I have heard this winter, was from a poor match-seller—a kindler, I should fear, of more destructive fires, than those which he lit by profession. I have seldom met with so singular a character as he appeared. Wretched and beggarly as was his first appearance, I felt astonished at the subdued tone of voice, and the correct fluency of expression with which he spoke. He said he was a traveller from Liverpool, and he went on to animadvert on the evils and abuses which he had seen on his way. The rich he represented as all haughty and luxurious; and the poor as, to a man, unmercifully oppressed, and wanting the food with which the gentry supplied their dogs. Such a state of things, he went on to tell us, could not exist long. The time was come for the people to exert themselves,—now that things were so bad, they must be mended. But it is in vain for me to attempt to describe the orator's manner. Having never heard any thing of the sort before, I was silent with astonishment; so confounded, that I did not answer a word: perhaps he flattered himself that I was a convert to the fluency of his rhetoric.

But the young woman in whose clean, but shattered cottage, I was sitting, had more sense than I. "Master!" answered she, and the colour rose as she spoke, "times are bad, that's sure enough; but we ought to recollect, that if we have a potato, it's more than we deserve by right; and when God afflicts us, it is for our sins, and to make us turn to Him; and if we all did that, times would be better;—that's what I think!" Well done! my friend Fanny! we should be a more prosperous nation I believe, if high and low thought on the subject of reform as she did.

But I begun by telling you, that I have been pondering

over Clarendon's history of the great rebellion, and since you must be by this time tired of these scenes in low life, we will take a glance at a loftier station, such a one as may well make us turn again cheerfully to our barren hills, and our stony lanes, and unpolished people, and bless God and be happy.

It was on the evening of the 28th January, 1649, that the Ladye Elizabeth was summoned to attend the King her father: she had been anxiously expecting, dreading, and yet longing for that summons all day; yet now when it came, she trembled so, that she could with difficulty rise to attend the call. But the Princess, though only thirteen years of age, had learnt in a fearful school to command her feelings. There was many an hour, when her exclamation might have been that of the prophet, "O that mine head were water, and mine eyes fountains of tears," when the Princess did not dare to weep. So she rose quietly; the blood left her cheek indeed, and her lips as white as marble, as she did so, and again rushed back, swelling the blue veins in her fair temples, and flushing the delicate neck and hands with an unnatural colour. Again she turned deadly pale, and stopped as if she could scarcely breathe; but she recovered herself, walked on, and said nothing. Who cared in those days, that the Ladye Elizabeth's heart was well nigh broken? She held her little brother by the hand, and entered her father's prison. I could scarcely show you a lovelier or a sadder scene. The monarch of a mighty land, violently thrust down from the throne of his birthright by the craft of a few designing men, acting upon the violence of an ignorant and turbulent people. Cast from his throne did I say, and into a prison? O the Ladye Elizabeth had not mourned thus, if that had been all. How joyfully she would have spent her life in that dreary room with her dear, dear father! She would have asked nothing else, have sought no amusement, have requested no gratification. Sunshine and flowers, such as the peasant children enjoy in every cottage garden, beneath every hawthorn hedge, in the green spring time, she would have been content never to have seen more; even the pure air, and the light which God freely gives to all, she thought she could have renounced for ever—too happy if, in the absence of all else dear to him, she had been permitted to share her father's undeserved distress, and to smooth his thorny path to a bloodless grave. But so it was not to be; and if you had seen her then, though the stamp of nature's nobility was on her graceful form and beautiful forehead— and though the robe which she wore was still that which beseemed a princess, and the pearls, her mother's last gift, worth an Earl's ransom; you would indeed have seen cause in a moment for the agony of grief, against which she could no longer struggle, as, throwing herself into her father's arms, she wept aloud, without attempting to utter a word. You would have guessed that the scaffold was erected, and the axe sharpened that was to be dyed in the blood, the sacred blood of the king. O you would have pitied her, you would have understood why her father's gentle and soothing tones only made her weep the more passionately, because she felt she was never after that sad evening to hear them more. Can you not fancy how, when at last she had composed herself, she sat gazing at him, almost unable to realize her awful condition—looked at the clear, mild eyes, the firm and manly form before her, and questioned herself as to the possibility that men would really be so iniquitous, so desperately cruel, as to tear her father from her? Other griefs, and bitter ones, the Ladye Elizabeth, young as she was, had known. The troubles of her native land had caused her to be separated at different times from her mother, her infant sister, and those dear playfellows, her brothers; and she had known what it was to listen all day with feverish anxiety for important tidings, and at evening to hear worse than even her most distressed imagination could have conceived. One after another, she had been parted from faithful friends; one after another, she had seen the survivors put on mourning, ever for the dearest and the best. But now, all other friends seemed of no value; all other troubles were nothing. "O!" thought she, as she fixed her eyes on her father, as if she desired never more to remove them again, "O that they would spare my father!" "Will they really murder my father?" and the fearful question rung in her ears, as if it would stun the voice of reason. But her father commanded her attention, and she had always obeyed her father's command. History has told us in a few words, what was the purport of that interesting conference. How the King charged her on her allegiance to him, and as she valued his blessing, to forgive her enemies—alas! that a child of her age should have any to forgive! It was a Christian message, and Charles had grace in his last extremity, to set his children the noble example. To her ladye mother, he sent a message of faithful affection and of true love, which had never swerved, and which is stronger than death. To her eldest brother, he charged her to pay all loyal duty, for he soon would be her sovereign lord the king; and to the Church of England—that church of which he died a faithful member, and which yearly commemorates her royal martyr with a mother's love—he bade her continue in firm and steady affection, recommending her, with calmness admirable at that time, such books as would enlarge her knowledge of its value, and increase her love for its ordinances. History has delighted to tell us, how composed the King was during that interview—that last interview with his children, until, surprised at the passionate answer with which his young son replied to his charge, "not to be made a king," he for a moment lost his self-possession, and burst into tears. It is a sad story, and you know it well. But history has not told us, it could not tell the feelings of the Princess at the moment of their separation; how again and again she endeavoured to promise her father a faithful attention to his desires, and again and again failed; and when for the last moment, she clasped her arms round his neck, and thought she had so very much, such a world of love to tell, she found no word of utterance, but the passionate and reiterated cry, "O my father! my father!" History drew a veil over the Princess during the next melancholy, and the next horrible day, and well it might! What a murder was perpetrated on the bloody scaffold at Whitehall, on the 30th of January, we all know too well. One murder the sun has seen of infinitely deeper atrocity, and but one.

It could not be, but that some tear of sympathy was shed at a view of that pale and troubled countenance, that uncomplaining despair; but sympathy with Elizabeth Stuart in those days was accounted a sin: no human voice comforted her when the last fatal news reached her, and no human ear heard the orphan's exclamation, "O that my turn was come!" A few months only passed, and the desired hour of rest came.

Years passed on, and, tired with a tyrant's reign, at last

P

the guilty nation returned to its allegiance. History loves the shout that rings round the triumphant car, better than the sigh which is breathed over a martyr's grave; and it tells us of such a shout that day as echoed from Dover cliff to Berwick, and from the Land's End to the Orkneys. It tells us of true and loyal hearts thronging to welcome their returning king, and of the song of the fair and lovely, who strewed May flowers on the shore where he landed. It tells us of broidered banners and of gilded oak branches, and in many a page we may read glowing and gorgeous descriptions of the pomp, the revelry, and the exultation with which the people gave a loose to their extravagant joy.—History may well love the sunshine of that day, and the sound of that heartfelt shout; and yet I wish one sigh had been breathed, and one tear shed over the low grave in the Isle of Wight, where the young Princess had been so long buried—over the grave of the gentle, the beautiful, the heart-broken Ladye Elizabeth. But it was no matter. Well for her, that meeting her sainted father so soon in heaven, she escaped from those evils, which indeed had brought her in the early spring of her years to an untimely grave! Well for her, that she did not live to see her country forget its mercies, and her brother trample on the laws of his father's God!

It matters not, since we trust her record is in heaven, that earth's memorials say so little about her, or that years passed after her heart was broken, before any one inquired for the low grave of Elizabeth Stuart.

*March 22, 1831.*

# ALICE GREY.

>  ...... What heart could spare
>    To the cold cheerless deep
>  Her flower and hope? but thou art with him there,
>    Pledge of the untir'd arm, and eye that cannot sleep—
>  The eye that watches o'er wild ocean's dead,
>    Each in his coral cave,
>  Fondly, as if the green turf wrapt his head
>    Fast by his father's grave.
>
>                                  KEBLE.

Is it not a pleasant thing to meet a sailor on his first landing, with his glad step, and his beaming face; carrying all his worldly goods slung in a bundle over his shoulder, and bearing cautiously in his hand the foreign basket that contains perhaps some token of remembrance for an expecting heart? He greets every landsman that he meets with a friendly word, stranger though he be. He is so happy, that he feels kindly to every one—for happiness is a very good-natured feeling—and of all grown men in the world, perhaps the newly-landed sailor gives one the best idea of exemption from care; as he leaps on shore how little burden he carries! There is a pleasure in his heart and his eyes—aye! and in the very waving of his blue handkerchief. And then the meeting—" Please God a week more of this wind, and he'll be at home," his mother has said week after week; but the wind has shifted often. "I trust they were not beating up channel last night," his father has thought on many a stormy morning; and his sisters have watched the weathercock and the clouds, and expressed, in various terms and tones, their anxiety about him. Very likely there may be somebody else who never mentions the weather or the sailor, and yet who spends more sleepless nights than even his mother, and longs for his return more anxiously, ah! ten times more anxiously, than his sisters do. She has sown her sweet peas and her lupins amongst the knots of boy's love and marjoram at the door, with a vague idea, which she never whispered to any one, not even to herself, that perhaps *his* ship may be safe in port when they blossom. She has trimmed her jessamine; and the French beans which she planted are grown half way up the bended willow wands that form her arbour in the corner of the garden hedge.

"Not," as she thinks to herself, "that very likely he will ever come into it again: but he did admire it once." At last he has really landed! His mother has held him in her arms, and his father has blessed him—and his sisters, how vociferous and how joyful they are; and that faithful one has met him too, how gladly, we cannot tell—because she never told.

And then, on Sunday, how pleasant a sight it is to see the sailor in the same seat which he occupied when he was a fair curly-headed child, and to feel that He who sitteth above the water floods has once more in mercy heard his church's prayer for "all who travel by land and by water." O it is a pleasant thing, and a profitable thing, to kneel where our fathers knelt, and to thank God in the words they taught us!

It is a troublesome world, but God has given us some moments of deep delight and of undescribed rapture. So poor Alice Grey thought as she received her husband on his arrival from the first voyage which he went after their marriage. She thought he was looking very well, and he was kinder, and better to her than ever.

There was but one thing to make her heart ache, and that was the thought of so soon again parting. The second voyage was a perilous one; and whilst on shore in Jamaica, Tom Grey had the yellow fever, and when yet scarcely recovered, he wrote his wife a very affectionate but very melancholy letter; a letter with which Alice never parted, but which she has since told me, seemed like a token of all that was to follow. But the sailor forgot his forebodings, and came home in good health. "Tom!" said his wife, "God has sent you back to me in his mercy when I did not expect you, now let us make any sacrifice rather than part again." She pleaded earnestly, but she was too late. The captain had already engaged the steady and active young sailor on whom he had much dependance, and Tom's wife knew that he never broke his word. "God prosper me this one voyage," he answered, "and then I never will leave you or your children again." His time was very short, but during it he made every arrangement that he thought could conduce to his wife's comfort. The Japan cabinet, not exactly of a piece with the rest of the English cottage furniture, which he had brought her, he put up with his own hands on the last day he was at home; and though Alice has wanted bread since, she would never part with that. He trimmed the willows at the hatch, and dug up her flower-beds, and white-washed her walls; but the memorial at which she looked oftenest, and afterwards with the saddest recollections, was a line that he cut at the side of the fire-place, to mark the height of his sweet little girl. " God bless her, and send me safe back to her!" said the sailor, and the tears sprang into his eyes " please God to give me a safe voyage home, and I never will leave you, Aly, nor your little maid more." Alice made no answer, but busied herself in arranging her little girl's beautiful curls, and as she did so the tears streamed silently down her cheek and fell on the baby's head; and it was in vain that the fingers stole up so quietly and dashed them off, they gathered again and again, and her husband vainly endeavoured to comfort her. Is there such a thing as presentiment in our marvellously constituted frame? I cannot tell, but it was with more than usual anxiety and distress that Alice saw the preparations for that voyage. His ship lay at many miles distance, but as if she knew it was to be their last journey together, she travelled with him, went on board with him, and they parted. " Neither of us," said she, "spoke one word." So the ship sailed, and she returned home with a heavy, but a submissive heart, and after a little while her wonted cheerfulness returned, her affairs seemed to prosper. The little business that she carried on succeeded. Her fair child grew presently above the mark that its father had made; and monthly, when Alice received the half of her husband's wages, it was with commendations of his determined and skilful conduct. " They may well praise him," thought she; " but if it please God to send him safe home this once, I'll be content to hear no more of his boldness and his skill. O it's little comfort for a husband to be praised for boldness that may leave his wife a widow and his children orphans!" His children? Yes! for Alice was again a mother.

She was pleased that her infant was a son, she should so

delight to call him by his father's name. There is a degree of superstition natural to us, and it is easier to account superstition folly, than to be entirely free from its influence. Yet I think the wakeful nights that poor Alice spent during her illness, and the exceeding lowness of spirits with which she was afflicted, was natural enough to one whose best friend was so far away, without being sure as the old nurse injudiciously told her, that it was a token there was bad news a coming. It was natural that a young and delicate woman, and a sailor's wife, should shudder at the sighing of the midnight storm, even if those about her had not excited her already fevered imagination with the idea that it was the voice of one wailing and lamenting.

And it was nothing very unaccountable, if, on the first Sunday in which she was well enough to appear at church, she became, as she knelt at the altar to return thanks, so weak as almost to faint. Yet the good women who gathered about her in the vestry, nodded one at another, and whispered loud enough for her to profit by the suggestion, their conviction, that all her agitation, her faintness, so naturally to be accounted for, was a warning—a sign—something—about poor Tom.

"Alice," said her mother-in-law the next morning, " I hear the ship is at Gravesend." "The ship at Gravesend," said Alice, "and no letter! But," she added, "I meant to take the baby to show them at the office, and then I shall hear for myself." Weak as her spirits had been before, at that moment, she says, she had not the slightest misgiving. A letter might come to her that day, or the next, or, better than all, her husband himself was on the road—her kind husband, who had promised never to leave her again. She had just received the half of his wages, and the thought that they might never be due to him again, was not likely once to occur to her. The next morning she dressed herself and her beautiful infant in their very best. It was a bright summer day; so she selected from her neat but scanty wardrobe, the light cotton gown which her husband had chosen, and which had been her best when she married. She crossed her gay orange silk handkerchief over her white one, and tied on her new apron. You might have looked far, before you had seen a gayer or a prettier party than Alice Grey and her children.

"I wish I could take Lizzy all the way," thought she, as having dressed her little dark-eyed girl she left her under a neighbour's care to wait her return; "yet I need not wish it, for Tom can't be there, yet, it is no use to think he will; and if he were, I must show him his boy first."

So she set out for the office, a walk of about three miles from her house, telling every one who inquired of her, that Tom, she supposed, was still at Gravesend, and that she did not expect him down for two or three days; and yet, poor thing, having dressed herself exactly in the clothes which she knew he liked best, and admiring her baby all the way, with the feeling of how his father would admire him, it was not until Alice reached the door of the office that her spirit failed her, and her heart sunk for a moment; but recovering herself, she went in. The kind old lady who was used to receive her on such occasions took her infant from her, made her sit down, and gave her a glass of wine. She'll need something to strengthen her, thought she, as she looked at her compassionately. Alice could not ask for a letter. "What a very sickly time we have had," said the old lady after a pause. "Have we ma'am ?" asked Alice. The air is fresh and pure on our hills, and Alice did not recollect any one who had been ill. "Why," said another female in the room, "have you not heard that the captain has been ill, and has lost two of the men ?" "I felt the word," said poor Alice, "from the crown of my head to the sole of my foot." "It is my husband!" said she, and without making one effort to support herself, she fell down in a fainting fit. It was with a kind intention, I dare say, that when they had brought her to herself again, the women deceived her into a belief that her husband was only very ill, not dead. But it is not right, and therefore never wise, to deceive. It is not a Protestant doctrine to do evil that good may come; and in this case—as I believe in all others—the evil being done, the good never comes. "We expect a letter to-morrow or next day, and then we shall hear how he is: but let some one else come," they said soothingly, "you are too weak." She was weak indeed; and as she sat listlessly gazing at her baby—her fatherless baby—so the sad whisper in her sinking heart told, you would have thought it impossible that she could have reached home that evening. But there is little knowing what the weak human frame can bear, till the hour of need comes, in which God's strength is made perfect in weakness. The next morning her mother offered to go the office, and make inquiry instead of her. "What! and I wait here? O I could not—I could not!" said Alice, passionately; and the next day, and the next, she went to hear the vague and deceitful comfort, with which her injudicious friends supplied her. Ah, poor Alice! she had vainly decked her infant's worked cap with the shining rosette of white satin, saying to herself, "This will be for his christening when his father comes." It would have made your heart ache; to see the look of deep unmurmuring despair with which, on the Saturday after she heard the dreadful news, she sat quietly unpicking the ribbon, and supplying its place with one of black love. The next day the mourning party appeared at church in the afternoon, and after service, Alice, her mother-in-law, and her brothers, carried the infant to the font—the fair child whose father might never glory in him. They called him by his father's name, but he may never hear the voice of a father's blessing. Well! the blessing of a mightier Father rest on the sailor's orphan child.

Affairs have not prospered with poor Alice—how should they?—since she became a widow. She has missed her husband's pleasant company, his ready assistance, and his kind words; but she has missed his wages also: and as her blooming children have grown up, she has denied herself many a meal, that they might not be stinted, and has sat up at work late, on many a night, "rather," as she says, "than Tom's children should not look something as they would have looked if he were there to see them." There are very few who know how hard she has struggled. "Some have pitied my trouble, and some that I thought I might have looked to, never took much notice." I thought there was something expressive in the phrase. There are too many in this selfish world, of whom the least reproachful thing that can be said, is, that they do not "take much notice of the grief that is consuming the very life of a fellow-creature.

There was one person, however, who did take notice of

poor Alice Grey's trouble. There was a young man whose business had called him on board of Tom's ship, within a day or two after it came into port. It happened that whilst looking round, a chest caught his eye, on which were rudely cut, the words, "Thomas and Alice Grey." Leonard looked again, for Tom Grey had been a favourite schoolmate of his. "Ah!" said an old man who stood by, "poor Tom's cutting! he was a favourite with every body!" And he went on to tell how one fair day, when the ship was at her moorings abroad, Tom and a shipmate of his got leave to go on shore.

"They went with light hearts," said Leonard, when he repeated the story to Alice; "but he that told me, said they were never the same men after they came back. It was burning weather, and it may be they over-heated themselves, or perhaps they made too free with the plentiful fruit that grew there; we can't tell—they came back to the ship, but they never looked up more." It was a sad tale for poor Alice to hear, but he who repeated it to her, pitied her from the bottom of his heart, as he spoke of the hopeless yearning with which the dying men pined for their native hills, and for the kind voices of home, as they loitered about the deck, shivering in the torrid sunshine. Alice wept as she heard how it had been her husband's last amusement to cut his own name, and hers, and the little girl's, in different parts of the ship. "But," concluded Leonard, "that was soon over; they grew worse and worse, and one died one hour and the other the next, and their shipmates sewed them up in their hammocks, and buried them in the waters, just when the ship had sailed three days." "Ah!" cried Alice, "that's the worst of it. Would God I had spoken with him but for five minutes. Would God I had followed him to his grave, where his father is buried in our churchyard!" It is a natural feeling, yet let poor Alice take comfort. That is a peaceable grave where God's blessing rests, and he sleeps as well in the tossing ocean, as if he were lying where the sun shines under the old chestnut tree.

Alice Grey was left a widow at little more than three-and-twenty. She was very pretty and very agreeable then, and I have thought sometimes, that, perhaps, there was something more than pity in the interest young Leonard took in her concerns. "But Tom's children are more to me," said Alice, "than any one else can possibly be. I love his children as I do my own life." She spoke positively, and I believed her; I hoped she never would: and now I am quite sure, Alice Grey will never marry again!

### LINES TO COMFORT THE SAILOR'S WIDOW.

O! happy those who rest
  In their own churchyard's shade;
With the green turf on their breast,
  And the old yew at their head;
Who knelt at their own altar's side,
And in their father's faith have died.

Our feet this fresh turf trod
  In childhood's pleasant hours;
Around this house of God
  Sprung up our fresh wild flowers;
The violets that we loved the best
Grew, where our kindred's graves are blest.

Dear is the hallowed ground—
  And there the tried and true;
A faithful band around
  With tears the grave bedew:
And pleasant is our hope to lie
With those we love, when we shall die.

Yet if your loved ones sleep
  In ocean's caverns wide,
Not thus despairing weep,
  For them the Saviour died;
His eye beholds that "coral cave,"
His Spirit guards that billowy grave.

Happy are they who rest
  In their own churchyard tomb—
Yet those shall be as blest
  Who sleep in ocean's gloom.
Their Saviour walks their grave beside,
If in his faith and hope they died.

*April* 21, 1831.

# THE CREW'S HOLD.

> "I have war and tempest seen,
> I've in many a peril been—
> Borne the tocsin and the strife
> Of a long eventful life—
> Hear then what I have to say
> Of the strange and devious way."

"THEN you have been in perils by land and by water!" I said carelessly, when old Thomas closed his sentence; for he had been talking in an unvarying tone for a long time, and my thoughts had wandered to very different matters. "Perils by land and by water!" repeated the old man, probably observing my apathy, and speaking in such a tone as instantly recalled my recollections, and made me feel ashamed at the selfishness which rendered me weary of what was so interesting to him. "Perils by land and by water! I wonder whether I have not or no? Why, I've walked three times from here to Portsmouth, and twice back again, and I've been in the Brazils, and I've served in North America, and I've been in a peace ship, but that was only to the West Indies; and that's some thousand miles. Perils by water! why, I've been weeks together seeing nothing but water and sky; and I fell over the side of a seventy-four gun ship once, and *He* saved me," and he looked upwards seriously—"and I served in the French war afore you was born. And perils by land! why, I have known some in my time. I worked once in the coal-pit, and got badly hurt there twice; and I have worked at smelting ore, and at the copper furnace, and the lead—the lead for four-and-twenty years; and till I was afflicted"—and he looked down at his poor deformed feet and hands—"there was not a better fireman the country round than I —and I've worked at the brass too. I've seen things in my time you'd be 'most frightened to hear—I have known perils, sure enough." "I should like to hear them," I said, thinking to make up for my unintentional slight; "I am very fond of old stories." "Are you?" answered the old man, and his pale face becoming instantly grave, and his

small grey eyes assuming a very shrewd look, he said, "I can tell you there's many stories told in the world, and," lowering his voice, "some that are not true." He evidently meant to give me a sort of certificate of the truth of what he should tell; but I pretended to take it to myself, and assured him that when I told his story over again it should be just as he told it to me. "O! I don't mean such as you," said he; "there is not any body in all this country, high or low, I can make more free with, than all you and your brother, and I know many here say the same." I was really pleased. Some of them are indeed very free, but if that freedom, coarse though it be, now and then, arises from confidence in our steady desire to be of use to them, we will be thankful that we have been able to inspire such a feeling. The hand that is stretched out to clasp mine, may be toil-worn and hard and rough, but if it is stretched out in gratitude and affection it must be false delicacy indeed, to shrink from the touch. It was not that I found in old Thomas's story much of connected interest, that I have taken the trouble of recollecting some things which he told me; but I liked to hear him talk, for he gave me, in the half hour I sat there, some striking particulars illustrative of the alteration in the character of our people, which I might not have met with elsewhere. He had been at an early age left to struggle with the world for himself, for his father died in the prime of life, leaving his widow with eight children, among whom he was one of the eldest. Then one brother went to sea, and I believe never returned, and, another a fine lad about sixteen, was killed in a coal-pit. "My poor mother had a *power* of trouble in her family," observed the old man. "That brother was brought home to us, poor fellow! about three hours after we had parted with him, so hale and strong in the morning. I mind it was one Friday about noon. I had a sister then, a young sprig of a maid, such another as you, and when she saw him brought home, and all of us crying and lamenting, she said, she could not cry for her brother, but she was sorry for him; and the next morning, Saturday morning, she died, and they were laid out on the bed, side by side—so you must needs think that was trouble."
O it was trouble indeed! The mower's scythe is not feared in the forest; but the fallen stone may crush at once the

springing foxglove and the wild anemone that grew at its
root. O dear, dear! it must indeed have been sad to see
the widow weeping over her poor children as they lay
there silent and still, in their decent white shrouds, strewed with that sad spring's primroses and rosemary! And
that poor girl, who can tell what suffering was her's in
those few brief hours of agony—what revulsion of blood to
the heart, what an overpowering thronging of the thoughts to
the brain, when looking on her dead brother, she could
find no words to express herself, only "that she was very
sorry, but could not cry." Who shall speak again of want
of feeling in the uneducated, when the poor collier's girl
died of grief at the loss of her brother?

Of the number who followed that doubly sad procession
to the grave, all beside are long since dead; but the tears
in the old man's eyes showed that he, the sere and one sur-
vivor of that once blooming group, yet mournfully remembered the untimely blasting of those two wild flowers.

But it was not the history of his private life that interested me so much, as the accounts he gave of my countrymen's wild and lawless manners at the time when he was a
boy. He could not recollect the insurrection of the colliers,
but his wife's mother, still living and enjoying all her faculties at the age of eighty-seven, could. She was little
more than an infant when it happened, yet the impression
made at the time was so strong, that she still remembers
her father's hiding between the bed and the sacking, on the
approach of the rioters, with whom he did not wish to join,
and who, making the common mistake of those who go
mad for love of liberty, compelled every one they met with
to join them, if not in heart, yet with hand, whether they
chose it or not. Old Mary recollects, or has heard the story so often, that she thinks she recollects, how the poor
misguided men came down the hill to the number of two
thousand, armed with pickaxes and clubs, stopped at every
pit, and every collier's house, to increase their number; and
at last collected on the spot, where now the church and the
quiet vicarage stand. She recollects how they tore down
the turnpike-gates, then newly erected, and marched down
to the city. Such an undisciplined force was of course
soon driven back, and no doubt it was from pity that a part
of their demand was granted to them; and that though new

turnpike-gates were immediately erected in the wild parts which they had been taught to call their fathers' and their own, the toll was lowered, so that the carriage of coal is still lower here than any other. To be sure, the grave companies of colliers whom I sometimes meet on their way, to and from work, and whom I seldom hear exchanging a word which each other, must be wonderfully sobered down since then; yet I like to believe, that all that they have lost is evil, and that they have as much intrepidity now, as when, in their vain attempt to force the prison where some of them were confined, their young companion was shot dead amongst them, and they gave three wild cheers as they took him up, and carried him home. "They must have been very bold men." I thought out loud. "They *are* very bold now," interrupted the old man: "why do you know, I have heard officers and admirals too say it, they had rather have Kingswood men for sailors, than any other; they are daunted at nothing."—"And do you recollect how the sailors used to come up here to hide from the press-gang?"

"The sailors! Don't I recollect it? Why I served in that same war.———Why," he added abruptly, breaking off, "I have stood as close to the king, this same king as ever is now, nearer than I am to this table." I do not know whether he accounted that as one of his "perils by land," but he went on with some very free remarks, which my loyalty will not allow me to transcribe, but which were admirably characteristic of the freedom with which my countrymen speak of every body. They are no respecters of persons. "The sailors!" continued Thomas; "there was never such work in all the world, as there was here then. Wild, wicked doings sure. But the people, for the most part, liked the sailors, and harboured them, and used the officers of the press-gang very ill." "I have heard," interrupted I, "about taking them down the coal-pits."— "And didn't I know two myself that they did take down— there was Jock Ward, and he deserved it," (some of the esprit de corps still in existence, thought I,) "and there might be several more."

Certainly that was a summary way of proceeding, and a very convenient method of taking revenge, for to themselves it could give no trouble, and yet left those who had given offence, to say the least, in a ridiculously helpless situation. And then it could do no great harm. For my own part, I have long had a desire to be initiated into the mysteries of those lower regions, and though I should not wish to be carried down, *vi et armis*, like Jock, I shall never think myself free of the parish till I have been. But Thomas allowed no time for my considerations. He was delighted that he could recollect so much, and that he had found some one who would listen to his recollections. "I'll tell ye something worse than that, they did once," said he; "they took the king's officers, and carried them blindfold down the copper furnace—you'd be frightened if you saw the place."—"I've seen the place where they melt lead," interrupted I,—" O," continued he, "it's ten times hotter than that. They tore down the door, and made them look down into the furnace, and threatened to throw them in, if ever they came that way again. You may be sure the poor gentlemen were terrified, and right glad to get away faster than they came."—" Well! after this, I must be patient when people speak ill of us. I am sure, I did not think we had ever been half so bad. I have heard it said too, that they fixed a cannon on the broken piece of rock, behind the white house, then one of the chief places of resort for the sailors, and threatened to fire at any vessel that came up the river to look after them."—" It is very like," said the old man: "why there's a large cupboard up-stairs, where two of the sailors were hid for a day and a night, and the officers were forced at last to go away without them."

You cannot be so interested in these strange recollections as I was, my dear reader; but in time to come, when a generation or two more have passed, if the gradual improvement which is begun here, should continue in the same progression, as I trust it may, people will not know the meaning of the name given to this part of our parish— "The Crew's Hold,"—for it has already degenerated into the unmeaning word " Screw's-hole." It is a singularly wild and poor part, yet we feel now not the smallest fear; and, indeed, as the old man concluded his reminiscences, by observing, "I don't think there's any body here now, that would hurt a child." We will go on a little further, then, fearlessly, for there is another spot which brings to my mind remembrances of very early childhood.

It is a long while—it is years ago, since we used to visit old Henry and Sarah Curtis, in the cottage nearest the river side. There is no harm now in telling their names, for they have been long in their graves, and there is not even the record of a head-stone to tell where they lie; and as for pointing out the house, it is so much altered, and all around it is so altered, that from my description of what I can once remember it, you would hardly trace it now. The precipitous bank beyond it, where there used to grow gaze, and furze, and broom, is excavated into a very large stone quarry. There are noble masses of stone, displaying every variety of colour, from pale brown to deep red, and from cold neutral tint to bright purple. An artist, describing it at sunset, when the red setting light streams up the river upon it, would find it difficult not to make his picture more bright than common observers would allow to be natural. But an artist must not paint, a poet must not write, for common observers: Nature is their gentle mistress, and they will do best who follow her most closely, with unequal steps, perhaps, but undoubtingly wherever she leads. The quarry, is in itself a fine object; but it has been the means of bringing a number of noisy workmen to what was once a comparatively quiet scene; and the fine elms that grew by the causeway, under the bank, have been cut down, and every day increases the depredations which are made on the picturesque underwood along the steep: for they have discovered that the whole hill side can afford stone, and soon, I suppose, it will be one huge quarry. They have done worse than this. They have built a steam-engine for raising coal on a spot, which we used to think quiet and pleasant; and where, until then, we could gather woodbine and blue violets. It was once a pleasure to us to walk there. Now, when we do so, it is a business and a duty, and we cannot help looking with a sigh at the shady woods and the soft fields on the opposite side of the river, when our feet are so tired with walking amongst stones and cinders. The elder hedge, inside the low wall, that surrounded the old people's garden, has been long torn entirely away, and for many years the wall has been much broken down also; and the house fell quickly into decay, as uninhabited houses are likely to do, in the midst of people who think it allowable to take all that can be taken, and amusing to destroy what remains. Lately, however, the wall and house have been partially repaired.

But the garden is altered indeed to what it was, when the neat and industrious old couple used to give us wallflowers, and clove pinks over the hedge; and the house, I cannot help thinking, from its outward appearance, must be very different from what it was when old Sarah had finished her whitewashing about Whitsuntide, and used to have us all—to be sure we were very little, or she could not have found room for us—into the small parlour in which she generally sat. I remember how loath we used to be to pass without her notice, and when we discovered the back of her neat mob cap as she sat in the window-seat, how we used to linger about the garden wall and talk louder; for we were not permitted to call to her, and throw stones into the river, to excite her attention; for it was a great treat to us to go into the house, because perhaps, it was so unlike all other houses that we had ever seen. It consisted but of one room on the ground floor, from whose corners a bedroom, pantry, and the little sitting-room were petitioned off. There was a large flue in the middle of the ceiling, at which we used to gaze up in wonder; and I remember old Sarah's trying to describe to us the apparatus which once belonged to it, and which was used, as far as I understood, for trying the qualities of ore. She had once lived in a larger abode, having many years before we knew her been mistress of the white house—the resort of the rebellious sailors of which I spoke just now, and when she came into a quieter line of life, with old Henry, who was her second husband, I suppose she sold some of her furniture, but certainly she had too much for comfort left.

The extra chairs were hung up against the wall, round the top of the room; and there were chests of drawers and corner-cupboards by the half dozen, and drinking vessels and tea things by the score. But the pictures I remember best; for whilst our elders were deeply engaged in conversation, we were obliged to sit still, and had nothing to do but to look about us. There was an hieroglyphic of the Tree of Life, with medals and mottoes all over it—a portrait of Whitefield, hanging beside a caricature of a mailcoach breakfast, and in company with two lamentable pictures, at which, awkward and out of drawing as the figures were, it would be a sin to smile, for there was depicted poor Lewis the Sixteenth taking leave of his family, and preparing for death. It is very likely, that when we were tired of sitting still so long, we began to wonder that the conversation should excite so much interest in the parties engaged in it; for then we were too young to understand how that redemption, which is a fit theme for the songs of angels, is permitted to employ the weak tongues of men. We did not then understand, how meet it is that they should give thanks, whom the Lord hath redeemed and delivered from the hand of the enemy; and old Henry and Sarah had many mercies to recount, for their journey had been long, and they had gone far astray, "had wandered out of the way, and found no city to dwell in." Then they cried unto the Lord in their trouble—blessed be his name, that trouble should sometimes bring us back to Him—and he delivered them, turned their feet into the right way: no wonder they loved to talk of him by the way, as he led them to their city of habitation. But there were subjects of conversation, to which we could listen with delight, and which we could fully understand. There were Sarah's long histories of all the "dumb things" she had reared. Children brought up in the country love "dumb things." To this day, I recollect the pleasure with which she told, and the wonder with which we used to listen to the story of her sow and its family of young ones, who, tempted by the fertile pasture, used, as I understood the tale, to plunge into the river one and all, swim across, and riot in the luxuriance of the meadow, much to the annoyance of the proprietor. Then there was her other story about a sick animal of the same noble species, of which she took, I was going to say, motherly care. She wrapt it up in her own red cloak, and then—I suppose the nights were cold and she was willing to pay all due attention—she brought the unaccustomed guest in a basket into her own bed-room. What the eye does not see, it is said, the heart cannot rue; so she thought it wisest not to mention the matter to her husband. In the middle of the night, however, the pig bethought it of the comforts and convenience of its native sty, and became impatient of its confinement, and struggled to be free, and the old man awoke in a great fright. "There's robbers," said he. "O dear no!" she answered. "It is," repeated he, "can't you hear?" But a convenient fit of deafness had come over her; at least she felt sure she did not hear *robbers*. One effort more, however, and away ran her invalid, struggling and stumbling over the red cloak, as it fell like ornamental trappings, sweeping the ground under its feet. "It is a spirit," said the old man—an unphilosophical idea of a spirit he had to be sure. "It is a spirit," he repeated, frightened out of his wits, and marvelling at his wife's self-possession, "what will become of us?" "Now don't be angry," said she; "there's no occasion to be frightened; it's nothing in the world but the pig that's ill, with my red cloak tied round it."

Then she had two or three very handsome cats, each, according to her account remarkable for some particular intelligence or affection; and, indeed, those who will condescend to observe such matters, will find that God has given to this lower order of his creation, faculties very capable of improvement, and that improvement is chiefly made, as indeed in the intellect of a higher class of beings, by benevolent treatment. I know that one of these poor creatures, which lived to be very old, evidenced the strongest pity for her mistress when she was in pain; running from a distant part of the room, springing on her knee, and licking her hands when she heard her sigh, and constantly sitting on her bed after old Sarah was confined to it. I am surprised that I can remember so few particulars of our visits; but the impression of the old people's kindness to us is very strong indeed. I recollect one cold winter day, when we could not stay to go in and warm ourselves, they handed us over the hedge a large bason of what then appeared to us the best pea-soup we ever tasted. Then the old woman more than once made us a cake to carry home; and as for sprays of rosemary, and strawberries, and roses, I believe we might have had all in the garden if we would. She was, I should think, naturally fond of children; but the circumstance of her having lost her only daughter in the bloom of youth, and two or three boys in early infancy, might, perhaps, have softened her manners, and made her more tender towards children, than her education or her appearance would have led you to expect. Yet, in many respects she was superior to her station. She had in her youth been in service in respectable families, and she had a mind capable of using the opportunities of improvement then afforded: the situation of mistress, to even the public-house at the "Crew's Hold"—bad as it was in important respects—had, from the various company with which she associated there, given a quickness to her perceptions, and a fluency to her expressions, somewhat remarkable in an uneducated woman. Perhaps she had been well looking in her day, for old as she was when we knew her, she had clear, dark, lively eyes, and a healthy, gipsy complexion; her black hair, until her last illness, shewed scarcely one tinge of grey; and being of a firm, square make, age never seemed to bow her down as it does most people. She continued upright, though not active, till her last sickness laid her on her bed. The old man was not to appearance so strong, yet from being of a slighter figure, he was more capable of exertion than his wife; and I remember nothing longer ago, than watching him after his long walk hastening up the field to church. For many years he occupied morning and afternoon that single seat under one of the south windows; and when he was afflicted with asthma, and could brave the steep hill but once in the day, there every Sunday morning saw him for years more. There was his delight, there he found comfort. I remember the strong expressions of well-deserved esteem and love with which he spoke of his pastor, and how delighted I was, when, during his last illness, he said he liked me to read the Psalms to him, because my voice reminded him of that dear and honoured one. O those are blessed feelings, which exist between a faithful shepherd and his flock! Can they be doing right, who are loosening the bands, the golden bands, that bound us together? I cannot help feeling it—I cannot help saying it: efforts are made on all sides—God knows with too much success—to lessen the shepherd's influence, and to scatter the flock. "Give peace in our time, O Lord! there is none that fighteth for us, but only thou, O God!" The old man died after, as far as I can remember, a short illness. His end was calm resignation, quiet confidence, perfect peace. If there was no ecstatic feeling of delight, (and who wonders, that when the sinner is walking through the dark valley of the shadow of death, there should be none?) there was yet no fear of evil, for David's Lord was with him, his rod and his staff did comfort him. I can recall very clearly our visit to

Sarah after the funeral—with what satisfaction she dwelt on the hope of a blessed immortality, which her gracious God had given—with what interest she detailed every word, every action of her departed husband, during the last day or two of his life, even to the most trivial particulars—to the morsel of food that she prepared for him, and to the last draught with which she endeavoured to quench his dying thirst. It does not do, to be in a hurry on such occasions: when people are in trouble, it is a greater kindness to let them "tell all about it," than it would be to give them a handful of gold if one could. I cannot say for how many months Sarah survived her husband; but I know she was for a long time confined to her bed, and that she bore her illness with great patience, and many expressions of gratitude and affection to the kind relations who came to live with her during her widowhood. She was very humble, having a deep and habitual recollection of the sins and offences of her youth; but the eye of faith had been fixed for years on the cross, and it pleased the God of spirits, that a naturally lively imagination should reflect vivid impressions of the affecting history which his own word gave of her lost state by nature, and her Saviour's mighty salvation. "I lie here at night thinking of Him," she once said, "till I almost fancy I see the fresh wounds in his hands, and in his feet, and his bleeding side; and his look to me is full of mercy, and his voice says, 'I cast out none that come;' and he looks and speaks to me, to me—and O! how many years I lived in rebellion against him." With such feelings, with such scriptural trust, she died; and certainly there is a pleasure in remarking God's fatherly dealing, in thus gently showing the sinner the error of her way, and forming such a contrast in the quiet death-bed of the aged believer, to the early life of the mistress of the riotous Crew's Hold.

But one particular of their history I had almost left out. I wonder I should have done so, because I know that, as long as old Henry lived, it was a constant subject of conversation. There was some estate to which they had, or fancied they had a right, and every small sum of money they could command was spent in carrying on a tedious, and, as it proved, useless lawsuit.

But the lawyers constantly held out fresh hopes, and the

old people as constantly believed them. Sometimes old Sarah would go so far as to tell us " no more was wanting but for the Lord *Chancel*," as she called him, " to put his hand to something,"—I believe she never knew exactly what—and then, the deeds were to be signed, and she should go to her beautiful estate, where we were to visit her. I always expected we should, and then, they were to have gold and silver to spare, and fruit on the garden walls, and filberts in the wood. But the lawsuit outlasted the old man's life. On earth they had no inheritance to leave, and obtained none,

"But the tinsel, that shone on the dark coffin lid,"

and the weeds that grew on the grave. But there is an inheritance incorruptible, undefiled, and that fadeth not away.

"There no delusive hope invites despair
No mockery meets—and no deception there."

Rust and moth corrupt it not—thieves cannot break through and steal. " It was reserved in heaven for them, through faith which is in Christ Jesus." My kind reader, is it waiting there for you and me also?

*May* 31, 1831.

# THE CONFIRMATION.

And oft as sin and sorrow tire,
The hallow'd hour do thou renew,
When beckon'd up the awful quire,
By pastoral hands—toward thee we drew.

KEBLE.

IT is certainly not a sacrament, but I know it is a means of grace, and I trust and believe, generally speaking, an efficacious means. And how simple the rite itself is; and how very natural in both its parts!

How natural it seems, that those to whom a gracious God has given life, and health, and happiness, and beauty, should, as soon as they are old enough to look round on the fair creation, amidst which they are placed as the fairest, desire of themselves to place themselves under the care of its beneficent God. Yet, alas! there I mistake my ground; that was man's natural condition once, when "God saw every thing that he had made, and behold it was very good;" but the case is entirely altered now; yet it is meet and right, that, if having been afar off, they have been brought near by the blood of Christ, sprinkled with the waters of baptism, and taken when unconscious of the privilege, into covenant with the most high God—it is natural, that if they have any feeling, any gratitude, they should desire to renew the vow, and enter into the covenant for themselves. And how simply beautiful our service is—how free from superstitious pomp, and unmeaning ceremony on the one hand—and on the other, how impressive, how solemn; how all things are done decently and in order!

We had yesterday as fair and lovely weather as ever June herself had to bestow; and to country people, on these occasions, the weather is a matter of some importance; because in a poor congregation, there will be several to whom the spoiling of the only decent clothes would be a matter of consequence, and at such a time one would gladly have every mind free from solicitude, that it may the more surely keep in view its grand object. We were in the church-yard some time before the church doors were open; and it was as well, as it saved all anxiety to those of our young candidates whom we had promised to meet; and on such a morning—the sun lighting up the ornamented buttresses and the grey niches of that most beautiful building; and the fresh air fanning the green leaves of the lime trees in the avenue, we could not have regretted the time, had it been as long again. Our little company came, in two or three separate parties, but presently we all met, and were conveniently seated in the places appointed for us; and during the time which elapsed before the service began, I was amused and interested by watching the other clergy bring in their separate flocks. Sometimes it appeared to me as if they had not met with all, and then I saw them go out and return again—perhaps with one or two in addition : that was a pretty emblem. Again, in recognizing the scattered members of their folds, it might be that an old man's eyes were dim, or a young man's thoughts might wander—but, I thought, when they meet these in heaven, before the throne of God—and O, that they may all meet there!—with what a glance shall they know each other!

It was not possible to look round on such a company as rose up when the service began, without feelings of delight mingled with something very like sorrow. What storms, one could not help thinking, shall blast, what blight shall fade these young flowers! Of all that number of untroubled hearts, how many must learn, by bitter experience, that here is not their rest; and otherwise, how many will be snatched away in the very spring-time of their years, "in pomp and pride of May," leaving vacant places among relatives and friends, never, never to be filled up. Which, I involuntarily asked as I looked round, which of these young and lovely ones is nearest the brink of the grave? O! we have seen it ourselves—the young, the healthy, come here in the full prime of life, and yet within the last month of their lives. Have we not seen eyes never yet dimmed by sorrow, and then suddenly dim in death! Yes, there he came the last time! I watched him during the ceremony. I saw the slight change of colour on the healthy cheek, as, first of our little company, he walked up to the altar. I observed his emotion when the bishop's hand was laid on him, and felt sure that grace would be given him to stand to the covenant. O! when I stood there then, how little likely it seemed that the old man should bestow his blessing, years after such a young man was in his grave. As we were on the road, my mind was full of these thoughts. It could not be otherwise; and as I glanced round our party, my eye rested on a small brooch that one of them wore, containing a lock of soft brown hair. I could scarcely restrain my tears. And is that all we have left of him? I thought. But I looked up toward the altar, and my thoughts became calm. There I stood watching him, as he went up a little before me, and knelt down at the rails.—Do I grieve that he is gone up a little before me now? Am I not content to see that, in this instance, my country's prayer has been granted; that my Lord defended that his servant with his heavenly grace, that he continued his, we humbly trust, to his short life's end, and was so soon safe in his heavenly kingdom.

The service continued, and though it so happened that the 39th Psalm was read, and that its funeral verses renewed in the mind every feeling of man's being in his best estate altogether vanity, yet we once more found that the service of our blessed church is well calculated to calm the fevered, and to heal the broken heart. The Communion Service was ended, and the other candidates being gone up, our parish was called—last, as it should be, for we are poorest and fewest ; and our date some centuries less ancient than any other. Never mind; let us remember, with deep solemnity, that "there are last who shall be first." Our orderly little party rose, and arranging themselves two and two, began very slowly to move forward. It was only the candidates who were summoned, but I could not have denied myself the pleasure of going up with them, on any account, and as the throng in the aisle only opened to allow space for them to pass, it was necessary that, to do so, I should join the procession. It was not exactly in order indeed; yet I think it was a privilege that might be fairly granted to the parson's daughter, and nobody disputed my right, so I went on. I do not wonder that there was no sound as the beautiful procession passed up the lofty and arched aisle, for it was a sight to fix the eyes, and engage the hearts of the lookers on. They passed amongst the tombs of their forefathers under the riven banners, and by the rusted armour of the mighty men of other days. Who

R

could look on, without seeing how moth and rust corrupt; and without being reminded of that spiritual armour with which these young combatants were to be invested, and praying that they might triumph and have victory? We moved on very slowly, and paused many times. Presently we passed through the iron gate that separates the nave from the chancel, and stood at the foot of the steps that led up to the altar.

"How beautiful it must seem to them!" I thought as I observed our young country girls' solemn look of wonder and delight, as the coloured light streamed through the stained window on the whole company as they stood still; and then another thought passed through my mind: If feeble man can raise a temple to the honour of his God—thus majestic and thus impressive—what shall that temple be which God has raised to his own honour? Eye hath not seen, nor ear heard! and O, if we may find entrance there, how shall the most refined, the most intellectual, pause at the threshold in wonder, more simple, more humble, and more deep, than that with which our country girls beheld for the first time in their lives so beautiful a work of art!

At that moment the question was asked, "Do ye here," the bishop began, "in the presence of God and this congregation, renew the solemn promise and vow made in your names at your baptism?" I had separated myself from the company of candidates, and stood a little apart looking at them. "Do they?" I thought, "here? where the dead in Christ are lying to rest around them; where the eye of God is in an especial manner upon them; where their ministers are watching as those who must give account, and anxious friends are looking on even with prayers and tears? Do they come *here* with true hearts, or dare they here to trifle? O let them turn back now! I almost said, let them not lie unto God!" or rather, here, as at the foot of the cross, let them accept the offered mercy of Him who waiteth to be gracious. Of all the thoughts that come into one's mind in looking on that lovely congregation, the saddest was the dread that some there perhaps, though charity hoped better things of all, had come carelessly, as to an unmeaning ceremony, and had not even then the sense to say, "Is there not a lie my right hand!"

But to look on the heart is God's prerogative, and it is

well for erring man to take what comfort he may from that which is lovely and satisfactory in outward appearance; and really the appearance of feeling and sincerity which was evinced by the whole company was cause of thankfulness, yet it did not need a very acute eye to trace shades and lines of difference.

Most of the company were in the very flower of their youth, but here and there might be noticed one whose youth had, perhaps, been given up to other masters, and who now came trembling to offer the less lovely, but blessed be the God of mercy, not the unaccepted sacrifice. Were those the bitter tears of remembered sin that he shed, on whom the prelate's hand was laid at that moment—and did the gentle touch remind him of the scorned blessing and the slighted counsel of a pious father, whose grey hair went down to the grave in sorrow? Is the sickness that makes his cheek so thin and pale, the effect of sinful riot and intemperance?

Weep on, poor prodigal! thy penitence is too late to be a comfort to the old father and the broken-hearted mother. Weep on, poor prodigal! but we who are watching thee will rejoice. Thy heavenly Father has met thee, and even now his words are sounding in our ears: "This my son was dead, and is alive again; he was lost, and is found!" Yet where sin has been, sorrow will unavoidably leave its trace also; and observe what a contrast that agitated sufferer forms, to the fair child who kneels beside him. All the other females have their heads covered, wearing neat caps or veils; but perhaps her mother thought her too young: look at her as she leans her forehead on the rail—her long shining curls hang round a face so fair, so childish, so innocent—you love to look at her. She is a little pale from awe, not fear; how should one of the little flock fear, to whom it is the father's good pleasure to give the kingdom? The solemnity of the moment has given an almost angelic beauty to features that seem never yet to have been ruffled by an earthly expression. As one looks at her, St. Paul's words to Timothy come into one's mind—"I call to remembrance the unfeigned faith that is in thee, that dwelt first in thy grandmother Lois, and thy mother Eunice, and I am persuaded that in thee also!" Blessed child of many prayers, the God of thy fathers make the rest of thy life answerable to this beginning! Rise up, dear child, be certified by this sign that "God's fatherly hand shall be ever over thee." Do not tremble so, for none but loving eyes are upon you, and look up, stand a little aside as you come down the steps, for see, who is being led up to your place! No wonder, the solemn look of reverence was so instantly changed to one of pity—his scarred cheek is indeed a contrast to hers.

The fair scene is a blank to him, for disease has made him blind; but you, poor blind boy, trust fearlessly the gentle hand that is leading you: kneel down there, Jesus of Nazareth is passing by, and if you have only faith to cry yet to him, "Thou son of David, have mercy!" surely you shall hear the gracious voice saying, "What wilt thou that I shall do unto thee?" Then the spiritual eyes shall be opened—nay, I doubt not they are opened now; and have patience with your blindness yet a little while, and you also "shall see the King in his beauty, you shall behold the land that is very far off."

I felt as if I could have stood there all day, watching the interesting train as they came up one after another, and then in the same order retired so quietly, so solemnly. My fancy framed a tale for many of them, but for one there the aid of fancy was not needed. Her pale cheek, her braided hair, and her close mourning cap, told her story of widowhood. It seemed strange that she had not presented herself there before.

It might be, that whilst she rejoiced in the shadow of her gourd, she had forgotten, like Jonah, that it was the hand of God which had prepared it for her, and perhaps it was not till the worm preyed upon its root, and the vehement east wind and the sun beat upon her head, "that she bethought her of Him who shall be for a hiding-place from the storm, a covert from the tempest, the shadow of a great rock in a weary land." Well, I trust she will find him now! blessing and comfort to her! She is indeed differently situated to all those who kneel around her.

It is a barren and lonely world—strange, though it be, to call the peopled world lonely—that lies before her; while to most of them it appears lit with sunshine and strewed with roses; but helpless, weak sufferers they must all be; they all need the same protector, the same guide. I trust they have found him. Surely, they will from this time cry unto him, "My Father, thou art the guide of my youth." From *this* time. How little they know what scenes are opening before them, but all through their lives, God grant that they may look back to this time with peace and satisfaction—to this bright 8th of June, in which they have so solemnly taken the Lord for their God, and stood to the covenant. Before they rose from the altar, I observed that the bishop's chaplain silently placed a tract in the hand of each, and I could not but hope, that the pages delivered at so solemn a moment will be kept as a memento of their engagement even to the last day of their lives—and that when they are invited, (as in these days of change, I doubt not they will be,) "also to go away;" the little book may lie before them, a token to remind them of their own mother's faithful care and love to them—and God in his infinite mercy grant that at last every faithful shepherd, shall count his flock safely into the heavenly fold, not one being left behind!

> Lord of that holy hour!—the sunny air
> Streamed like thy blessing through that house of prayer,
> On the cold marble stone, up the long aisle,
> And shone on ancient tombs, like Mercy's smile;
> Casting a ray of hope where'er it gleamed,
> 'Till on the holiest place, the glory streamed:
> Down, upon young pale brows untraced by care
> In breathless reverence bent and waiting there—
> Waiting to hear—thy promised blessing given,
> Strength for the weary way and hope of heaven.
> Lord of that summer hour!—nor cloud, nor storm
> Dared with a shade to dim thy sunbeam's form;
> But storms we know must come, and tempests lower,
> Then, Lord, on every heart shine forth in power.
> When winds and waves awake, say, "it is I!".
> And to the people's prayer, reply! reply!
> In thee we trust and hope—our shield, our sun,
> Guide these, the rough dark road that they may run.
> Till where no cloud can dim, thy temple fair,
> Each, after each, O Lord! shall enter there—
> Remembering that blest hour when the bright air
> Streamed like thy blessing, through the house of prayer!

*June 9th*, 1831.

# THE WOODS.

> They love the country and none else, who seek,
> For its own sake, the silence and the shade.
> 
> COWPER.

THERE is little need that I should remind you of that summer walk, for I do not think either of us likely to forget it. But it would be strange if, having written so much for my own amusement, I should hesitate to attempt, at least, any subject proposed by you. Yet pleasant though the theme be, do not think that it is without its difficulties. The beautiful woods are too beautiful for my weak powers of description, and I am likely to make mistakes, for I was a stranger in a strange place. This at least is not a scene in our parish; and you and others know every step of the ground so well, that the most trifling mistake will be evident.

Yet such considerations shall not influence me. Others, indeed, may see what I write—but it is to please friends—for the few who understand me—for those who

> " Know my raptures are not conjur'd up
> To serve occasion of poetic pomp :"

for those that I write, who can trace steps trodden at my side, occurrences that befel us in each others company; to please such, that is my first design. I cannot refuse a remembrance of that walk, since you have asked it, for who understands me better than you?

" Her merchants are princes," said the prophet when he spoke of Tyre; and as we stood on the bank of the river which bears riches from all quarters of the world to your city gates—as we looked up at the long splendid rows of buildings, the houses, so very like palaces, we thought the words applicable enough to the merchants of our own day. Yet knowing so little of the world's business as I do, I hear enough of the uncertainty of great men's possessions, not to envy them; and thinking of my country in general, if it is "righteousness that exalteth a nation," the Christian may tremble for its prosperity indeed. But the stately scene before us, the grand buildings ranged so loftily in the sunshine, one above another, spoke to the outward view, at least, of wealth and glory. A noble, a princely scene, yet it touched no answering chord in my heart—it awakened no deep feeling—no thought of peace and home—the world glitters too brightly for me, for I have been used to the shade, the thronging and the press make me giddy, the noise stuns, and the glare confuses me,—with what delight we turned into the deep and silent shade!

I knew that the woods were beautiful, for I had heard them described often, but that so near such an immense population, and trodden so constantly, there should be so little to show the neighbourhood of avaricious man, I did not think possible: for I cannot help feeling, that man seldom lays his hand on God's fair creation, but he leaves a blot on the page. As yet, however, he has not done so here. Up to the very top of the steep ascent here grow untrimmed, uninjured, the delicate birch, and the aspen, trembling as the sun displays the glittering silver of its leaves. No rough hand has torn the wild climatis: it is not yet in blossom, but its luxuriant verdure, ornaments well the pure, pale tassels of woodbine, whose sprays at this time of the year are more "copious of flowers" than of foliage. We turned out of the accustomed path, pushed aside the tangled hawthorn boughs, and the swaying branches of the latest dog-roses, and seated ourselves on a little open space, which commanded a view of the deep way beneath, and the wood-covered hill opposite. Those lovely trees! O can you see them in your mind's eye, and if not, I could not describe them to you. How they tower one above another, each beautiful, exactly with its own peculiar grace, and all grouping together. O how the divine Artist has grouped them—grey, and green, and silver, deep green and pale, blue and brown, and copper colour! By that slight, quivering aspen, look at the broad oak, whose rugged trunk and massive form contrasts with the lively colour of the young leaves; and those again are well relieved by the slender dark sprays of ivy, which twist and hang and cling about its firm branches, as lovingly, as if it felt how much it needs support. Perhaps it is a feeling natural to one who has seen very little; but as I looked, I wondered how there could be any thing more beautiful in the whole world. Every soft shadow seemed thrown exactly in the situation most fitting to bring into full relief some form of exquisite elegance and grace; and every sunbeam streamed just where it showed most of might and perfection: how could it do otherwise, since it streamed from heaven? But the hand of an omnipotent Artificer was evident also in the small flowers that sprung amongst the deep moss on which we sat. We could yet see the folds from which His hand had that very morning unbound the tender leaves of the fairy cistus. He also had instructed the glad birds that sung so joyously round us, and he had provided for the merry rabbits that scouted by us. Do not think I am forgetting the dignity of my subject. O no! I am sure of that, since the pen of inspiration has not disdained to inform us, who it is that maketh the "high hills a habitation for the wild goats, and the stony rocks for the coneys."

We had stayed, not as long as we could gladly have done, but as long as time permitted, and we descended to the shadowed pathway again. You pointed out to me traces of the handy-work of former days. There are the remains of a Roman road, and we paused to see how little was to be seen. Yet what skill was displayed once in planning—what energy in carrying forward—what ability in completing the work; and it was the work of the mightiest of men, of those who boasted their citizenship, and obtained their freedom from the greatest city in the world. And this is all that is left to show of it—a foot or two here and there of rough pathway—a yard or two of shattered wall, which n one but an antiquary's eye cares to trace. Yet the vanity of earth's distinctions need not raise a sigh in their hearts, who humbly trust that their citizenship is in heaven. We stopped to rest once more amongst the green trees at the top of the wood. It was a lovely spot, in the full pride of summer. The softest thyme and moss beneath, and leaves, and garlands of climatis and woodbine and ivy, the greenest above us. We were in the midst of earth's loveliest and most fading things, and we talked, as it was natural enough we might, of others that we had known, lovely and fading. It was an interesting conversation, and I remind you of it, because it

turned afterwards on the epithet "Sentimental," and I
said, I was anxious not to deserve the charge, and, if it
might be, to escape it. And here, as others, who do not
understand me so well, will very probably read these remembrances, I will just say, that I mean by sentimental
writers, such as give way to morbid melancholy, and who
express deeper feeling of this world's worthlessness, than
they really experience. The sentimentalist views things
in a false light. When Charlotte Smith asks, in such a
despairing tone,

"Ah! why has happiness no second spring!"

I think she is sentimental. She ought to have known,
that happiness cannot, for the honour of God's justice be
a native of a sinful world; and the happiness that, for the
honour of his mercy, descends from heaven, she might
have experienced if she would: to blossom after the spring
and summer of youth are past, more lovely in the grey
autumn of life's decline, all through the frost of age's winter, and shining on the grave of death. Charlotte Smith
ought to have recollected, that

"It is not wise complaining,
If either on forbidden ground,
Or where it was not to be found,
We sought without attaining."

But I do not think that can justly deserve the charge of
sentimentality, if there is such a word, or perhaps I shall
be understood better, if I call it false sentiment, or morbid
feeling, which, although it views the world as one cursed
indeed for its sin, and abounding with thorns and thistles;
yet traces throughout it, a path marked by divine mercy,
by the side of which there are "quiet resting-places" for
God's people, from whose parched rocks flow streams in
the desert. It is natural, sometimes, to shudder at the remembrances of the storms and tempest through which one
has passed, and which we know may darken our sky again
at any moment; but it is not sentimental to do so, if faith's
bright and steady eye is fixed on the rainbow that shines
for ever about the throne. And surely no one will venture
to call me sentimental for speaking, once now and then, of

withered flowers and riven blossoms: for then the voice which said, "Cry, all flesh is grass, and the goodliness thereof as the flower of the field," will be charged with sentimentality, and the prophet who wrote it down, and the apostle who repeated it, will be called sentimental too.

It was time for us to go on; and so much singular and majestic scenery, such strange masses of fallen rock, such aged and picturesque trees, so fantastic roots propped up, they seemed, with huge stones, and garlanded with ivy by the hand of Nature—such bright and graceful foliage, detained us to admire and wonder every moment, that, after all, we had time to look at but half that we longed to see. Those stones must have been hurled from the top ages ago, and with what a crash, with what a tremendous fall they must have come down! There they lay, the immense branches that they broke in their fall, withering about them, and shadowing with their decaying leaves the red and brown masses of freshly severed stone.

By degrees, the vivid red and brown became less distinct, as the weather stains drove against them, and then the lichens, the grey, and afterwards the yellow, slowly spread upon the surface; and as they mouldered, the seeds of innumerable small plants, wafted there by winds, or carried there by birds, grew up luxuriantly in the healthy shade; and now the large stones which lie all down the steep bank, as if they had been borne there by the current of a strong stream, are covered with fern and thick feathery moss. There is one much larger than the rest. It is lofty and square, like a huge altar tomb. You might well fancy it the grave of a minstrel, for here were gathered together all mute nature's sympathies to bewail him. I remembered Sir W. Scott's lines,

> "Call it not vain: they do not err
> Why say, that when the Poet dies,
> Mute nature mourns her worshipper,
> And celebrates his obsequies."

I need not write down that passage—who does not know it, and delight in it? But that singular stone, and the romantic scenery around it, reminded me also of a sad story of modern date, the death of the poor sculptor Deare. It was in some such spot possibly, but beneath the cloudless sky of Italy, on such a chilly couch, that he chose to rest; only his was the block of pure marble, which he had just procured, and on which he determined to sleep; fancying that in such a situation, sublime dreams might present forms to his imagination, fit subjects for the superior beauty of the mass of marble which was to employ his chisel. Do you recollect the story? He slept there the whole night: who can tell the enthusiast's feelings, but those who have felt such? He dreamt as only genius dreams. The proud spirit felt, and exulted in its unearthly might; but the night wind had chilled the weak mortal frame, and the young sculptor awoke, fell sick and died.

> "There will I rest to-night," the artist said,
> "Place my pure marble by the myrtle tree,
> And if as hard as Jacob's be my bed,
> Visions, as Jacob's bright, shall come to me—
> Beautiful marble! gathering over thee—
> My touch to thee immortal fame shall give,
> And thou shalt breathe my marble, and shalt live!"
>
> It was a passionate energy—alone
> He lay, to rest on that majestic stone;
> He laid him down, when in the deep, blue sky
> Keeping its sleepless watch, each star shone high;
> Whilst stately lilies, born to grace that land,
> Breathed their pure incense in the clear moon's ray,
> Soft, odorous gales his burning temples fann'd
> As on his cold and dazzling couch he lay.
>
> Then came fair visions round him—such as keep
> Watch, mighty Genius! o'er thy fitful sleep:
> Beauty was there, with spring's fresh roses crown'd
> Her locks loose floating, and her zone unbound—
> Her white feet glancing in the pure moon's light,
> Her sweet voice singing to the listening light.
> Thither, descending with bright wings unfurl'd,
> Came Hope exulting from a fairer world;
> And mighty Strength on massive club reclin'd,
> And Joy, whose bounding feet outstripp'd the wind.
> And hark! and hark! Fame's trumpet blast,
> As on the glorious pageant past;
> High beat his heart, exulting at the sound,
> But darker forms his midnight couch surround—
> A voice of terror on his slumber broke,
> Death threw his cold arms round him, and he woke!

The path was steep and slippery which we had to descend as we passed these singular stones, and the spot so sheltered that last year's leaves still lie heaped up and rustling under our tread. As we paused there, we caught, through the tops of the trees, a glimpse of a broad, sunshiny road at a little distance. We could distinguish the passing of varied forms, and the glitter of gay equipages. Oh, how unlike "the silence and the shade!" But it is a world for action and exertion, not for musing only, I know; and therefore we will uncomplainingly go back again: ever remembering, or trying to remember this, that where the path of duty lies, be it in the hot glare or the pleasant shade, there only God's blessing rests, and there only shall we find happiness.

*July* 13, 1831.

# THE DAY'S WORK DONE.

> "It matters not, so the work is done,
> At what hour sets the declining sun—
> If shadows come o'er him at noon of day,
> Or if he shine on to the evening grey."

It was the evening of a long summer day. The sun, which through all the waking hours had shone so brightly, had burned yet more brilliantly when he approached the horizon. The sweet peas, and the roses that had glittered all the noon and the afternoon, were now folded up, and the tall evening primrose, and the June jessamine opened, as the fresh dew descended, and the still moonlight arose upon them. The last heavy wagon had passed. The last bustling sound had died away in the street—only now and then, the silence was broken by the lonely footstep of a late traveller. The very breeze that shut the convolvulus, and shattered the pure gum-cistus leaves on the mown grass, told that the day's work was done.

We had been a walk that evening, and had stopped on our way, to look at Joyce's herbs, and were startled by her abrupt intelligence. "The dear old man's dead," she said; "the old man whose place you looked out in his book on Sunday."

"The old man dead!" we repeated. "The old man who sits at the top of the aisle? Why," I said, not caring that Joyce had made the same observation, "I found out his place last Sunday; he looked very well then." "Aye, so he was," said Joyce, "he was well at breakfast-time this morning, so they tell me; and he died just after." "What? he was quite well on Sunday, and this is only Tuesday?" Ah! what wonder is that? How long shall we be in learning, that in the midst of life we are in death. We could think of nothing else during our walk. The old friend was gone, whom we had been taught to love and reverence from our early childhood. We had learnt to consider it an honour to shake hands with him, or to talk to him, and so indeed it might well be; for we knew him one of a race of kings, nay, a son of the King of kings, and if a son, then an heir of God, and joint heir with Christ. What a stupendous title, and how suddenly he had been called to his inheritance!

Notice for the celebration of the sacrament had been given in the morning—and as I thought of the small company whom I hoped to see there, old John naturally presented himself first. He had knelt in the same place at the north end of the rails, years before I was born; and since I had been admitted to a participation in the blessed privilege, I had never missed him there, and no doubt he fully intended to be present next Sunday. We shall be there, I trust, and we will think of him when we pray for grace to follow their good examples who are gone before. But his labour is ended, he no longer needs refreshment by the way, for he has reached the city of habitation—his day's work is done! Death is at all times an awful thing, because it is a mark of a righteous God's displeasure against sin; but in some favoured cases, the enemy appears so entirely a conquered enemy, the sting is so taken away, that our grief is exchanged for joy, and bursts into the involuntary exclamation, O death! where is thy sting? O grave! where is thy victory? Thanks be to God who giveth us the victory! And we prolong the shout, Victory—victory! through our Lord Jesus Christ!

The master of the vineyard in the parable, we know, gives to his labourers each of them a penny—to him who has wrought one hour only, as well as to him who has borne the burden and heat of the day; but I think that belief does not at all discredit the idea that an additional blessing of peace and comfort is permitted to those who have sought Him in the days of their youth—that, with regard to such as He has brought from their youth up, He will in an especial manner prove, that when they are old and greyheaded, he will not forsake them.

Our friend has been in an eminent degree an instance of such support. In his early days he learnt to know the God of his fathers, and even to his old age that God said, "I am He," and to his grey hairs, "I will carry thee!" It was the foolishness of preaching that was made strong for his salvation. And may I be pardoned here, for referring to the venerable man—venerable for his worth as well as his grey hairs, and rendered yet doubly an object of interest by his blindness—who in this instance, and so many others, has been made the instrument of such incalculable blessing? Will it give him an additional subject of thanksgiving to learn, that one of whom he perhaps never heard on earth, loved and reverenced him as his best blessing, thanked God that he had ever heard him, and cherishing a deep, perhaps it might be thought, a romantic attachment, even to the place where he had at first heard the message of salvation, to the last Sunday of his life attended the morning service there, though the distance was considerable, and received the sacrament there every first Sunday in each month—our own festival day being always on the last. Perhaps, if the old man had expressed them, he might have told us of some particularly sublime feelings in his mind last Sunday, when, for the last time, he knelt in the place where the riches of the gospel were at first made known to him; when he joined the worship of the church militant so very few hours before he was admitted into the general assembly and church of the first-born, the innumerable company of angels, in the church triumphant.

As I told you when I mentioned him before, in my account of Whit-Monday, it had long ceased to be a matter of any importance to him, who preached, he had for many years been so completely deaf; but he has often said to me, looking up at our church walls, "It is my Father's house; I love to be there!" and O, that house of his Father's which he has entered now; those walls not reared with hands eternal in the heavens—how he must love to be there!

The religion of Jesus Christ is the one thing in this wearying world that ought to make people happy; yet unfortunately, owing, not to want of power in that religion, but to man's want of faith in that power, it has not often its full effect; but old John always seemed as happy as possible. To the last week of his life he was an active and industrious man, and activity and industry are the second great causes of happiness. Not that he had for years been capable of a day's work, but what he could do, he did joyfully. It is but six weeks since that we were surprised by seeing him, uninvited, join our haymakers, and work diligently on the top of the mow for a long time. We did not think it right he should be there, but he only answered our expostulatory signs (for we could not make him hear) with a merry laugh and increased exertion; and it was not till he had laboured for four hours that at last he was prevailed on to come and rest in our kitchen. It was wonderful to see his energy; and in answer to the kind expressions addressed to him, implying fear that he had done too much, he answered, "It is what I always did love—hard work—but it's 'most done now—I've been round since to look at my grave in your churchyard. It's all ready now, and I'm ready—my work is 'most done!" The tear would come into his eye in a moment, when he expressed gratitude either to his God or his fellow-Christians, but his habitual tone was one of joy. He had much comfort at home; for his excellent daughter, over whose childhood he had watched vigilantly, repaid his care by constant attention and kindness in his old age. It was natural that she should make every effort to procure for him each blessing that affection could provide, whilst she felt that her neat and orderly household was blessed like Pharaoh's, for this Joseph's sake.

Some years ago, he had a severe illness, from which no one thought he could recover, and he rejoiced and triumphed in the prospect of death, but he had then yet longer to wait. His work was not then done, and I remember the pleasure and respect with which more than one of the congregation welcomed him to his place on his recovery. It was a long walk for an invalid, and after church we used to take much pains to prevail with him to come in and take some refreshment.

When he did, his gratitude generally expressed itself in simple and earnest prayers for us, but he could not bear to intrude, as he called it; and would so often escape our importunities, by going out at one door when we were looking for him at the other; and so often, when we did overtake him, he excused himself in various ways, that at last we pressed him no longer, only leaving, I hope, the impression on his mind that we felt it a pleasure to do any thing for him. Yet I well recollect how fervently, with closed eyes and lifted hands, he would thank God for what we set before him, and the courteous and almost graceful manner in which, before he drank, he used to wish us health and happiness. Indeed the old man's pleasant manner was one of his characteristics. I cannot understand how a Christian can be otherwise than careful never to give offence, and such care is the foundation of real politeness. O, Cowper made no mistake when he said,

> "———Smooth good breeding, supplemental grace,
> With lean performance apes the work of love."

There was more of real politeness in that old man's manner when he once attempted to congratulate me on an event of some importance to us—and the tears rose to his eyes, and he broke off abruptly, saying, "Well, God bless you! God Almighty bless every one of you!"—than ever the envious world would have expressed.

There was more of deep sympathy once on another occasion, when on looking at our morning party, he attempted to offer no consolation, but he wept as he lifted up his eyes and raised his clasped hands in prayer to Him whom he knew by long experience to be a sure hold, in the day of trouble; more than the thoughtless world could ever have offered. How should the gay and selfish world know the meaning of sympathy?

There is some charm in religion to still the passions, yet there is also something that keeps the feelings tender, even in extreme of age; and therefore it was, I suppose, that our old friend was so easily moved, that he always seemed so glad to see us, and received us with such a cheerful tone of kindness. It was difficult to hold any vocal communication with him, for having lost all his teeth; one could scarcely understand him; and as at the same time, it was almost impossible to make him hear, he was so far prevented from any exchange of sentiment on earthly subjects, that his conversation might almost literally be said to be in heaven.

There was, however, no possibility of misunderstanding him, when holding your hand affectionately, he would smile as he looked up to heaven, and pointing upward say, "Going home, going home!" There was no mistaking when you met him in the churchyard, and he pointed to the spot under the chestnut tree, and told you in the same glad tone, "I shall be there soon, very soon:" and if you happened to pass through the church three quarters of an hour or an hour before the service began, and you found him in his place; his broad old-fashioned hat and his stout walking-stick laid beside him, as he looked up from his large printed bible at you, and understood your look of wonder at seeing him there so early, the light and gladness in his clear blue eyes told, if his broken accents had failed to do so, " It is my Father's house! Here my Father's children meet—I love them—I love it—It is good to be here!" But my old friend had another way yet of expressing his feelings. His bible lay always by him, and sometimes, without attempting to make you understand him by words—an attempt which he had often found to fail—he would readily turn to whatever portion of the sacred page best suited him at the moment. I think I see him now, as he sat in his comfortable chair with his back to the window, so that the full light streamed over his grey head, and on the holy page of his bible, which lay open upon his knees. Sometimes he had fallen asleep—"the spirit was willing but the flesh was weak," he had arrived at that time when "the grasshopper is become a burden," —he was eighty-five years old; and then the expression of calmness and composure was really beautiful; you recognized the stamp of "perfect peace," and lifted up your heart to God, acknowledging "because he trusteth in thee." But oftentimes he was awake, and then, one after another, the variety of shades of thought and feeling that passed over his countenance were most interesting. The last time I remember seeing him at his own home, he beckoned to me, and turning over his bible leaves rapidly, pointed me to that verse in the 29th chapter of Isaiah,—"In that day shall the deaf *hear* the words of the book."—"Ha!" said the old man, laughing for joy, "*hear* the words, *hear* the words! no deafness then!" It was no wonder, if such a one was happy. He felt that the hand of a mighty God was with him, to keep him in all his ways, and consequently could know nothing of anxiety, and every blessing he received as coming from the kind hand of a merciful Father, and therefore was at peace.

"If I woke in the night," said his daughter, "I often overheard him praising and blessing God! If he came in tired from a walk, he would kneel down on his chair, and thank God for the rest he could take in it. If he did but take a draught of water, he would lift up his hands and eyes, giving thanks for it." It was only last Friday, that his daughter heard him in his prayer thanking God for a mark of kindness that day conferred on him by his pastor. Only last Friday, and O, how far he is beyond our assistance now! What a little dim world this must seem to him! On Sunday as I told you, he went to a church at some distance in the morning, and came to his own corner where we have so loved to see him, in the afternoon. It will be long, indeed, before two neater or more respectable old men are seen in our aisle than those we have so suddenly lost— for I forgot to tell you, that good old Jacob, who stood godfather to poor Isaac's last child only on May-day, has been dead and buried more than three weeks. Well! at sermon time on Sunday, John came as usual and handed his great bible, and I marked the text—" They all with one consent began to make excuse." Dear old man! it did not apply to him. Monday passed as usual. "I had no thought of it," said his son-in-law, "when I passed through his room to go to my work at half-past five—he was sleeping like a child. He breakfasted early with his kind daughter, and some time afterwards, as he was accustomed, took his bible with him, and went to lie down on his bed. And there, a little after, his daughter coming up accidentally found him. He had sunk down by the bed-side, and his bible had fallen from his hand, only at the moment in which he had no longer needed its guidance. He had obeyed his master's direction, and his day's work was done. "So" as prays the pious Bishop Hall, "when I have worked enough, lay me to rest; and when I have slept enough, awake me, as thou didst thy Lazarus!"

"We much wish to bury him on Sunday," said his daughter, "but the weather has been very hot, and it was found necessary that the funeral should take place on the second day after his death." In our climate such a necessity does not often occur; and the impossibility of getting her mourning ready, added much to poor Hannah's grief, as it prevented her paying the last mark of respect—that of following the last friend to the tomb—which our people here are always anxious to pay. It was in consequence, a small, though very orderly funeral. The youngest grand-daughter was the only female present, and she cried as if her heart would break; but the men were only serious, not distressed. Why should they? Themselves for the most part old and grey-headed, they cannot have long to wait before their work also shall be done. O, that it may be as well accomplished! that there may be as sure hope concerning them, as they enjoy with regard to this their brother, and then what need to weep? O, when the last shock is borne in its season to the garner, ought it not to be with a shout of joy and thanksgiving?

But I have just been looking at our young gardener's favourite tiger iris, one of our most splendid and most short-lived flowers.

It is but just eleven o'clock, and already the tips of the crimson leaves are beginning to flag. The clear golden spots are as pure, and the polished centre as bright as it has been at all, yet a shade of decay has passed over it, which will every moment become more and more dense, and at noon its beauty will be entirely gone; and in one hour after, long before evening, it will be dried up and withered—and O, I have lately seen something so very like that!

Yet who regrets the iris? It lives for the time its Creator has appointed. It praises him by its beauty. Solomon in all his glory was not arrayed like it; and then, whilst the cloudless sun shines brightly on it, whilst every eye gazes at it with admiration, in the joyous noon-light, it folds itself up and it is gone, and the place thereof knows it no more. Poor Mary Ann! I could not help thinking of her as I looked at it. She had not yet come to a third of the appointed age of man. The eyes of love and of affection, watching over her with their own deep and unvarying interest, saw her fade away—so gradually, yet so hopelessly—procured every support, every assistance—just, as you, my dear Susan, tied up the head of your beautiful flower when it began to droop—but it was of no use. It is pleasant to think with how much of peace and comfort it pleased God to bless her short life. An only daughter, her kind parents had procured for her a better education than fell to the lot of many in her circumstances, and her gentle and agreeable manners showed how much she had improved her advantages.

Just about this time two years, she married. I used to like to see her walk down the garden, leaning on her husband's arm, and stand at the door to watch him as long as she could as he went down the road. I thought she seemed so much attached to him: and, poor thing! the tears that came trembling into the full, glistening eyes, and the flush that passed over the pale cheek and brow, at the mention of his name, the very last time I ever saw her, told that the deep and pure love had continued unabated. "I really dread his coming home," said she; "I don't know how he will bear it," I don't know how he has borne it. It was a sad welcome for a sailor to his native land, to learn, as the first news, that his young wife was dying; to come home but just in time to receive her last farewell. Yet I am glad he came home in time even for that, "I was obliged to turn comforter," she said, "but it was a hard trial for him." I think poor Mary Ann knew where to find comfort herself. She told me that she made it her constant prayer that God would teach her to say from her heart, "Thy will be done!" and she added, "I hope he will," but she could never restrain her tears as she said, "It is so much worse for them than for me. I'm afraid poor mother will sink under it! indeed, no one in all the world I think ever had dearer friends to part with than I." And then, there was another, unconscious of her loss indeed—but poor little dear, she has sustained an irreparable loss. There is the little delicate child. A sweet, gentle-looking creature, but there is something in the dove-like eyes that always gives me an idea of sadness. I saw her yesterday in her black gingham frock, and her clean white pinafore: something had troubled her, a trifle perhaps—yet the tears in the little orphan's eyes almost brought tears into mine. Poor Mary Ann! she had every prospect that her station could present of earthly happiness, much to make her long to rest here, at least for a little while; and seeming better after her husband's return, she had even mentioned to a neighbour the possibility of her changing her place of abode. O what charm is there in consumption that makes it so insidious a foe! Saturday she was taken worse, but had strength enough to pray constantly in earnest, though broken petitions, to Him who never fails to hear. When we think how much change there is in this mortal life, we must certainly own those to be blessed who die in the midst of friends that love and delight in them. The most tender of relations had wept beside her all night, and at dawn she raised herself up in her bed, threw her arms round her mother's neck, and died. She had much to make life desirable, but she has been cut down in the flower of her age; and may those who mourn her, not sorrow as others which have no hope—may they learn the value of that redemption which we gladly believe she sought and found—may they practice that resignation which the Holy Spirit of God alone can teach, and which we rejoice to believe he had taught her. May they look up from the grave where they have laid her, to that heaven whither they trust she is gone; and seek and find the way to it—the way consecrated to the blood of the cross. We cannot look on such a company of mourners—young companions, who miss one from their gay circle—a father and mother who have lost from their quiet fireside the only daughter who made that hearth so bright and so pleasant—the husband who must bear wind and tide, stormy nights and torrid suns again, but without hope of the kind welcome that has hitherto cheered him. We could not look on them without deep feelings of sympathy; without an earnest prayer, that He who does not willingly afflict, nor grieve the children of men, may cause the affliction to work out for them "a far more exceeding and eternal weight of glory;" and in remembering her, it is not because her life has been what the world calls innocent and amiable—though God forbid that we should not feel the true loveliness of those lovely things; not because of these that we think of her with comfort, but that feeling herself in the eye of a holy God a sinner, she had asked, "What must I do to be saved?" and being told, "Believe on the Lord Jesus Christ and thou shalt be saved," had answered like one in the gospel, "Lord, I believe, help thou my unbelief." Such comfort is sufficient. If the servant is ready, if the day's work is done; it matters not at what hour the Lord cometh, at noon-day, at midnight, or at the cock crowing, or in the morning.

> With voice of thanksgiving and praise,
> Meet for the ripen'd harvest days
> Beneath the broad moon's silent rays,
>    Bind the last sheaf!
>
> With praise to Him whose hand of care
> Has made so frail a thing—so fair—
> Whilst noon-day fades its colours rare,
>    Watch the bright leaf.

The God of autumn's loaded vine—
He guards the good man's calm decline,
And bids on him his blessing shine,
     At evening light!

He bids with years his hope increase,
He gives the way-worn pilgrim peace,
And signs, at last, the longed release
     From toil and night.

And He, the summer's choicest boon,
The iris flower, that fades at noon—
O, say not that it fades too soon
     In that bright sun!

He reared it but to show how well
His Spirit works the hidden spell;
His mercy and his might to tell—
     Its work is done!

*August* 8, 1831.

# A VISIT TO THE OLD COURT.

Song, hath been here with its flow of thought
Love, with its passionate visions fraught;
Death, breathing stillness and sadness round,
And is it not——is it not, haunted ground?
                                    Mrs. Hemans.

You will recollect the morning, my dear Mary, in which we set off for our interesting and pleasant walk. It had been one of the gentlest Aprils I ever remember, for April, bright as she frequently is, generally partakes something of the boisterous passions of her brother March, and is even more wayward than her changeable sister, beautiful May. But this April, from the calm and holy Friday on which it begun, all through the pleasant Easter, and to nearly the latter end of the month, was singularly unvarying in its beauty. We had been expecting rain then for several days. There had been a thundery weight in the air, and for two or three successive evenings a gathering together of heavy grey clouds, that as night drew on became more and more purple, with a heavy portentous colouring over the eastern hills, that seemed to us to foretell the coming of the red storm. But the first of May was fair and sunny, as a May day should be; and the second rose brightly and beautifully, and gave no reason that our long-intended walk should be any further delayed.

Decay, that silent dweller in every garden—in the newly-reared bower, as well as in the shadowed churchyard—reminds us of its presence less at this time of the year, perhaps, than at any other. The snow-drops, indeed, we have lost; but that is so long since, that the brown petals are quite hidden amongst the slender rush-like leaves, still fresh and green, and every thing else is but beginning to come forth in beauty.

Some of the sycamores are but just unfolding the delicate and polished cinnamon-coloured leaves, which the sun and air will presently render so much deeper and brighter. Another sort only opened its long pendant clusters of fairy-green flowers in the sun of yesterday; and the first bees which have ventured out of their southern hives, are visiting the various lilacs, whose early bloom hastens to contrast its beauty with the gueldre rose and laburnum. All is just now life and freshness. And we look at the butterfly that is revelling in the luxurious weather with deeper interest than at all the rest, for we see it a type and emblem of our own best hopes.

> Thou! who wast born on earth to dwell,
>   Spread thy bright wings and soar to heaven,
> Burst! burst thy shroud! Leave! leave thy cell,
>   Joy in the light thy God is given.
>
> Far, through spring's clear and sunny air,
>   Where blossoms wreathe the topmost bough,
> Mine eye shall greet thee—wanderer! there,
>   And I rejoice to be, as thou.
>
> A little while, with thee to creep,
>   Shrouded awhile, like thee to lie;
> Then, then, to burst, the bonds of sleep,
>   And up toward heaven, like thee to fly!

All is just now life and freshness, but who can look upon it without remembering the change, the quiet and gradual change, that is passing like a shadow or a blight over it. Who looks at the flower, without remembering, "In the evening it is cut down?" On that morning especially we could not, because the purpose of our walk was to visit an ancient family mansion, and now family and mansion both are declining into gradual and sure decay. Those who are constantly used to visit the same spot, and look upon the same scene, feel pleasure in the discovery even of an unexplored lane, or a new field, which such as live in a varying circle can little understand. The merest trifles may be made sources of pleasure. Perhaps we gather blue bells finer than our own; or there is a little specimen of the more rare orchis, delicately striped with green on the outside leaves; or, thanks to an intelligent companion, we learn the name of some weed which we had long wished to know, and which even Joyce could not tell. But we had now yet further reasons for enjoying our walk, for nature had delighted herself in that quiet spot; there, for ages she had reared her stately trees, and there she had poured her silver water. We crossed a sloping field, shadowed on one side by a pretty coppice, in which dark fir-trees mingled well with willow and lime. We paused and looked round us, for still and retired as the spot appeared, it has not always been such. Fancy may throng this green valley with knights and ladies, and she does not wander so far from truth as sometimes, in doing so. It may yet tell a loftier tale, for once when the whole gallant company stood here, on this very turf, every head was bared as the lord of the fair domain, kneeling, did homage to his sovereign liege the king. Under which of these old trees did the royal party stand? Ah! we mistake in saying, under one of these very trees. So many have been cut down for the sake of the timber, and though many graceful, and many noble, are yet left, we cannot look on these massive remains that so frequently impede our footsteps, without viewing them as tablets on which is inscribed, in legible characters, a tale of glory and of decay.

But if there are a few days, in which our thoughts are led to the bright side of things, and our imagination is little checked in its range amongst that which is fair and gay, this day might have been one, and as I looked down the soft valley again, the gorgeous train of other days passed before me, and the times of chivalry returned. O, if these old trees could speak, if the wild flowers that grow just in the same spot, where they sprung five hundred years ago, could but tell us, what traditions would they not certify, and with what intense interest we should listen to the record! But they may not be. Fancy shall people the fair scene for us, and we will gaze with unquestioning belief on the visions she bids pass before us.

\* It was the morning of some such day as this, a bright summer day, the day of an earl's bridal, and the day appointed for a tournament.

Here was the fair field prepared; seats were arranged here for the noble spectators, and there the lists were made ready for the gallant combatants. There, around tents erected for the knights and squires, hung the bright shields, glittering in their various blazonry against the morning

---

\* The following scene is founded on the history of Mary, Countess of Valentia, grand-daughter of Edward III. foundress of Pembroke College, Cambridge. See Wilson's Memorabilia Cantabrigiæ.

sun, and there the waving of lordly plumes and the fluttering of emboidered banners was reflected in the quiet stream. What does the quiet stream reflect now? The clouds drifting over the untroubled heaven, and the swaying of the willow-bough; but, as in water face answereth to face, so the heart of man to man; and amongst that company, were some things which the varied course of five hundred years has not altered. "Human hearts were there." There was the throb of ambition—the bound of pride—such as man's heart feels now—and O, deeper feelings, the quiet bliss of requited affection, the love of a happy heart was there. For there, in the midst of her bridemaids, the admiration of the gorgeous circle, sat the Ladye Mary de Valentia.

The canopy over her head was of cloth of gold, for royal blood flowed in the Lady's veins. Her robe closely fitting her small and delicate form, was of white satin fringed with gold, and embroidered with fleur-de-lis of gold and silver. The circlet round her waist was adorned with diamonds, whose value befitted her high station, and clasped with massive ornaments of wrought gold. All that art could do, to add grace to an almost perfect form, and to arrange around a more than lovely face the soft profusion of sunny hair which indeed little needed such assistance, had been done that morning; but the veil of silver gauze fell in such broad folds about her from head to foot, as whilst it dazzled and deceived the eyes of the spectators, yet drew them with but more interest toward her. The Lady of Valentia was that morning a bride. Of the splendid ritual of the church of Rome in those days, on so lofty an occasion, I can tell you but little.

> The bells had been rung,
> And the mass had been sung—
> And censers of incense around them swung;
> And the holy blessing said—
> And gifts had been offered both rich and rare,
> And to Virgin and Saint they had knelt in prayer,
> That honour and wealth on the noble pair,
> Might in measure full be shed.

Of all this I have read little, I have seen nothing, and therefore I cannot describe it to you; but a woman need only look into her own heart to know the exultation with which the Lady Mary beheld all eyes turn with admiration on the lofty bearing and gallant appearance of her own knight, the noble Lord Andemar, as with his three esquires he enteredt he lists. A woman will not marvel, that though it was not the fashion of that day to be nervous, and the ladies were trained to look on scenes which the firmest amongst us now could scarcely behold, without a shudder, the Lady Mary's cheek blenched, and her eyes involuntarily closed, as the words of admiration, "Good steed!" "Brave lance!" hailed the first course that her noble bridegroom ran. But the second time she was more bold, and with a flush of joy and pride, and unshrinking eye, marked and gloried in his success. The third time her pulse beat higher, and her heart bounded yet more exultingly, and as other voices cried, "O brave knights, bright eyes behold you!" the lady almost unconsciously leant forward from the gallery, waved her white scarf, and repeated, "On! on!" There was a moment's pause of intense interest—a shock of encounter, a heavy fall—a shriek from the gallery as the lady burst from those who would have detained her, exclaiming, He's fallen, he's fallen! and I urged him on! O my Lord! my Lord! my own Aymer!"

But I said that we viewed the moss-grown remains of the trees as tablets whereon was inscribed in legible characters, a tale of glory and of decay. Such an account also we learnt from the difficulty with which we obtained admission. The porter was long ago dismissed, and the ploughboy in his smock-frock, seemed, by the astonishment he displayed at seeing a party of strangers stand outside the iron gate, little used to his office. We did not regret the length of time which it took to find the key, as it gave us an opportunity of considering the architecture of the old gothic chapel, and of looking through the archway into the gardens, whose abrupt descent, prevents you from knowing where it terminates, and leaves your imagination to roam on, through sunny meadows and valleys, for many a mile beyond. There is a luxuriant ivy growing within the arch, which itself all beauty and freshness, (for the shelter afforded by the situation, has brought forward the large delicate leaves far beyond the size of any we can find in the open air,) contrasts beautifully with the grey and hoar appearance of the arch about which it clings. We entered at length, but it was only to see on every side marks of decay. In the spacious hall panneled with dark oak, at the end of which was a raised seat for the magistrates—for it had formerly been a court of justice—there had been many fine family portraits. Now very few are left. One would not ask questions; but lawsuits of many years standing cannot be carried on without great and ruinous expense. There had been fine tapestry up-stairs, but we were not asked to see it, probably it is no longer there. There was something in our visit, if not quite of a melancholy, at least of a grave nature. One felt the worthlessness of all that earth has to give—riches make wings and fly away—but one thought not of wealth and fame and glory alone, but of lovelier things than these: the deceitfulness of love—the changeableness of affection—the vanishing of hope. The bound of very children's feet has been heard brought this lofty hall, I thought, in their happy play—where are they all now? Here the feast was spread for friends and retainers, when the young heir came of age—but the revellers are gone! Down that broad staircase, the veiled bride has come from her chamber, and waited, with varying thoughts of hope and fear, for her mother's last kiss, and her father's blessing, before she left the pleasant home of her childhood. "But their love, and their envy, and their hatred hath now perished; neither remaineth there now any portion to them for ever, of any thing that is done under the sun!

> He till'd the lands his fathers till'd,
>  She rear'd her children fair,
> Who joy'd and wept, did plant and build,
>  Have now no portion there!
> Beneath the old grey tower they lie,
> Their low tomb stays no passer by;
> On other graves the sun hath shone,
> But these, their very graves, are gone.
>
> Her thought by day—her dream by night—
>  Her watch in twilight bower!
> Her tone of love, her smile of light,
>  Her prayer at waking hour.
> 'Tis past, the wish—'tis hush'd, the sigh,
> Closed and forgot the beaming eye;
> The panting heart rests still and dead,
> For woman's love hath perished.

T*

> The warriors met with glance of fire,
> Fiercely they fought and well:
> With thought of hate, and word of ire,
> That hour the barons fell.
> Far, in the arch'd cathedral's gloom,
> Their sons inscribe each noble's tomb—
> Illegible to learning's gaze,
> That pompous epitaph of praise—
> The faithless marble kept it not,
> The memory of them is forgot.

Who dwells here now? Nay, the family is so dispersed, one can scarcely tell; and the last heir of that ancient house . . . . . . . . . We saw all that we might of the mansion, and walked between the clipped hedges of yew to the end of the straight garden, and round the old statue of Neptune, which stood in the middle of a bath once; but the course of the stream having been diverted, and the bath filled up, the image occupies an inappropriate situation now, in the centre of a flower-bed.

We had been enjoying the solemnity of the dark and plain chapel, and came out again into the porch. There had been a shower, but it was past, and a few drops only hung glittering from the bright leaves. The sun burst out gloriously, as we set out on our walk home. I cannot give the least idea of the scene, as we reached the top of the hill. I never before saw so wonderful a contrast as the intense darkness of the purple clouds before us, and the burning brightness of the sunshine behind. As we came toward the lime trees, then just in the early greenness of their soft foliage, it seemed as if the whole light of heaven concentrated itself to fall on them.

They shone against the angry sky, like a group of angels—like the angels that hurried Lot out of the darkness that was gathering over the devoted city. The cloud and mist grew more dense over the whole wide valley below; but still the undimmed sunshine streamed on the graceful trees—still lit up the mossy path along which we were to go, with so lovely a brightness, that how could we be in haste to leave it? How could we think the storm would so soon fall there? As we lingered, however, the first low-toned thunder was heard, and the first broad drops fell.

The shadow passed on the shining lime trees, and the storm burst upon us. Might it not have made us think again of the thunder-cloud of wo, that had so suddenly darkened the Lady Mary's noon-day of happiness? A wide meadow lay before us, but there was a low hut at the end of it—and toward that we hastened. The path became more and more slippery at every step, for it poured heavily, and our wet clothes clung around us and impeded our progress. Still we pressed on, for shelter and rest were before us. We ran to the cottage door, but it was shut; we called, but no'one was at home. We walked round, but there was no other door, not even a shed or a corner that could afford shelter. I shall not soon forget our disappointment. We returned to the lee side of the hut, and stood in despair leaning against the wall. I need not tell you how long—for you cannot have forgotten, how, for a little while, our umbrellas kept a little of the rain from us; and then they began to drip, and we should have been as well off without them; and then they streamed, and really we should have been better with none. I need not tell you how, in the next ten minutes, bonnets and bonnet-caps, shawls and frills, and shoes and stockings, and a long list of *et ceteras*, were wet through, and yet, there we stood, for it would have been even worse to have braved the violence of the storm. At last it abated; and you will recollect what a plight we were in, slipping and splashing through the ploughed fields. You cannot have forgotten the difficulty with which, drenched as we were, and laden with our wet umbrellas, we clambered the five-barred gates, and descended heavily in the mud of the road. I need not tell you how philosophically we bore it all; for your good-humour helped to keep up that of the rest, and when we reached our kind friend's home, you know who provided the poor wanderer, with

"Rest and '*dry clothes*,' and food and fire."

Fitz James scarcely needed them more.

I laid my sketch of our visit to the Old Court aside, and I forgot it. The varying spring passed, and the sweet summer—so pleasant a summer that I would fain pause one moment and take farewell of it.

  Farewell! on yonder distant hill
  Thy latest light is shining still,
  And where thy flying feet have pass'd,
  Lingers thy dearest rose—thy last.

Farewell! in thy forsaken bowers
Faint perfume breathes from fading flowers,
And trembles from the jessamine bough
The solitary blossom now.

Thou art here no more with thy flowery train,
Thy burning sun and thy glittering rain—
Thy thunder tone on the solemn night,
When the dark vault was riven with the flashing light.

Thou smilest no more on that pleasant scene,
Where glides the still river her banks between ;
Nor lingers that placid eve to see,
The joyous group by the holly tree ;
For already the wreaths that thy fair hands twined
Grow sere in the early autumn wind.

Farewell! with every blessing fraught,
Long shalt thou dwell in memory's thought—
For 'mid thy calm and pleasant hours,
Few were the thorns, and bright the flowers!

Now blessings to Him, who has sent thee here,
With thy smile of light and thy voice of cheer;
Sickness has sighed in other bowers,
But the voice of joy has been heard in ours,
And we know it is mercy alone has made
Thy sunshine so bright, and so calm thy shade.

E'en whilst I gaze, the gleam has died
Upon the distant hill's blue side,
And as all earthly joys must be,
Thou art passed whilst yet we said, "Hail to thee!"
—Yet may I not mourn that thou art gone,
Sweet summer! thou hast helped me my journey on ;
My journey on—to that land of light
Where glows one season for ever bright,
Where sunshine comes not to yield to shade,
And bright flowers blossom, and not to fade.

Now that I am writing, it is autumn: mild, soft, and pleasant, but still grave autumn. The smoke rises slowly from the tribe of low houses that I see from my little window, in thin upright columns. There is not a breath of air to curl it, nor to stir the dark leaves whose colour is yet unchanged, even on the early falling acacia, the aspen and willow: and every now and then, when some single yellow leaf whirls down, it is not because the frost has sered it, or the wind torn it; but only as if it had lived long enough, and came down of its own accord, wishing to be at rest.— The pale sunshine lights up the clustering mass of fading climatis flowers, which nearly cover the grey bark that the first chill rains have begun to streak with green lichen. The unwithered nasturtium spreads its large round leaves and its golden flowers on the damp thatch and round the arched door of our forsaken bower. Without it is all beauty, but within, cold and out of order. The moss with which we lined it, now much of it strews the unoccupied seats and table; the water is dry in the cocoa-nut shells, which we hung up there for flower-stands; and the last nosegays that we arranged there are dead; but it is a quiet retreat still; and still there are beauties every where around us. Scarlet cardinals and late sweet peas, red Virginian creeper leaves, and budding laurustinus. Tokens of decay are here, but decay in its softest and least distressing form.

My thoughts had been called back to the tragical story of the tournament, and I could not help drawing a comparison between the latter days of the Lady of Valentia's life, and that calm, still October afternoon. Upon her husband's death, says the short historical notice that I have been able to obtain of her, she devoted herself to acts of piety, and founded a college which long bore her name. Whether her life— her disappointed, solitary life, was prolonged to old age, my memorial does not say; or whether the sunshine being overcast, the white rose was blighted in its early blossoming, I know not. But so far charity delights to hope, that the bond being so rudely rent asunder which held that weak heart to earth, it rose unwaveringly to heaven; and we will believe, for it is a pleasure to do so, that through the mist and errors of a perverted faith, His mercy pointed out to her the good and the right way; that He made the broken heart a contrite one also, who has said, "Let thy widows trust in me!"

# EXTRACT FROM A LETTER

### DESCRIBING

## A COUNTRY FUNERAL.

The day drags through, though storms keep out the sun;
And thus the heart will break, yet brokenly live on.

BYRON.

"You recollect John Rider at the mill. You cannot forget him, for many Sundays you and I used to watch him, walking up and down the green, waiting to catch the first glimpse of his old vicar, as the quiet couple, the grey haired priest, and the slow-paced steed, entered the distant avenue. We used to feel pleased at the respect and readiness with which John's services were tendered. Cannot you recall now the manner in which he so carefully assisted the infirm old gentleman to dismount, and then quietly took the bridle, and led the sober steed to his father's stable? You said he gave you exactly the idea of what a young English yeoman ought to be; and since that day I never looked on his tall well-made figure, his handsome sunburnt face—I never observed the buoyancy of his step, the simple good-humour of his expression, without a feeling of pleasure at the thought, that he was my countryman; and I remarked his constancy in his place at church—his orderly behaviour—his attention, with a yet deeper feeling of interest—of hope that England has many such. These were but outward signs indeed, such as might deceive; but hope is a blessed thing, and we have need of all the comfort hope can give now. Poor John is dead! his illness was raging fever, brought on by over exerting himself in the anxious time of a stormy hay-harvest. I had known of his illness only two or three days, when on Wednesday I called to ask after him. I shall never forget the terror of his little sister's look, or her sudden burst of grief, when she heard her mother answer my question with an unnatural composure more affecting still—'God help us!' said she 'the doctor can do no more for him!'

"As I turned to leave the house, and passed the projecting angle of the barn, my eye rested on a face that showed more despair than his mother's, more agony than his sister's. There stood poor Amy Miles; she had evidently heard the news which had been told me—had been lingering about, I suppose, for the purpose of hearing it.

"She did not speak, but hid her face in her apron, and passed me like lightning. It struck me at the moment, that the last time I had seen poor Amy was one fair moonlight evening, standing in the little copse, that leads to her father's cottage; that the moment after, I met John in the lane. I remember too, that I had been puzzled at the occurrence. You know these sort of matters always had a great charm for me; for I knew that the miller and the cottager were at law at the time: and beside, John Rider was a person of much more consequence in our little world, than poor Amy Miles. Well! I was awakened on Thursday morning by the bell tolling muffled for John. It would exceed the bounds of my letter were I to attempt to describe to you the sad feelings of the survivors of our little circle, on this melancholy occasion. In so small a village as ours, you know, we feel something like one large family; and for poor Rider in particular—every one had known him from a child—every one could remember some good of him; and then, he was his father's only son—and the grey stone under which he was laid yesterday, bears a long list, the names of his respectable ancestors from the date 1583: but when John's name and his father's,—how sadly out of place after that of his healthy son—shall be engraved, there is not one left to continue the race. ''Tis all well!' said the old man, as he turned from the grave yesterday, 'there's never been any stain on the credit of my family, the last,' he looked towards the open vault, but could not bring himself to name his last child,—'the last has carried a fair name to his grave with him—there can be none to dishonour us now.'

"It was the most affecting of the many affecting funerals that I have witnessed. Our little school-girls, generally careless enough on such occasions, stood now linked hand in hand, gazing on the flowers that were scattered about the pall, as seriously as if they felt the similarity between those withering beauties, and him who had come up and been so suddenly cut down. The poor father and mother were objects of deep pity to the whole congregation. The father never shed a tear, but stood with his eyes immoveably fixed on the letters of his poor son's name on the coffin-plate, as if he felt it necessary to read the melancholy inscription over and over again, in order to convince himself of its truth. The mother, the poor mother! her behaviour was quite a contrast to what it had been on Wednesday. The flood-gates seemed to be opened, and the full tide of sorrow flowed forth. Her very heart seemed bursting. The maidens, who, according to our country custom, attended as pall-bearers in white hoods and scarfs, were much affected—as well by the mother's intense distress as by the melancholy cause of their assembling; and as I looked at the young graceful forms so bowed down with unaccustomed grief, the bright eyes so strangely dimmed with tears, a thought crossed my mind, silly enough, that perhaps he had left, as Cowper says, 'a heart-ache to one of them for a legacy.' But at that moment—when that most touching part of the service preparatory to the corpse being laid in the grave was read—just as the old clergyman's voice trembling with emotion, and yet so deep and solemn, that every word touched the hearer's heart, said, 'Man that is born of a woman, hath but a short time to live, and is full of misery'—Full of misery! O what true words! At that moment there was a sudden movement amongst the attentive throng. The little children shrunk back in fright, as a pale girl, not dressed in mourning—the world recognized no right that she had to mourn—but O, custom cannot bind heart-felt sorrow; she rushed up the churchyard, through the aisle; her dark hair loosened from the haste of her motion, the tears streaming down the pale cheeks, the whole dress disordered. She passed the mourners; the old clergyman paused in pity and astonishment, as with a wild and passionate cry which has 'sounded in my ears ever since, she sunk upon the coffin. Poor, poor Amy! God comfort her!"

# REMEMBRANCES OF AN ORDINATION.

> Spirit of light and truth! to thee
> We trust them in that musing hour,
> Till they with open heart and free,
> Teach all thy word in all its power.
> KEBLE.

"THEY shall not bring gifts unto me, saith the Lord, of that which has cost them nothing." I looked around me with a rejoicing feeling, for the beautiful proportion of the arches, the delicately carved ornaments, told me that the rich men of other days had not refused him ought that the thought of genius could plan, or the hand of skill might execute. As I stood considering what makes an acceptable sacrifice, how few have gold, or spices, or myrrh, to offer, yet how many shall praise thy name, O God, because it is so comfortable! and every one can give "an offering of a free heart"—a full burst of thrilling music pealed down the aisle and reverberated through the distant cloisters. "There is another offering in which I cannot join," I thought. And that is a feeling which always pains me when I hear beautiful music. Why may I not swell the chorus? Why do I not understand its mysteries.

> "In vain with dull and tuneless ear,
> I linger by sweet music's cell."

When those thrilling tones touch as it were my very heart-strings, why is my weak and tuneless voice so utterly unable to respond to the emotion? O, are not these pantings after a superior state! how one longs at such a moment,

> "As with a cherub's voice to sing,
> To fly, as on a seraph's wing!"

And for the moment all one's thoughts and hopes seemed borne away by that strong tide of music from earth to heaven. It was only one moment—the procession came from the cloisters up the nave, and my thoughts and eyes followed it. The bishop took his place, and the candidates ranged themselves in the long seats near the altar.

Again the text crossed my mind. "They shall not bring gifts unto me, saith the Lord, of that which has cost them nothing." O they have not! they have not! Here were come to offer themselves for the service of the sanctuary, the children over whom parents had watched for many years. The first-born son, perhaps, of whom his mother had spoken, "The Lord has granted the voice of my request, therefore as long as he liveth he shall be lent unto the Lord." Young men in the vigour of their age came to devote their strength to the guide of their youth. Learned men were desirous to enlist all their wisdom under the banners of the cross, and in deep humility to take Him for their teacher, whose name was to the proud Jews a stumbling block, and to the learned Greeks foolishness. Perhaps among that group of the younger candidates in the grave dress appointed for the deacons, may be one, the youngest brother of some large family, over whom his elders have watched with deep anxiety, from the time when he was a likely child, on through his merry boyhood, and to his becoming a brilliant and much-admired man. They have seen the strong passions gradually subdued, have known the vain wishes overcome, and all the abounding energies devoted to the service of his God.

No wonder they watch him with delight—it is so natural to delight in the youngest of one's family; but there may be some who look on with a more thrilling interest still— for those whom God has blest with many brothers, can little guess the trembling earnestness of that affection with which sisters hearts cling to their only one.

But though, doubtless, many a heart there had a deep private feeling of interest in the sight, it was sufficient for the larger part of the congregation, that before them stood those to whom was about to be committed the charge of God's church.

It was sufficient to know that in these turbulent and trying times, when, because iniquity abounds, the love of many waxes cold, here stood the men, who, through evil report and good report, must gird on the church's armour and combat at her side. The Socinian may sneer, and entering into her holiest places, lay his destructive trains under her very altar. These men must minister them fearlessly. The Papist exults to see his converts increasing, his wealth accumulating, his power strengthening; and he owns in his heart that his motto, as of old, is "still the same." Look at these young men; by God's grace they shall be the same also—Protestants, as their martyred fathers were. Yes! look upon them—there are eyes that see storm and cloud gathering all around our horizon—there are those who believe that the judgment is about to begin at the house of God: and God give grace and strength sufficient for their day to those whom he may be about to try; but I will believe when the danger is nearest, there is not one of these young men who shall not say with Nehemiah, "Should such a man as I flee?"

There was dignity in the bishop's manner when, turning toward the crowded congregation, he pointed to the candidates as they were presented to him at the altar, by the grey-haired archdeacon, and commanding in the name of God, that any who could allege reason why they were not worthy to be admitted to holy orders should come forth and show the cause. And if men will so perjure themselves as in such a manner lightly to undertake so awful a responsibility, is it not right by every possible means to put hindrances in the way of those daring Uzziahs who will presume to lay unhallowed hands on God's ark? But we know where there fitness lies: "We will lift up our eyes unto the hills, from whence cometh our help." And on this day there was a solemn voice of prayer, and surely it shall be answered. Was there any heart that day that did not feel the petition—"That it may please thee, to bless these thy servants, now to be admitted to the order of deacons and priests, and to pour thy grace upon them?" *Thy Grace*, O God, what can they do without it! and with it, what can they not accomplish! "that they may duly execute their office to the edifying of the church and the glory of thy holy name." Could any fail to respond, "We beseech thee to hear us, good Lord!"

The prayers were ended, and again the candidates became the sole subjects of attention. They were standing round the altar when the oath of allegiance was administered to them, and it is well: faithful servants to the King of kings can never be unfaithful to his anointed servant. It is a gentle command, "Submit yourselves to every ordinance of man, for the Lord's sake." It has not been given in vain. History's page has proved to us in the behaviour of a Hall and a Ken,* how loyal to their earthly king those can be, who bear unshaken fealty to their Master who is in heaven. It is not my intention to dwell long on the various parts of this service. Those who have never been present on such an occasion cannot know how solemn and how affecting it is; and those who have not listened as we did for the voice of our dearest—almost our dearest on earth—as mingling with those of others, it made the sincere and humble replies to each solemn question—" It will so do by the help of the Lord." "I will apply myself thereto, the Lord being my helper!"—cannot feel the thrilling interest of that moment, when the congregation were desired to offer up their secret prayers, and silence was kept for those applications for a space. They cannot tell the touching interest of the moment when the bishop's voice was again heard alone, in the quaint but expressive language of former days,

"Come, Holy Ghost, our soul's inspire!"

and the clergy who surrounded him and the people took up the stanza,

"And lighten with celestial fire."

None others can feel the beauty of that hymn, especially the lovely verse,

"Keep far our foes—give peace at home,
Where thou art guide, no ill can come."

We have found the truth of it, as a nation, as a church, as separate families. God grant that we may do so still! But less can one who has never been present, and present under such circumstances, conceive the beauty of the group formed by the clergy in their simple but slightly varied dresses, as they gathered round every kneeling candidate,

* I mention Ken because his conscientious opposition to James in one particular, renders so much more striking the affection which induced him to refuse to transfer his allegiance to William.

laying their hands with those of the bishop, on each bent head separately. Who could tell all the feelings of delight and anxiety but those who beheld amongst that kneeling train, a beloved son, perhaps the only remaining son, or those whose eyes were gazing through their tears on the dearest playfellow of childhood, the kindest companion of youth, the chosen comforter in trouble, the most disinterested of friends! It was a sight on which one might well love to look. A sight to which the heart shall often recur in the quiet shade of the distant garden, and in the still watches of the night, and again and again our prayers shall be offered for them, and faith shall renew for each, and affection take up the strain.

### TO A CANDIDATE FOR ORDINATION.

There is a blessing on thee! go thy way,
   Strong in the Lord and in his Spirit's power—
His shield be o'er thee in this evil day,
   And his high name be thy defence and tower.

Rise, and go forward, warrior! though the fight
   Gather around, and foes from earth and hell—
Upon thy brow descends the Spirit's might,
   And hosts of heavenly legions guard thee well!

There is a holy shadow o'er thy head,
   A pillar'd fire, that hath before thee gone—
Darkness and fear, amidst thy foes to spread,
   But to give light to thee—arise, press on!

Grasp thy bright sword, young warrior! Take thy shield,
   Follow the road thy conquering Lord hath trod!
Stern contest waits thee in the battle field,
   But go and prosper in the name of God!

They still remained kneeling around the altar for the appointed emblems of their dying Master's love—the broken bread and the wine poured out, were spread for them; and as unwillingly we followed the retiring throng, we could not help once again turning to look at them.

O! if there was one expression of earnest desire more passionate than another, by which we might, like Jacob, wrestle with God for a blessing, on our church and these members of it in particular, would we not have used it? "The Lord bless them and keep them; the Lord make his face to shine upon them, and be gracious unto them; the Lord lift up the light of his countenance upon them and do them good."

The clouded sun of the cold winter day was set, twilight was fading into dark evening when the bell of the old cathedral once more summoned us.

There was little noise in the streets, for it was evening of the day of rest, and there were few passengers abroad, for it rained heavily. The large drops fell from the leafless tree in the square, and plashed on the worn paving. O! the rain of a January evening is very cold and chill: but what a contrast to the comfortless world without, was the scene that presented itself at the descent of the broad stone steps that lead down into the ancient church! The beauty of the building never appeared half so great to me, as that moment when I saw the distant arches, and the lofty pillars, and the silent tombs, partially illumined by the lamps which the grey-haired beadle was just then lighting. How safe it looked—how sheltered—how peaceful—an emblem how easily understood?

> "Forth from a dark and stormy sky,
> Lord, to thine altar's shade we fly!"

The congregation was small—in a large proportion composed of the candidates whom we had seen ordained in the morning. According to a usual and natural custom they had dined with the bishop—sons should find a place at their father's table—and came once more, as was fit, to the house of God before they parted. And to my mind, as after the service I stood in the shadowed nave, the partings were very affecting. I observed many of the young men meet, converse for a few moments, give each other the right-hand of fellowship, and separate. It was the sending forth of shepherds, each to his little fold, to seek the lost, to bind the broken, to recover that which is gone astray. Who will be faithful among them, caring for the flock committed to him?

It was the parting of servants each to his appointed station, whose Lord shall come at the hour when they think not. Which of them shall hear the glad words, "Well done, good and faithful!" It was the hastening of soldiers each to his own place in the forefront of the battle, in the moment after each had sworn fealty to their captain, whilst the enemy's war cry is heard, and the hostile trumpets are sounding; each has girded on his trusty sword, is longing to be gone, and has only time to say to his comrade, God speed! And how shall I wish them God speed better than in the sweet lines that follow those with which I begun—

> When foemen watch their tents by night,
>   And mists hang wide o'er moor and fell—
> Spirit of counsel and of might!
>   Their pastoral warfare guide them well!

# ONE PAGE IN MY LIFE

### RECORDED ON THE 31st OF OCTOBER, 1831.

> O! for a lodge in some vast wilderness,
> Some boundless contiguity of shade,
> Where rumour of oppression and deceit,
> Of unsuccessful or successful war,
> Might never reach me more. My ear is pained,
> My soul is sick, with every day's report,
> Of wrong and outrage with which earth is filled.
> 
> COWPER.

SOMETIMES when I have chosen a subject on which to write, it has been said to me, "There is not incident enough; it will not be generally interesting;" but now, one page of my life has been so crowded with incidents—so full of intense and varied feeling—there has been in a few short hours so much of quiet enjoyment, driven from our remembrance by so great anxiety and terror—such thrills of hope and fear—such a discovery of the worthlessness of earth's possessions; and yet such an increase of love to some of them, through the very knowledge that they might soon be snatched from us; that our hearts yet tremble with the strife, and your heads yet ache with the recollection. It was the morning of the last Sunday in autumn, our sacrament Sunday. We had heard of tumult indeed, but reports so often exaggerate, that we paid little heed, and all around us was so peaceful. There sat old Eleanor upon the rail by the leaping-stock, an hour and a half before the service began, waiting till the church doors were open. The children in various parties were running down the road to school. In the quiet room we found a larger number than usual, for it was a very calm day: there stood my own class, all the orderly feet to the line, and there sat my good little Betty, teaching them till I came in. Poor things! how quiet and well behaved I invariably find them! They have yet to learn—but, alas! it is a lesson easily taught and readily learnt—to treat with disrespect those whom God has seen fit to place above them. In the boy's school, one very little fellow belonging to the hospital took my attention: he was admiring the shining white buttons on his new brown coat, and smoothing the smooth fur of his smart cap. "Nice warm clothes," I whispered, "quite new!" "Yes ma'am," answered the child, blushing with delight, "quite new!" and he looked up in my face with a beautiful smile of pleasure, which made me say to myself, "England is a happy country after all, where the poor friendless child, whose father and mother have forsaken him, is supplied with every necessary comfort for his body, and means for the salvation of his soul."

Poor England! is it a happy country? Twelve hours after, I could not have said so. The morning passed on, and we knelt at the sacrament. The wind sighed through the withered leaves, and swept the long grass in the churchyard. There was no other sound except "the gentle footstep gliding round." O blessed moments! Surely it is right to tell how the appointed means of grace are made capable to effect the ends for which they were ordained: to give peace to the troubled conscience—to purify from the love of sin—to supply strength for the time of need. I believe we all returned home that day, fitter for what we had to bear, though we knew not then that the trial was coming. Towards evening rumours spread, and reports became alarming; but I always make a point of doubting ill news: every one looked very grave—but here at least we have peace; and we settled ourselves to enjoy the quiet and holy evening. I read my last chapter, "The ordination," to a friend. I believe my prognostics appeared to him unnecessarily gloomy, and I hoped they might be so myself.

Then we were told that the city jails were on fire, we ran to the windows, and with that unwonted and fearful light, the certainty presented itself to us. We could deceive ourselves no longer.

There under the dark outline of the western hills, the strange fires blazed up—three, four, five at once. O who had kindled them? There was no need to believe, that there are times when, as our fathers used to say, the spirits of the air have more than usual power. It was Allhallows Eve, and sometimes fancy might have amused herself with playful terror, but not now: we saw too plainly the awful power of sin at work, to trifle. The prince of this world seemed to have assumed a visible power; and though we knew that He who was on our side, was greater than all that can be against us, we could not but tremble. The whole western sky bore a livid and red appearance—how unlike the calm autumn sunset!—and we could even distinguish the wavering of the mighty mass of flame. The dark and damp trees stood out from the strange back-ground. There were hasty feet passing in the road, and confused voices mingled. It was not, however, from the terrified passers-by at that hour, that we could expect correct information. We were content to wait until morning. There is some comfort in putting off bad news. The hour for evening prayer came, and we found peace and comfort where we knew we could not fail to find it—in placing ourselves under His protection, who "stilleth the madness of the people." It was just when we rose with minds somewhat calmed that our faithful friend from the school (generally our first reporter of news, and one of our cabinet council) came in. He told us much more than we had been willing to believe of the state of rebellion and uproar in the city. Our clerk and he kindly offered to sit up in our kitchen that one night, as much as possible avoiding giving us alarm, by merely saying, that many bad people were about, and no one knew what they might be tempted to do. So much he told us at the time. In kindness he concealed what we heard afterwards, that they had sworn to burn down our church and our house; and it was said, that the mob having, as we plainly saw, set fire to the jail nearest us, were even then on the road. But who had sworn it? Who are our enemies? If we did but know, possibly some defence might be made against them. And are we really obliged to keep watch in our own country, as if we were in an enemy's land? Having given no offence, are we beset by the violent and blood-thirsty, so that we cannot lie down and take our rest? Lord! wilt thou not judge? wilt thou not defend us? Are we really come to such times as those, in which Falkland used to exclaim with a breaking heart, "O Peace! peace!" It was little wonder, if, as I looked round our dear party, I should have seen none but pale cheeks and serious faces; yet, there were spirits that through those dreary nights and days never flagged—hearts, that seemed to bound all the more lightly, like gallant ships when the waves are tossing; and we will not look back to those memorable three days, without expressing our gratitude to that God, who in supplying us all with strength for the time of need, gave to some amongst us double vigour and energy for the comfort and support of the rest. Some slight preparations were needed for this unexpected way of spending the night. The parlour fire was piled anew, and some put on additional clothing, for terror made us chilly. "It is well," said one to me, whose white lips told that if the spirit was strong, the body was weak: "It is well to feel that we are ready for any thing." There is a preparation, a readiness, of which only God is judge. He knows who amongst us sought and found it that night; but if calmness in a time of unparalleled agitation was a true witness, the whisper of one of that circle spoke for all: "I have been where strength is, and now I am afraid of nothing!" It was not possible that in such an hour of terror, any regular train of thought could be carried on; yet it was curious to observe the various workings of differently constituted minds, as displayed in their choice of subjects of meditation. When under the influence of any one overpowering feeling, the mind is satisfied with a repetition of some phrase or verse that expresses that master sentiment, the calm and firm faith of one, would on such an occasion, speak for itself in the beautiful lines that claim

"God" as "our help in ages past,
Our hope for years to come,
Our shelter from the stormy blast,
And our eternal home!"

repeating them so often that the mind wondered it was not wearied. Another of more timid spirit could only dwell on the touching complaint, "O that I had wings like a dove, then would I would I flee away and be at rest. I would make haste—I would make haste to escape: I have spied unrighteousness and strife in the city!" A third perhaps in the very bloom of youth, thus early brought to a feeling of the misery of this troubled world, dwelt constantly on the lovely hymn beginning,

"Lord! have mercy and remove us,
*Early* to thy place of rest;
Where the heavens are calm above us,
And as calm each sainted breast."

Who joins in the affecting petition? O when our youngest was *early* removed from us, how passionately we grieved after him; but now, having the hope that we have concerning him, would we recall him to take his dangerous post in the strife and the storm? Our various thoughts were often interrupted by the awful and agitating news that every fresh messenger brought. There were two hundred rioters on their way to burn down the church, we were told.— Why should we doubt it? when the flames within a mile and a half showed how near they were bringing the work of destruction. A friend who was come immediately from the scene of desolation, entered, and from him we learned that the bishop's palace was in flames. My mother covered her eyes with her hands, but did not speak. It seemed to us now as if our doom was sealed. We understood why they should burn the jails. The convicts there would be helps meet to strengthen their bands. Political feeling might give some shadow of a reason for the outrageous and misguided attack on public buildings. We questioned our informant again. "I have seen the bishop's palace burning," he repeated; and the mob are shouting for "the king, and no bishops!" Ha! we have lived to strange times—men are so mad for freedom, that none but their own party are to dare to be free, and our property is ruined, and our lives in danger, because we act according to the dictates of a conscience which dares to differ from theirs. Their conscience? poor, wretched, misguided creatures; when they burnt the bible on the communion-table in the chapel, to show their contempt, as for the servant so for the master—when they drove women and children from their homes, and delivered the houses of those who had no thought of evil toward them, to fire and plunder—what consciences have they? But a sense of our immediate danger pressed upon us. Have we lived to perilous times? Then let us recollect where strength lies, and let our spirits rise to the emergency. Our bishop is an old man, and at the consecration—and it was a peaceful and pleasant consecration, two days ago—his voice trembled, and there were tears in his eyes, as if he knew of a gathering storm; but now in the time of need he has found strength, and set us an example, which, by God's help, we will follow: and our children's children shall learn, with the seven bishops of the days of James, to join the name of good bishop Gray, whose palace was burnt at Bristol, and who, being urged not to preach, because the infuriate people were mad against him, answered, (and how should a bishop of the Church of England have answered otherwise?) " I will preach if I die there?" I cannot be charged with time-serving *now*, to write thus. The parson's daughter shall from her heart thank the God of might, that in these days of trouble, and reproach, and blasphemy, he gives strength and energy where they are needed; still raising up in the persecuted church, whose trust is in Him, some rulers who are willing to suffer for conscience sake, and are followers of them, who through faith and patience, inherit the promises. But our danger recurred to our mind, and our hearts sunk. The bishop's palace was burnt—then the houses of the clergy would presently follow. One we already knew to be in flames, and our own was singled out.

It was not a time for connected prayer. The tempest, the loud sighing of the northern wind, according to Bishop Taylor's beautiful and well-known simile, beat the poor bird back, and it was forced to sit down and pant, and stay till the storm was over; shall it ever rise again and sing? What a mercy to feel the hand of a Father leading, when one's voice trembles too much to ask his guidance! We sat looking at each other. Every fresh intelligence seemed something worse than the last. The candle-light glanced prettily on the mirror and pictures, and our pleasant room shone with a cheerful fire. We thought how soon a fiercer and intenser light might be blazing round it. The portentous silence was often broken by dear voices, whose most melancholy tones were yet comfort to hear. O what different sounds might a few minutes bring there!—and as the eye of love glanced from one pale cheek to another, an awful feeling sunk in the throbbing heart of the possibility that before morning some amongst them might be paler still!

We were sitting thus in feverish and anxious expectation, when a little after one, the bell was rung violently, and the door shaken as if it would be broken down. We sprung from our seats. "There they are!—come!" It had before been agreed, that no resistance should be attempted—what could half a dozen unarmed men do against a mob? If money would satisfy them, money they were to have; and if they resolved to come in, they must come; and the will of the Lord be done! At that moment when those we loved best went down the dark steps into the garden to face we knew not what fearful dangers—when the pleasant home we loved so well, was perhaps to be ours no longer, in the expected wreck of all most dear, most holy to us, how did we feel? I cannot tell what effect sudden terror may have on most minds. For myself it is stunning and stupifying, like that I suppose to be produced by a violent blow. I tried to realize my situation, my own danger, and the danger of my dearest relatives and friends, but could not. I tried to lift up my heart in prayer; but in any thing like connected prayer, in vain. I endeavoured to repeat some verse, some psalm, but my mind seemed a blank. At that moment, one single text filled my soul, elevated my spirit, strengthened my heart. I repeated to myself over and over, and over again, and had the rioters entered that moment, I believe I should have questioned them with it. "In the Lord put I my trust, how say ye then to my soul, that she should flee as a bird unto the hill?" And who ever did trust in him and was confounded? Refuge and strength thou hast been to us, O God, and a present help in time of trouble. The alarm was past. Who ever they were, that, at such a moment, thought it worth their while to add to the terrors of an almost defenceless family, we know not. We have asked few questions, and we have forgiven them. They were gone on, before the door was opened; our own party returned, and we sprung to meet them. That deeper injury was intended for the ensuing night, and yet deadlier evil meditated against us, we know well. However, the alarm was over for the moment, and our spirits rose with the feeling of safety; so by way of changing the scene, we walked round the garden. It was Monday morning, wearing on toward two o'clock, quite dark and cloudy, and a little rain fell at intervals. We could scarcely distinguish the outlines, not at all the colours of tree, and shrub, and autumn flower; but we knew them all very well. They were like friends, companions to *us*, whose life had been spent amongst them.

We had played at paying visits to each other under these sycamores, and we had hung wreaths of jessamine against the thick privet edge, which then formed the fancied wall of our house. We have run races down this broad path, and with companions whose feet shall never bound here any more. Here was the rude seat under the laurels, where the robin, already tamed by the approach of winter, comes so duly to be fed.

Nothing but thoughts of peace were brought to our minds; but at that instant, just as we passed the shadow of the first chestnut tree, where it waves over the grey tomb of the last inhabitant of what we for the present are permitted to call our dear home, the increasing light from the burning city flared upon us. We went silently into the church-yard, because from thence no trees would intercept our view. O, in what peace the dead are laid to rest around us! Under the first little mound that we passed, sleeps a child, whose death I remember at the time to have thought very melancholy. She drank laudanum, which had been inadvertently left in her way, and having been long asleep, awoke and died. There were those whose hearts ached at her untimely death; but now, whilst sounds of fear are coming nearer and nearer, whilst this awful and unwonted light glares across her low bed, and she sleeps well, who would have the little one awakened? There too just taken in good time, out of evil in which so many of his age will ruin body and soul, worn out with lingering consumption, which for six months he bore with unmurmuring patience, young James has been lying a few weeks. Here sleep the little twins, and there blind Samuel and his infant sons; and yonder, safe from the scene of wickedness which would so have grieved his spirit, pious old John. We looked from the dark, damp mounds, amongst which our feet stumbled, toward the blazing city.

The broad mass of yellow flame cast a strong light through the thick atmosphere, and then suddenly assumed a redder and more terrific appearance, as if some warehouse containing peculiarly combustible materials just then caught fire. Even then, through the deep stillness of the scene around us, we seemed to hear the shouting of the inflamed and guilty people. The terrors of the scene presented themselves to the distressed imagination. The dismay and grief of those, whose lives and whose children's lives were in danger, and whose property was thus wantonly sacrificed,—the evil actions on which the pure eye of

God looked that night, and the words of sin which he registered. We shuddered at what we could see of the spectacle, but the multitude around us were still. We looked up at the church, to-morrow it may be a heap of smoking ruins; but in these graves, at least, the wicked cease from troubling, and the weary are at rest. O blessed! blessed are the dead that die in the Lord! We left the wet churchyard, and returned sadly into the garden, and after prolonging our walk, we re-entered the house. My story would be too long if I attempted to describe all the feelings of that lingering and well-remembered night. In order to pass the time, some of us took our work, and some of the party endeavoured to amuse the rest by singing. It must have required not a little self-denial, I think, at such a moment; but there are those, whose feelings never interfere when the wishes of others are to be consulted. It was sweet music, yet so little in unison with our agitated thoughts, that it almost failed to please; and as the richly-toned and melodious voices mingled, our heads involuntarily turned, as if our ears expected to catch other and less gentle sounds. But, thank God, the terror was over for that night, and at four o'clock we parted. Yet it was only trust in an Almighty guardian's protection, that allowed us to lie down even then; and before we did so, anxious looks gazed out towards the east, longing for the dawn.

Morning came, sleep had refreshed us all, and I ran down-stairs with a lightened heart, believing that the worst was past, and resolving to credit only half the bad news I should hear. All were assembled earlier than usual, but my first glance round the circle made my heart sink. They had heard news which I did not know; and if they believed only half, it was evidently of evil import enough to sadden the most cheerful amongst them. I asked no question, but my look, I suppose, was one of inquiry, and it was instantly answered: "They intend burning the ships and all the churches, and this church is to be down before night. The Mayor's chapel is on the ground, and the cathedral is now burning." * "The cathedral!"

---

* It may be necessary to remark, that the latter part of this information was incorrect. The attempt to burn the cathedral was frustrated, and the Mayor's chapel, I believe, not attacked. Yet at the time the report reached us, we had no reason whatever to doubt its truth. The

echoed two or three terrified voices at once. At that moment, a message came that some one would speak to us. It was poor Hannah, old John's daughter. I told her what I had just heard, hoping she would say something that might alleviate our fears; but she was more agitated than we were. All I said of ill news, she knew, and by her manner much more. " They have threatened to burn the church to-night," I said in a tone which I believe almost implored her to tell me there was no such fear..

But there was no earthly hope in her voice as she answered, " I know they have, but the Lord God of your fathers deliver you! "

She continued in a broken and agitated tone to commend us all to the mercy of God our Saviour, in an earnest and solemn manner, which showed she thought we had no secondary ground of confidence.

I was afraid to trust myself with her, for all the calmness we could command was needed, and her simple affection was very touching. I made no excuse to leave her, saying, that it was prayer time, and shook hands with her, thinking that perhaps it was for the last time—and she is one of my oldest friends, and had been kind to me, making me cakes, and giving me pears when I was quite a child. I turned to go away, but again she took my hand, kissed it affectionately, and said, in a voice trembling with emotion, whilst the tears ran down her cheeks, " Comfort yourself, my dear lady! remember there is a new heaven and a new earth, wherein dwelleth righteousness." Dear, kind Hannah! God make me worthy to meet you there. I must not linger on the separate and well-remembered hours. " We sought the Lord, and he heard us, and has delivered us, for the present at least, from all our fear." There were some people in the vestry who had been accustomed to pay a few pence at a time, for the purchase of clothes, blankets, &c.

As it was nearly the end of the year, we had now almost twenty pounds of this money by us, too large a sum to be risked in the event of our being obliged to leave the house; so I paid those who were present, and sent word

smoke concealed the cathedral tower, and for hours the news rested on our minds as tremendous certainty.

that I was doing so, as speedily as I could, by them to their neighbours. Employment is generally desirable in times of distress, yet to have to arrange and settle money matters at that moment, was painful in the extreme; and whilst I sat waiting for one and another, and looked through the open door into the church, as the tremendous thought weighed down my mind, "They will burn it to-night!" I could not restrain my tears. I felt as if my heart would break. The people looked compassionate and civil enough: but I felt too miserable to talk, and I was grateful to them for not troubling me with commiseration.

My duty there was ended, and I thought I would once more walk around the church. I passed the lowly altar where I first knelt, where I have knelt in peace so often—and with such comfort only the day before—O how long ago it seemed! I looked into the seat, where I have sat, Sunday after Sunday, in the midst of my little brothers and sisters in my early childhood: where I had first heard the message of salvation, and first learnt, "How amiable are thy dwellings, O Lord of Hosts." I looked up to the pulpit. Some whom I had seen stand there, were gone to give an account of their stewardship; but those, the dearest, the most highly honoured, whose right it is to deliver, as ambassadors for Christ, the message of my hope and salvation—who shall dare to take that right from them?

My heart bounded, but sunk again almost in despair. I passed the poor children's seats, and the pretty font, and turned to the narrow north aisle. I looked down on a grey unlettered stone. "This time to-morrow, the heap of ruins may lie here. Those who clear them away, may not trouble themselves to distinguish this grave—there is no marble to mark it—not one word, no name; but we shall never forget it. Trouble and dismay shall never erase from our hearts the memory of the sleepers there. Dear pious grandmother! resting after the toils of threescore years and ten—dear sister! of whom I remember little, but whom I humbly trust to know better in heaven—and you, with the remembrance of whose loss our hearts yet ache—you, whom we missed whilst the song of your dear voice was ringing in our ears, and whilst we watched the bounding of your glad steps—you, our youngest, our most light-hearted, darling and pride, brought home to your grave on the very day in which you had bidden us expect you return with joy. O my brother! my brother! from what evil has God seen fit to snatch you! "He calls them earliest, whom he loves the best!" O, at such a moment, how natural it is that our hearts should long to hear, and obey the call also ; and yet, shame on us! how they sink again, how they cling to earth again, the moment the storm passes. The quiet of that melancholy hour was too deep to last long: a friendly hand was laid on my arm, and a kind voice breathed a prayer for us—so, simple so passionate—and it has been answered. We returned home. But I did not then, nor could I, sufficiently realize the terrors of our situation. It seemed but a dream to me, when I met the different members of our household, busied in packing up, and removing such articles of clothes, &c. as could be disposed of in haste. " I hope we are taking labour in vain," said our clerk, kindly endeavouring to comfort me; "but any thing you'd like, you'll please to bring directly— we want to fill up this pit as soon as we can." How strange it seemed to see the bundles of clothes and handsome books, piled into the wet pit in the dirty fowls' court. O, of how little value any thing in the world seemed then! I thought, I shall not give myself any trouble about it. Yet there are a few even inanimate things to which we find the heart clings. One puts on at such a time the little ring, or broach, less valuable for its pearls and gold, than for the love which gave it, or the lock of hair which it encircles, and which, it may be, clustered on some fair brow, long hidden in the dust. Another looked with tears on the speaking miniature, so carefully guarded till then, and hesitated long before trusting it to that unsafe hiding-place. And you, my poor manuscript, bear on the very page on which I am writing, a soiled mark to tell of your adventure, for you found a picturesque and appropriate place of refuge in the hollow bank under the foot of the old cross. It was just whilst we were all so very busy, that we parted with a dear friend. She did not leave us, because she does not know how to comfort those who are in trouble, but her own family were anxious for her safety, and for us, it was uncertain how long we might have a home to share with her. So we bid her farewell, and told her to hope for better times, and one of us gathered her the last spray of jessamine, sweet, but faint and pale, like the smile that tried to come as we parted. It was after she left us, under the escort of our faithful collier, Isaac and his wife, that the reports as to the number and intention of the rioters were again and again brought.

We traced every quarter of a mile of their approach by messengers arriving all the morning long. Yet we could do nothing—what could the assistance of a few unarmed men, faithful and steady as they were, avail us against a mob? We wandered from one room to another, looking at every well-known article, and certainly more astounded than terrified. There were the pictures whose progress we had watched,—the handy-work of a skilful and beloved hand—the plants which we had reared—the Narcissus roots that blossomed so splendidly last spring, and are just now putting forth the green leaf—and there by the parlour fire, which has been his place for ten years and a half, lay my father's favourite, poor grey tabby, in a state of most enviable unconcern; but I felt the tears in my eyes when I stroked him at parting, and told him he would never have a better master. At length our last informant, one who had been brought up at our school, and whom we felt pleasure to see, had not forgotten us in our distress, came to urge our leaving the house; and the noise at the door told us that for the female part of the family it was time. So we went down through the lower garden, not knowing whither we went; and another of our former school-boys, married last Christmas, ran after us to say that Betsy " had put every thing in order, and would make us as comfortable as she could." We shall never forget all the kindness we met with on that trying day.

So not knowing how, or when we might return, and leaving our faithful friends to do the best that circumstances permitted, we wandered mournfully down the field—stopping often and looking back. For myself I am sure I speak truth in saying, expecting every moment to see the windows filled with ruffian forms, and the fire blazing round our dear home. And why was it that the shout which rung in our ears the instant after, did not tell us that their frightful work was begun? Why was it that, maddened as they were, they did not accomplish the worst of what those who had incited them could have desired? It is true, they were in number not above a fifth part that we had been told to expect ; their party had thinned at the very numerous public houses on their way, and those who remained were incapable of acting on any regulated scheme. Yet enough remained to work us irreparable mischief. It is not to secondary causes that we will attribute our preservation from that dreadful calamity. If, not knowing their own strength, they feared the resistance that our small party could have offered—we will recollect who alone can make one [man to chase a thousand. If their misguided rage was changed into a foolish mirth, which made it easy to manage them with money, we will remember who turned the counsel of Ahithophel into foolishness, and who restrains the remainder of wrath. And when the door was once more secured after them, and we returned to the home lent us yet for a little while—if it was with peculiar gratitude for our renewed mercies, and yet of deep feeling of their uncertain tenure, we will pray that such impressions may be abiding, even if we should live to a state of things less awfully reminding us of the fact, than at present seems possible. Hannah came a few minutes after our return. She had been home to put her neat house in yet neater order for us, had arranged her clean bed-furniture, and came to offer us all she had, and with all her heart. She said she would do any thing for us, and we are sure she would ; and whilst acknowledging our gratitude to the God of all consolation, we will also with thankful hearts, remember not the wide ocean only, but the pure streams also.

One word I think it a duty to say with regard to the colliers, of whom I observe people in general form a very false opinion. To the present time, 17th December, they have been quite peaceable—I pray God to keep them so. I do not mean to say that no individual collier joined the rioters—I know of none who did ; and as a body of men, the colliers of this parish did not on those two days leave their work at all.

And now, my dear reader, I cannot but feel that an apology is due to you for detaining you so long over this melancholy page. I will not weary with an account of another weary night of watching, and two long days more of fear. But it was a remarkable passage in our lives, and this record is the only testimony I have to offer of gratitude to our

Almighty Preserver, for his interposition on our behalf.—May he give us grateful hearts! Joyful ones they cannot be at present. The last words of Pitt ring for ever in our ears, "O, my country! my country!"—and we can in some small degree understand the feelings of a greater patriot than Pitt, who wept over the coming desolation of his own Jerusalem. "A great country in ruins," says the most interesting of letter writers, "will not be beheld with eyes of indifference, even by those who have a better country to look to. Well, all will be over soon! The time is at hand, when an empire will be established, that shall fill the earth. Neither statesmen nor generals will lay the foundation of it; but it shall rise at the sound of trumpets?" Dear reader! do not lay aside my chapter till you have answered the question, "Will that trumpet be a sound of joy to me?"

## HYMN FOR A TIME OF COMMOTION.

*Written Sunday, 30th October, 1831.*

In time of terror and dismay
  Saviour and Lord! to thee we fly—
Safe are we, if thou guard'st the way,
  And sheltered, though the storm be nigh.

O mighty Lord! in wo and fear
  We hear of war and strife begun,
Leave us not! leave us not! be here—
  In strife our shield, in storm our sun.

We cling to thee, whilst doubt and dread
  Tell each to each the appalling tale;
Thou art the banner o'er our head;
  Our weak hearts bound—Thou canst not fail.

Despair and desolation come,
  The flames are blazing fierce and high—
Remind us of that heavenly home
  Where there is rest eternally.

O! that our heavy hearts were there
  O! for a land of calm and peace—
Where all the weary rest, and where
  The troublings of the wicked cease.

O! hear the voice of our complaint,
 The fluttering spirits turn and cheer;
Might of the weak! we shall not faint—
 Come war! come death! our God is here.

Our present help in trouble's hour,
 Early, O Lord, thy aid shall be;
Refuge! and might! and shield! and tower!
 O, safe are they who trust in thee.

# CONCLUSION.

Happy if full of days—but happier far
If ere we yet discern life's evening star,
Sick of the service of a world, that feeds
Its patient drudges with dry chaff and weeds,
We could escape from custom's idiot sway,
To serve the Sovereign we were born to obey.

COWPER.

WELL we have lived through this fearful winter, and now we must prepare to part. I should be sorry if I could now bid you farewell without some peculiar feelings of anxiety for *your* welfare, who have taken such kind interest in my sketches. I have seen very much this melancholy winter to rouse my desires to be of lasting benefit to you, for I have beheld in colours as strong displayed as is possible on earth, the folly, the guilt, and the wretchedness of sin. O, if I might by any means show you "the good and the right way that leads to peace and to heaven," by what passionate entreaty, by what earnest persuasion would I not urge you to follow it. I should indeed be hard-hearted, if, believing that all these commotions, these troubles, these perplexities, amongst which we live, are signs of the approaching wrath of God upon an ungodly world, I were to neglect to use my feeble means of entreating you to flee from the wrath to come! If I failed *now* to say, "There is no peace saith my God to the wicked"—and to remind you that the word of inspiration classes together "the wicked," and those that only "forget God," I should have had a near view of this winter's frightful scenes in vain. I should have heard of the tremendous sudden deaths when God took the sword of vengeance into his own hands; the slow-coming justice taken at last by human law, and the more appalling suicide, in vain. I will not dwell on tales with which you cannot but be too well acquainted. The newspaper accounts of these sad and sinful transactions have been full enough of horror: but it is the detail of human misery that touches the heart; and we, who saw the poor little orphans stand at their nursery window for hours watching for their father to come home, when he was coming home no more—who knew the more than Egyptian darkness of a grave which no Christian hope illumines, as the most melancholy of funeral processions set out in the gloom of a cheerless winter dawn—we cannot pass on our way as lightly as those who have heard of such things but at a distance. We cannot but charge it earnestly on our own minds, and press upon the minds of others, to seek the Lord while he may be found, lest, having called and we refused, He should mock at our calamity, and laugh when our fear cometh. He is a jealous God, he visits the sins of the fathers upon the children. But it is not by the terrors of the Lord only that I would attempt to persuade. He is a God of love, and all through these gloomy months, if we have had to speak of judgment, we have had to tell of mercy also. He has kept our poor people patient and peaceable during this time of peculiar distress; and he has graciously remembered us with regard to the weather. One poor sufferer remarked to me to-day the great goodness of God in this respect. "I really think some of us should have perished," said she, "if the weather had been as we have sometimes known it, but He is merciful in the midst of our great trouble." Yes, He stayeth the rough wind, in the day of the east wind. There has been since the riots, so great a stagnation in every branch of trade, that our men are to a sad number out of work.

Some of these poor fellows have walked to distant parts of the kingdom, vainly seeking employment, and come back disheartened, and weary and pennyless and foot-sore. Others yet more hopelessly set out early every morning, asking for work for miles round the neighbourhood, and come back at night hungry and without means to supply their own or their children's hunger. "I might say he's walked hundreds of miles," said Poor Patty, looking round with tears in her eyes at her husband, who sat on a low stool against the wall, gloomily leaning his head on his hands—"and now he's so weak for want of necessaries, I don't think that he could do a day's work if he had it—and indeed his shoes are quite worn out."

But do you think I have nothing to do but complain? O no! we have had assistance this winter of which we had no expectation. Friends, of many of whom we never heard until now, and of some of whom we do not now even

w

know the names. Probably such are now reading my farewell. Let them accept as earnest, as grateful an expression of thanks, as I have it in my power to offer. Their bounty has enabled us to give away, or to sell at very low prices, more blankets and rugs and flannel, than we ever had before, and we have established a soup shop; and these kind friends would, I am sure, feel amply repaid, if they could stand with me at the crossing, and watch the people thronging there twice a week with their strange varieties of pitchers and pipkins. They might see Joyce coming for the little sustenance still necessary for her dying husband, and though she would curtsey civilly and smile as she passed; the unwonted sadness of her broad and bronzed features would prove the truth of what I heard her say to him the last time I was there. "I shall be melancholy when you're gone, John!" We might see Miles's little dark-eyed maids coming far enough for all their suppers, and if the friend was there who ought to know of it, I would stop them and bid them tell what warm and comfortable articles of clothing her kindness has provided for him, and how thankful he has expressed himself to God and her. And Patty will be there, and well she need, for her husband and herself, and her four girls have had no bread in the house for several days, and of their winter stock not one potato left; and the "children lie about the room," said she, "faint and almost famishing, and when I get the soup it gives us all new life again." O my dear friends, you do not know what you have done for us. And there would probably be another ; a tall pretty young woman with what used to be merry black eyes: but she cannot look mirthfully now on the little thing that she carries in her arms: for it came into this sad world four months after its poor father had left her a widow: two others too young to be left at home totter after her, one boy is at school, and the eldest of the five earns a penny a day for leading a horse in a mill. This time twelvemonth she and her husband were struggling together against such hardships as others are bearing now; but some constitutions sink speedily; and when poor Joseph had known hunger and cold all through the winter and had taxed his failing strength to over-exertion, his health gave way. I have known him undertake a day's work gladly when he had not a morsel of food to take with him. He worked hard all day, from six in the morning to six at night. Twelve long hours, dear reader, in which you and I probably have had three or four meals. But Joseph worked hard all day without saying he was hungry, and it was not till his employer witnessed his eagerness to receive some broken meat offered him, in addition to his day's wages, that he had any idea that Joseph had not tasted food that day. It was no strange thing to him—but are not ours patient people? He was taken ill and carried to the infirmary—lay ill two or three weeks, and I saw the shabby funeral procession wind its way down the road on the first Sunday in May. How sadly poor a mourning party it was, you may fancy, when I tell you that it was long before the poor widow could collect eightpence to pay for turning the rusty silk of the bonnet and binding it with crape. But I should detain you too long if I waited to point out a kind neighbour carrying home the comfortable provision for blind Sarah and the sailor's widow, who you will be happy to hear are still living to set us an example of gratitude and contentment; and there are acquaintance from the Crew's Hold, and a party from the Holms and from the glen, where the brook divides the parish at its north-eastern extremity; we could not stop and gossip with all. But you that have assisted us will now know that the blessing of many a fatherless one and many a widow is upon you, and that you bear with you the thanks of the parson's daughter. I have been so much struck with the condescension expressed in that beautiful passage, " Inasmuch as ye have done it unto one of the least of these ye have done it unto me ;" that I have thought the subject over in verse, applying it as well as I could to our benefactors. Will they kindly accept my parting offering?

Thou! who with might and majesty hast crown'd thee,
Thou! whose gold girdle binds thy white robe round thee!
We cannot climb the heaven where thou abidest,
Nor overtake the whirlwind car thou ridest—
How shall we minister to thee, Holiest and Highest?
We seek thy gospel word, and thou repliest!

" Go to the couch of pain,
" Hear the weak voice complain,

"His sorrows see,
"Whose lot it is to know
"Heart-ache and want and woe,
"There thy kind aid bestow,
"'Tis done to me!"

Ancient of Days! the enraptured prophet's story
Might not proclaim the half of all thy glory—
We know thy brow with many a diadem crown'd;
We know the name inscribed thy vesture round;
The mighty name that on thy thigh thou bearest,
And dipped in blood the shining robe thou wearest.
Thou! who in glory art gone up on high,
How may we minister to thee? reply—

"Go to the dungeon cell
"Where sons of sorrow dwell
"Waiting for thee!
"Take in the stranger guest,
"Compose the sick to rest,
"And be the naked dress'd!
"'Tis done to me!"

Lord! we believe the word that thou hast spoken,
Thy covenant of love is never broken;
Thou seest when no human eye may see
The holy deeds thy people offer thee—
Thou own'st the cup to slake the pilgrim's thirst
Own'st, for thy sake the helpless orphan nurs'd—
Behold thy servants who thy voice have heard,
And be it to them, Lord! according to thy word.

Once more, kind companion, farewell! Use this world as not abusing it. Redeem the time because the days are evil—You and I must meet again. May it be with joy at the right hand of God. Farewell!

*Saturday, March 3d, 1832.*

BOSTON LIBRARY

NEW RELIGIOUS BOOKS, FOR GENERAL READING.

## J. & J. HARPER, NEW-YORK,

HAVE NOW IN THE COURSE OF REPUBLICATION

THE

# THEOLOGICAL LIBRARY.

THIS PUBLICATION WILL BE COMPRISED IN A LIMITED NUMBER OF VOLUMES, AND IS INTENDED TO FORM, WHEN COMPLETED A DIGESTED SYSTEM OF RELIGIOUS AND ECCLESIASTICAL KNOWLEDGE.

### THE LIFE OF WICLIF.
BY CHARLES WEBB LE BAS, M.A.
Professor in the East India College, Herts; and late Fellow of Trinity College, Cambridge.

THE CONSISTENCY OF THE WHOLE SCHEME OF REVELATION WITH ITSELF, AND WITH HUMAN REASON.
BY P. N. SHUTTLEWORTH, D.D.
Warden of New College, Oxford.

LUTHER AND THE LUTHERAN REFORMATION.
By Rev. J. Scott. In 2 vols. Portraits.

### THE LIFE OF CRANMER.
BY CHARLES W. LE BAS, M.A.;
Professor in the East India College, Herts; and late Fellow of Trinity College, Cambridge.

HISTORY OF THE REFORMED RELIGION IN FRANCE.
BY EDWARD SMEDLEY, M.A.
Late Fellow of Sidney Sussex College, Cambridge.

## FAMILY CLASSICAL LIBRARY.

"A greater desideratum to the English reader cannot well be brought to public notice."—*Bell's Weekly Messenger.*

"The *Family Classical Library* may be reckoned as one of the most instructive series of works now in the course of publication."—*Cambridge Chronicle.*

"A series of works under the title of the *Family Classical Library* is now in the course of publication, which will, no doubt, arrest the attention of all the admirers of elegant and polite literature—of that literature which forms the solid and indispensable basis of a sound and gentlemanly education."—*Bath Herald.*

"We are inclined to augur the most beneficial results to the rising generation from the plan and nature of this publication; and we doubt not that under the able superintendence of Mr. Valpy, the value of the present work will not exceed its success as a mere literary speculation. It ought to find a place in every school and private family in the kingdom."—*Bristol Journal.*

"The design of this publication is highly laudable: if it be patronised according to its deserts, we have no hesitation in saying that its success will be very considerable."—*Edinburgh Advertiser.*

"If we had been called on to state what in our opinion was wanted to complete the several periodicals now in course of publication, we should have recommended a translation of the most approved ancient writers, in a corresponding style. This undertaking, therefore, of Mr. Valpy's, most completely meets the view we had entertained on the subject. We strongly recommend the production to the notice of schools, as its perusal must tend to implant on the minds of the pupils a love for ancient lore. In Ladies' Seminaries the series will, indeed, be invaluable—the stores of antiquity being thus thrown open to them."—*Plymouth and Devonport Herald.*

"Economy is the order of the day in books. The *Family Classical Library* will greatly assist the classical labours of tutors as well as pupils. We suspect that a period is arriving when the Greek and Latin authors will be more generally read through the medium of translations."—*Cheltenham Journal.*

"We avail ourselves of the earliest opportunity of introducing to the notice of our readers a work which appears to promise the utmost advantage to the rising generation in particular. There is no class of people to whom it is not calculated to be useful—to the scholar, it will be an agreeable guide and companion; while those to whom a classical education has been denied will find in it a pleasant and a valuable avenue towards those ancient models of literary greatness, which, even in this age of boasted refinement, we are proud to imitate."—*Aberdeen Chronicle.*

"The *Family Classical Library* will contain the most correct and elegant translations of the immortal works of all the great authors of Greece and Rome; an acquaintance with whose writings is indispensable to every man who is desirous of acquiring even modern classical attainments."—*Liverpool Albion.*

"This volume promises to be an invaluable acquisition to those but partially acquainted with the Greek and Latin languages: each of the fair sex more especially as direct their laudable curiosity in the channel of classic literature must find in translation the very key to the knowledge they seek. The mere trifle for which the lover of literature may now furnish his library with an elegant and uniform edition of the best translations from the classics, will, it cannot be doubted, ensure the *Family Classical Library* a welcome reception."—*Woolmer's Exeter Gazette.*

"This work will supply a desideratum in literature; and we hope it will meet with encouragement. The translations of many of the ancient authors, who may be looked on as the great storehouse of modern literature, are out of the reach of the English reader; and this publication will render them accessible to all."—*Yorkshire Gazette.*

## Recommendations of the Family Library.

The following opinions, selected from highly respectable Journals, will enable those who are unacquainted with the Family Library to form an estimate of its merits. Numerous other notices, equally favourable, and from sources equally respectable, might be presented if deemed necessary.

"The Family Library.—A very excellent, and always entertaining Miscellany."—*Edinburgh Review, No.* 103.

"*The Family Library.*—We think this series of books entitled to the extensive patronage they have received from the public. The subjects selected are, generally, both useful and interesting in themselves, and are treated in a popular and agreeable manner: the style is clear, easy, and flowing, adapted to the taste of general readers, for whom the books are designed. The writers are mostly men of high rank in the literary world, and appear to possess the happy talent of blending instruction with amusement..... We hesitate not to commend it to the public as a valuable series of works, and worthy a place in every gentleman's library."—*Magazine of Useful and Entertaining Knowledge.*

"We take the opportunity again to recommend this valuable series of volumes to the public patronage. We know of no mode in which so much entertaining matter may be procured, at so cheap a rate, as in the Family Library."—*N. Y. Daily Advertiser.*

"The Family Library should be in the hands of every person. Thus far it has treated of subjects interesting to all, condensed in a perspicuous and agreeable style......We have so repeatedly spoken of the merits of the design of this work, and of the able manner in which it is edited, that on this occasion we will only repeat our conviction, that it is worthy a place in every library in the country, and will prove one of the most useful as it is one of the most interesting publications which has ever issued from the American press."—*N. Y. Courier & Enquirer.*

"It is needless at this late period to commend to public attention and encouragement the collection of delightful works now in a course of publication under the appropriate title of the Family Library."—*N. Y. Evening Journal.*

"We have repeatedly expressed our unwavering confidence in the merits of this valuable series of popular and instructive books. The Family Library has now reached its sixteenth number, with the increasing favour of the enlightened American public; and we have heard of but *one* dissenting voice among the periodical and newspaper publishers who have frequently noticed and applauded the plan and the execution of the Family Library. A censure *so entirely destitute of reason* cannot injure a class of publications pure in sentiment and judicious and tasteful in composition."—*The Cabinet of Religion, &c.*

"The names of the writers employed are a sufficient surety that the merit of the Family Library will suffer no decline."—*N. Y. Evening Post.*

"The Family Library is a collection which should be sought after by every one desirous of procuring the most valuable new works in the cheapest and most convenient form."—*N. Y. Daily Sentinel.*

"Those who condense and arrange such works for publication, and they also who promulgate them, richly deserve the thanks and patronage of all enlightened communities in the country. The Family Library promises to be a most useful and cheap repository of the most important events of profane, ancient, and modern history..... A series of volumes, well conducted, and published with such stirring contents, cannot fail to surpass all dry encyclopedias, or diffuse and elaborate histories or biographies, miserably translated, and extended to the very stretch of verbosity."—*Philadelphia Gazette.*

## HARPER'S FAMILY LIBRARY

Nos. 1, 2, 3. Milman's History of the Jews. With plates 3 v.
4, 5. Lockhart's Life of Napoleon Bonaparte. Plates.. 2 v.
6. Southey's Life of Nelson 1 v.
7. Williams's Life of Alexander the Great. Plates.... 1 v.
8. Natural History of Insects 1 v.
9. Galt's Life of Lord Byron 1 v.
10. Bush's Life of Mohammed 1 v.
11. Scott on Demonology and Witchcraft. Plate....... 1 v.
12, 13. Gleig's Bible History.. 2 v.
14. Discovery and Adventure in the Polar Seas, &c..... 1 v.
15. Croly's Life of George IV. 1 v.
16. Discovery and Adventure in Africa. Engravings .. 1 v.
17, 18, 19. Cunningham's Lives of Painters, Sculptors, &c. 3 v.
20. James's History of Chivalry and the Crusades.... 1 v.
21, 22. Bell's Life of Mary Queen of Scots. Portrait 2 v
23. Russell's Ancient and Modern Egypt. With plates.. 1 v.
24. Fletcher's History Poland 1 v.
25. Smith's Festivals, Games, and Amusements ....... 1 v.
26. Brewster's Life of Sir Isaac Newton. With plates... 1 v.
27. Russell's Palestine, or the Holy Land. With Plates 1 v
28. Memes's Memoirs of Empress Josephine. Plates.. 1 v.
29. The Court and Camp of Bonaparte. With plates 1 v.
30. Lives of Early Navigators 1 v.
31. Description of Pitcairn's Island, &c. Engravings.. 1 v.
32. Turner's Sacred History.. 1 v.
33, 34. Memoirs of celebrated Female Sovereigns...... 2 v
35, 36. Landers' Africa........ 2 v.
37. Abercrombie on the Intellectual Powers, &c...... 1 v.
38, 39, 40. Lives of Celebrated Travellers............... 3 v
41, 42. Life of Frederic II. King of Prussia. Portrait .... 2 v
43, 44. Sketches from Venetian History. With plates... 2 v.
45, 46. Thatcher's Indian Lives 2 v.
47, 48, 49. History of India.... 3 v
50. Brewster's Letters on Natural Magic. Engravings. 1 v.
51, 52. History of Ireland..... 2 v.
53. Discoveries on the Northern Coasts of America.... 1 v
54. Humboldt's Travels....... 1 v
55, 56. Euler's Letters on Natural Philosophy ...... 2 v
57. Mudie's Guide to the Observation of Nature...... 1 v.
58. Abercrombie on the Philosophy of the Moral Feelings 1 v.
59. Dick on the Improvement of Society, &c .......... 1 v
60. James' Life of Charlemagne 1 v
61. Nubia and Abyssinia..... 1 v
62, 63. Life of Cromwell .... 2 v
Several *historical* works in press

### CLASSICAL SERIES.

1, 2. Xenophon. (Anabasis and Cyropædia.) Portrait.... 2 v
3, 4. Leland's Demosthenes... 2 v.
5. Rose's Sallust. Portrait.. 1 v.
6, 7. Cæsar's Commentaries.. 2 v.

### DRAMATIC SERIES.

1, 2, 3. Massinger's Plays.... 3 v.
4, 5. Ford's Plays............. 2 v.

---

### Theological Library.

1. Life of Wiclif............. 1 v. | 3. Life of Luther ............. 1 v.
2. Consistency of Revelation. 1 v. | 4. Reformed Religion in France 1 v.

---

### Boy's and Girl's Library.

1. Lives of the Apostles, &c. 1 v. | 9, 10, 11. American History.. 3 v.
2, 3. Swiss Family Robinson.. 2 v. | 12. Young Crusoe............ 1 v.
4. Sunday Evenings 1st vol.. 1 v. | 13. Sunday Evenings, 2d vol. 1 v.
5. Son of a Genius............ 1 v. | 14. Perils of the Sea.......... 1 v.
6. Uncle Philip's Conversations 1 v. | 15. Female Biography........ 1 v.
7, 8. Indian Traits............ 2 v. | 16. Caroline Westerley...... 1

CPSIA information can be obtained
at www.ICGtesting.com
Printed in the USA
BVHW041622070819
555319BV00013B/355/P